"Thank you to all who contributed to this absolutely necessary book that tells too-often ignored stories of resistance and rebellion from real people—working class people, indigenous people, people with dirt under their fingernails and rage and sorrow in their hearts, as well as a deep and profound love for the land where they live—who are fighting for their lives, for their communities, and for their landbases against the grinding of the creeping fascism of the corporate state." —Derrick Jensen, author of *Endgame*.

"The stakes are high, in the so-called 'Red States,' as corporate America, the defense establishment, and an array of minions battle against the biodiversity of 'the heartland.' In this book, Joshua Frank and Jeffrey St. Clair skillfully present a diverse set of rebels who defy reckless policies and greedy profiteers. It's easy to feel enthusiastic gratitude for this collection of stories. Matching the principled stance of the narrators, however, presents a sharp challenge." —Kathy Kelly, co-coordinator, Voices for Creative Nonviolence.

"No myth is more urgently in need of debunking than the notion that the 'enlightened' residents of so-called Blue states are inexorably pitted against the 'backward' masses of so-called Red states. Joshua Frank and Jeffrey St. Clair have woven together a collection of gripping stories of these struggles, large and small, that are transforming the political landscape from the bottom up." —Sharon Smith, author of *Subterranean Fire: A History of Working-Class Radicalism in the United States.*

"Those of us who are tired of being laid claim to by right-wing politicians and tut-tutted over by coastal liberals can now brandish a copy of *Red State Rebels* and declare, 'This is the real story out here!'" —Stan Cox author of *Sick Planet: Corporate Food and Medicine.*

RED STATE REBELS

TALES OF GRASSROOTS RESISTANCE IN THE HEARTLAND

RED STATE REBELS

TALES OF GRASSROOTS RESISTANCE IN THE HEARTLAND

Edited by Joshua Frank and Jeffrey St. Clair

AK PRESS

EDINBURGH · OAKLAND · WEST VIRGINIA

Red State Rebels: Tales of Grassroots Resistance in the Heartland

© 2008 Joshua Frank & Jeffrey St. Clair
This edition © 2008 AK Press (Oakland, Edinburgh, West Virginia)

ISBN 9781904859840

Library of Congress Control Number: 2007939199

AK Press
674-A 23rd Street
Oakland, CA 94612
USA
www.akpress.org
akpress@akpress.org

AK Press
PO Box 12766
Edinburgh, EH8 9YE
Scotland
www.akuk.com
ak@akedin.demon.co.uk

The above addresses would be delighted to provide you with the latest AK Press distribution catalog, which features the several thousand books, pamphlets, zines, audio and video products, and stylish apparel published and/or distributed by AK Press. Alternatively, visit our web site for the complete catalog, latest news, and secure ordering.

Printed in Canada on acid free, recycled paper with union labor.

DEDICATION

I was born to rock the boat
Some may sink but I will float
Ain't no room on board for the insincere—
You're my witness
I'm your mutineer

—Warren Zevon, "Mutineer"

To the memory of:
Jeanette Rankin, Edward Abbey, Mary Dann, Leroy Jackson, Evel Kneivel, Tootie Montana,
Emmett Rufus Eddy, Karen Silkwood, Anna Mae Pictou, and all the other red state rebels.
Let the mutiny commence.

TABLE OF CONTENTS

INDIAN COUNTRY

SOUTHLANDERS

CODA

WE SHOULDN'T EXIST: PRELIMINARY NOTES FROM NO MAN'S LAND

By Jeffrey St. Clair and Joshua Frank

WE ARE NOT SUPPOSED to exist.

According to the political Steinberg map of the nation, we come from no man's land, fly-over country, the unredeemable middle, where political progressives are as rare as a Hooters in Provo, Utah.

We are children of the wasteland. The rural outback. Where folks carry guns and use them. Where fenced compounds and utopian communes exist side-by-side with a cyanide heap-leach gold mine. Out here cell phones don't work. Not yet, anyway. And some of us would like to keep it that way.

Frank grew up on the wheated plains of eastern Montana. St. Clair hails from the humid cornfields of central Indiana. These states span the glaciated heart of the continent, a region carved and ground-smooth by the weight of ice. From a distance, the terrain of the Great Plains appears homogenous. From a distance so do its politics and demographics. You must look closer to discover the diversity, the radical nuances.

Even the Republicanism of Indiana, sired as it was by the rigid Lutheranism of German immigrants, is wildly different from the libertarian, anti-government Republicanism of Montana and the Rocky Mountain Front. They are not one. Except on the two-color map of American politics, or Barack Obama's electoral playbook, which writes off this vast region almost completely.

Neither of us fit in the geo-ideological matrix contrived by the mainstream political establishment. Neither do thousands of others, left, right and anarcho-libertarians, who reside in the forgotten midsection of the nation.

And not all of us are children of Ken Kesey and Ed Abbey. Some follow in the footsteps of David Koresh, Reies Tijerina, Randy Weaver, Elvira Arellano or Mary Dann.

A Red States rebellion is breaking out. It's been going on for some time. Since Reconstruction in the South and even longer in the West. The true West of Wyoming and Utah, Idaho and Arizona. Where the stakes are high and the odds are long. And the battles are waged over the essentials of life: water, food, wilderness, human liberty.

Take abortion. Largely cast as an urban issue by the flyover press, the real crisis and militant resistance is happening in Utah, South Dakota, Mississippi and Idaho-states where unwanted pregnancy rates are high and abortion clinics are sparse and marked for extermination.

Consigned to death row, the loneliest and most forbidding place in America? Fighting for your life against the conveyor-belt execution industry of Texas is qualitatively different from the struggle in Illinois or California where activists and Ivy-league trained litigators are lined up to give aid. In the grim chambers of the row of interior America you can't expect to enjoy the right to a competent lawyer, a fair judge or crusading journalism students. It's just you against the death machine.

Or try being an environmentalist in the toxic towns of Libby, Montana or Tonopah, Nevada, where cancer rates are soaring, the death threats don't stop at prank calls and the cops are more likely to kick your ass than rush to your defense. It's a lonely and dangerous struggle. But people are doing it. Thousands of them. Fighting as if their lives depended on it—which, of course, they do.

Out here, there are no fixed blueprints for resistance. No organizational flow charts for how to plot a rebellion. No focus groups or pulse polls or field-tested PR strategies or genteel formalities for grant applications. Marx would be confused. The human spirit is the best guide. When Peabody Coal announces its intention to evict your grandmother, dynamite her hogan and strip-mine the family sheep pasture, you don't have time to consult Weiden and Kennedy for how to spin it to your advantage or wait around for a year on the infinitesimal chance that Pew Charitable Trusts might drop you a few bucks. You must act. As a group if you can, unilaterally if necessary—militantly if you must.

While the Forest Service sparks a chainsaw in the outback of Wyoming, no progressive from Vermont is going to stop them from ravaging the countryside. That job is left to the people who inhabit the places that are under assault day in and day out.

When the ATF or FBI come busting through your kitchen door, rousting you at gunpoint from your bed, roughing up your children, accusing you of being a rightwing crazy, an illegal immigrant or an animal liberation terrorist, the ACLU isn't likely to speed to Wallace, Idaho to bail you out of jail and make your case a *cause celebre* for constitutional rights. In fact, the FBI could burn down your house, incinerate dozens of women and children, and good liberals in New York and San Francisco will say you had it coming. They already have. See Waco and Ruby Ridge; Cove-Mallard and Wounded Knee.

This is the game plan the Feds have used since the inception of our so-called constitutional republic, and there have always been bloody consequences. Smoke out the non-conformists, or better yet, murder them. Of course there is a silver lining for the rest of us, and that's that these brave rebels are the true heart of the nation. The people who bring about real change. They are the freedom fighters. They are the sons and daughters of César Chávez and Leonard Peltier. Without them, the government's assault on its citizens and the environment would largely go unchecked.

Voting on Election Day, seen as one of the only ways to democratically vent our collective disgust, doesn't always do much good. In fact most of the dissidents in Red America don't vote at all. And for good reason. They know the system is rigged. Besides, they don't trust the government or its policies anyway. They see what it has done for their families and loved ones, and it's not much. They recognize they didn't enjoy the benefits of those federal tax cuts. They know their hardware shop went under because Wal-Mart moved to town. They see that their Grandpa lost the family homestead because industrialized farms began receiving huge subsidies from Washington. And they sure as hell don't trust the so-called liberal establishment. Why should they? Life under Hillary's husband wasn't any better than it has been under Bush.

The resistance in these places isn't always about revolution; it's about maintaining a semblance of dignity in a world where such a thing is in short supply.

That's why there has been a resurgence of organic farming in the Red River Valley of North Dakota where farmers like Todd Leake are fighting Monsanto and supporting their families through farmer's markets and community supported agriculture. If you want to learn about the negative effects of genetically modified crops, you don't need to consult a study by a scientist from Berkeley, just talk to the Nelson family of Amenia, North Dakota who stood up to Monsanto after the company sued them for patent infringement.

Or take a trip down to Colorado where feisty environmentalists are fighting the moneyed interests of billionaire Red McCombs who is trying to build yet another sprawling ski resort in the heart of the Rockies. These radical greens are fighting McCombs in the courts and may soon plant their bodies on Forest Service roads to block his bulldozers. Since we're here, may as well take a trip due west to the outback of Escalante, Utah, where Tori Woodard and Patrick Diehl routinely receive death threats for their environmental activism. A few years back, a band of local yahoos vandalized their home, threw bottles of beer through their front windows, kicked in the front door, trashed the garden, and cut the phone line to their house. It takes real guts to stand up in the distant belly of the beast, where defending the Earth usually results in a face-to-face confrontation with a bulldozer, a taser or a shotgun.

Down in Texas, not far from where the government torched the Branch Davidians alive, anti-death penalty advocates spared the life of Kenneth Foster, who was to be put to death for a murder he didn't commit. Or traverse Interstate 10 to New Orleans where passionate groups of local citizens, without much help from the federal government, are slowly rebuilding their forgotten neighborhoods. Many lost everything in the devastating, preventable Katrina floods of 2005. But they refuse to give up. Since we are in Louisiana, why not roll on over to the tiny town of Jena where protests rage on over the racist incarceration of six black youths who were unfairly jailed for beating a white kid.

This book offers a just a few snapshots of the grassroots resistance taking place in the forgotten heartland of America. These are tales of rebellion and courage. Out here activism isn't for the faint of heart. Be thankful someone is willing to do the dirty work.

Nope, we're not supposed to exist. But here we are, in the flesh, with mud on our boots and green fire in our souls—living examples of what Greil Marcus calls the Invisible Republic. Deal with it.

PART ONE: FLATLANDERS

Chapter 1

HOGWASH: FECAL FACTORIES IN THE HEARTLAND

By Jeffrey St. Clair

I GREW UP SOUTH of Indianapolis on the glacier-smoothed plains of central Indiana. My grandparents owned a small farm, whittled down over the years to about 40 acres of bottomland, in some of the most productive agricultural land in America. Like many of their neighbors they mostly grew field corn (and later soybeans), raised a few cows and bred a few horses.

Even then farming for them was a hobby, an avocation, a link to a way of life that was slipping away. My grandfather, who was born on that farm in 1906, graduated from Purdue University and became a master electrician, who helped design RCA's first color TV. My grandmother, the only child of an unwed mother, came to the US at the age of 13 from the industrial city of Sheffield, England. When she married my grandfather she'd never seen a cow. A few days after the honeymoon she was milking one. She ran the local drugstore for nearly 50 years. In their so-called spare time, they farmed.

My parent's house was in a sterile and treeless subdivision about five miles away, but I largely grew up on that farm: feeding the cattle and horses, baling hay, bushhogging pastures, weeding the garden, gleaning corn from the harvested field, fishing for catfish in the creek that divided the fields and pastures from the small copse of woods, learning to identify the songs of birds, a lifelong passion.

Even so, the farm, which had been in my mother's family since 1845, was in an unalterable state of decay by the time I arrived on the scene in 1959.

The great red barn, with its multiple levels, vast hayloft and secret rooms, was in disrepair; the grain silos were empty and rusting ruins; the great beech trees that stalked the pasture hollowed out and died off, one by one, winter by winter.

In the late-1960s, after a doomed battle, the local power company condemned a swath of land right through the heart of the cornfield for a high-voltage transmission corridor. A fifth of the field was lost to the giant towers and the songs of redwing blackbirds and meadowlarks were drowned out by the bristling electric hum of the powerlines.

After that the neighbors began selling out. The local diary went first, replaced by a retirement complex, an indoor tennis center and a sprawling Baptist temple and school. Then came a gas station, a golf course and a Mc-Donald's. Then two large subdivisions of upscale houses and a manmade lake, where the water was dyed Sunday cartoon blue.

When my grandfather died from pancreatic cancer (most likely inflicted by the pesticides that had been forced upon him by the ag companies) in the early 1970s, he and a hog farmer by the name of Boatenright were the last holdouts in that patch of blacksoiled land along Buck Creek.

Boatenright's place was about a mile down the road. You couldn't miss it. He was a hog farmer and the noxious smell permeated the valley. On hot, humid days, the sweat stench of the hogs was nauseating, even at a distance. In August, I'd work in the fields with a bandana wrapped around my face to ease the stench.

How strange that I've come to miss that wretched smell.

That hog farm along Buck Creek was typical for its time. It was a small operation with about 25 pigs. Old man Boatenright also ran some cows and made money fixing tractors, bush hogs and combines.

Not any more. There are more hogs than ever in Indiana, but fewer hog farmers and farms. The number of hog farms has dropped from 64,500 in 1980 to 10,500 in 2000, though the number of hogs has increased by about 5 million.

Hog production is a factory operation these days, largely controlled by two major conglomerations: Tyson Foods and Smithfield Farms. Hogs are raised in stifling feedlots of concrete, corrugated iron and wire, housing 15,000 to 20,000 animals in a single building. They are the concentration camps of

American agriculture, the filthy abattoirs of our hidden system of meat production.

Pig factories are the foulest outposts in American agriculture. A single hog excretes nearly 3 gallons of waste per day, or 2.5 times the average human's daily total. A 6,000-sow hog factory will generate approximately 50 tons of raw manure a day. An operation the size of Premium Standard Farms in northern Missouri, with more than 2 million pigs and sows in 1995, will generate five times as much sewage as the entire city of Indianapolis. But hog farms aren't required to treat the waste. Generally, the stream of fecal matter is simply sluiced into giant holding lagoons, where it can spill into creeks or leach into ground water. Increasingly, hog operations are disposing of their manure by spraying it on fields as fertilizer, with vile consequences for the environment and the general ambience of the neighborhood.

Over the past quarter century, Indiana hog farms were responsible for 201 animal waste spills, wiping out more than 750,000 fish. These hog-growing factories contribute more excrement spills than any other industry.

It's not just creeks and rivers that are getting flooded with pig shit. A recent study by the EPA found that more than 13 percent of the domestic drinking-water wells in the Midwest contain unsafe levels of nitrates, attributable to manure from hog feedlots. Another study found that groundwater beneath fields which have been sprayed with hog manure contained five times as much nitrates as is considered safe for humans. Such nitrate-laden water has been linked to spontaneous abortions and "blue baby" syndrome.

A typical hog operation these days is Pohlmann Farms in Montgomery County, Indiana. This giant facility once confined 35,000 hogs. The owner, Klaus Pohlmann, is a German, whose father, Anton, ran the biggest egg factory in Europe, until numerous convictions for animal cruelty and environmental violations led to him being banned from ever again operating an animal enterprise in Germany.

Like father, like son. Pohlmann the pig factory owner has racked up an impressive rapsheet in Indiana. In 2002, Pohlmann was cited for dumping 50,000 gallons of hog excrement into the creek, killing more than 3,000 fish. He was fined $230,000 for the fish kill. But that was far from the first incident. From 1979 to 2003, Pohlmann has been cited nine times for hog manure spills into Little Sugar Creek. The state Department of Natural Resources estimates that his operation alone has killed more than 70,000 fish.

Pohlmann was arrested for drunk driving a couple of years ago, while he was careening his way to meet with state officials who were investigating yet another spill. It was his sixth arrest for drunk driving. Faced with mounting fines and possible jail time, Pohlmann offered his farm for sale. It was bought by National Pork Producers, Inc., an Iowa-based conglomerate with its own history of environmental crimes. And the beat goes on.

My grandfather's farm is now a shopping mall. The black soil, milled to such fine fertility by the Wisconsin glaciation, is now buried under a black sea of asphalt. The old Boatenwright pig farm is now a quick lube, specializing in servicing SUVs.

America is being ground apart from the inside, by heartless bankers, insatiable conglomerates, a president who lies by remote control.

We are a hollow nation, a poisonous shell of our former selves.

Chapter 2

THE NEW NORTH DAKOTA POPULISTS: THE RED STATE REBELLION AGAINST CORPORATE HEGEMONY

By Ted Nace

IN THE NEW LEXICON of politics, with "red" denoting rural and conservative, and "blue" denoting urban and liberal, the Red River Valley of North Dakota seems aptly named. This is football-on-Friday-night country, where Clear Channel Radio sets the tone, and patriotic themes blend smoothly with corporate ones. Broad and pancake-flat, with topsoil measured in feet rather than inches, it possesses some of the most prized agricultural land in America. The roads run straight, the pickup trucks are big, and the immense Massey Ferguson tractors that ply the fields come equipped with global positioning system guidance, satellite radio, and quadraphonic speakers. In 2004, George W. Bush carried North Dakota with 63 percent of the vote. It seems like the last place one might go looking for a revolt against the powers that be.

Nor does Todd Leake seem like the type of person to participate in any such uprising. Extreme traditionalist might be closer to the mark. Lean and soft-spoken, Leake has spent the past 28 years farming the homestead established by his great-grandfather, a Canadian immigrant who arrived over 120 years ago. Leake even farms the same crop as his great-grandfather: hard spring wheat. "I guess you'd describe me as an umpteenth-generation wheat farmer," he says. "Because as far back as we can tell, on both sides of the family, it's been farmers. And as far back as we can tell, it's also been wheat."

On a crisp, windy, November day, Leake takes time out to reflect on the events that turned him into a thorn in the side of the agribusiness establishment, especially Monsanto. It's the time of year when farmers, having completed the harvest, begin overhauling their machinery and making plans for the next spring's planting. From Leake's kitchen, the view to the east is unimpeded thirty miles of Red River Valley farmland, an utterly flat landscape that must have looked like paradise to refugees from rocky eastern Canada.

Leake gestures toward two symbols. The first, just visible through his kitchen window, is the outline of the North Dakota Mill, the only grain-handling facility owned jointly by the citizens of any state. "Sort of the epitome of farmers cooperating," he notes.

The other symbol a less inspiring vision, one of farmer fragmentation and disempowerment. It is a simple refrigerator magnet inscribed with the words, "Monsanto Customer Support 800-332-3111."

"They call it customer support," says Leake, "It's actually a snitch line. Where you report that your neighbor is brown-bagging. Or where somebody reports you, and a week or two later you find a couple of big guys in black Monsanto leather jackets standing in your driveway."

Brown-bagging is an old term in rural America. It refers to replanting seed from your own harvest, rather than buying that seed. Until recently it was simply a word to describe a common agriculture practice. But in the last decade the term has come to possess a second meaning, that of a crime, a consequence of new laws and Supreme Court decisions allowing private corporations to own patents on life forms, and of the aggressive enforcement of those laws by patent owners.

When Todd Leake first became aware of genetic engineering in the mid-1990s, the prospects sounded enticing, including heady promises that new biotech crops capable of producing industrial chemicals and even pharmaceuticals would expand agricultural markets and thereby raise farm incomes.

But the technology, when it actually arrived, was more prosaic. "When they finally came out with actual product," he said. "It was all about selling more Roundup."

Roundup is the product name of an herbicide based on the chemical glyphosate, Monsanto's leading product. By using genetic engineering to encode glyphosate resistance in common crops, Monsanto made it feasible for farmers to apply Roundup directly to fields, killing weeds without killing crops.

By 2000, Monsanto had successfully introduced "Roundup-ready" corn, alfalfa, canola, soybeans, and cotton. Meanwhile, the company pursued research on hard spring wheat. To Leake, the lag in the introduction of wheat opened a unique opportunity for farmers to ask questions and possibly rethink the whole notion of genetic engineering.

When Todd Leake talks about wheat, the tone shifts subtly, becoming almost reverential. "Wheat's an amazing plant," he notes. "It's a combination of three Middle Eastern grasses, and that gives it a huge genome."

He goes on, "In many languages, the word for 'wheat' is the same as the word for 'life.' There's a 10,000-year connection between wheat and human beings, each generation saving seed. Now it's in our hands."

For Leake, brown-bagging is more than a mere convenience, more than the crucial link in an inter-generational trust: it's a human right.

Of course, other farmers might regard Leake's attachment to brown-bagging as esoteric or sentimental, and for them Leake is prepared to offer more pragmatic arguments. One is the issue of whether Europe and Japan's "Frankenfood"-averse consumer markets would reject GE wheat, causing a collapse in the price. That issue became real when North Dakota soybean farmer Tom Wiley reported that he had lost an estimated $15,000 when a shipment of non-GE soybeans under contract to a Japanese buyer was rejected due to tests that showed trace amounts of GE contamination.

The other concern to many farmers was Monsanto's aggressive tactics to enforce its patents. As part of purchasing GE seed, farmers enter into detailed agreements allowing Monsanto to make unannounced and highly intrusive inspections. In addition to actively monitoring their own licensees, Monsanto polices other farmers as well. Non-licensees whose crop is found to contain even a minor element of patented genetic material, such as Canadian canola farmer Percy Schmieser, are hauled into court. Schmeiser had never purchased GE canola and had only planted seed saved from his own fields; apparently, Roundup-ready genes got into his crop either through spillage or wind-blown seed or pollen drift.

In January, 2000, Leake began raising the GE issue with various organizations, including the Dakota Resource Council, a statewide network of local groups working on environmental issues ranging from coal strip mining to industrial hog operations. Among the activists of the DRC, Leake found a sympathetic ear, but the question remained: what tactics should be adopted, what objectives should be pursued? A reasonable political strategy might have been to do everything necessary to protect markets for non-GE wheat by means of strengthened protective regulations. They might have accepted that GE wheat would soon be a presence in fields, freight cars, and elevators; hired specialists to write new regulatory fine print improving grain segregation and testing; then hired PR and lobbying specialists to get the new rules enacted. All this technical tweaking of the grain handling and marketing system could have been done by traditional grain marketing and farm service organizations.

But Leake and the DRC opted for a more militant approach, an outright ban on GE wheat in North Dakota until all outstanding concerns are addressed—and here a bit of a digression is in order.

Like so many other things in rural America, the "red state" impression one first gets of North Dakota, especially that aspect of conservative ideology most friendly to the agendas of corporate America, is deceptive. Beneath the state's conservative veneer are surprising layers of history, some quite radically divergent from the course of mainstream America. Evidence of this is everywhere, especially in the distinctly non-corporate character of many farm service businesses. Farmers see nothing extraordinary in buying gas from a cooperative gas station, buying electricity from a rural electric cooperative, borrowing college money from the publicly-owned Bank of North Dakota, and selling their grain or milk to a producer cooperative. For them civic participation means not just participating on political bodies such as the county commission or the school board, but also taking part in running economic institutions such as the local electric coop or grain elevator. The theme of non-corporate economics pervades the state, extending even to agricultural processing cooperatives handling everything from noodles to buffalo meat to tilapia.

Things, of course, weren't always this way. Like so much of the settlement of America, beginning with the original Jamestown colony (which was organized by the London-based Virginia Company), the settlement of North Dakota was largely a corporate project. Having been granted three million acres of North Dakota grasslands by Congress in the 1864, the Northern Pacific Railroad sent its agents as far as Central Europe to recruit settlers to buy the land and break the sod. For decades thereafter, the state was run as a virtual colony of out-of-state corporations, with crucial decisions arrived at by business executives in meetings at the Merchant's Hotel in St. Paul, Minnesota. Farmers complained bitterly that the system was rigged against them, making them easy prey for gouging at the hands of railroads and for rampant cheating and underpayment by corporate grain merchants. Their options, of course, were nil.

That attitude of defeat changed quite dramatically when a populist uprising swept the state from 1915 to 1920. Tradition holds that the spark that ignited the revolt was a comment by a state legislator named Treadwell Twichell, who reportedly told an assembled group of farmers seeking relief from the state: "Go home and slop the hogs."

One of the farmers present, A.C. Townley, couldn't go home to his hogs; he had already lost his farm in bankruptcy court. Instead, Townley and his friend Fred Wood sat down in Wood's farmhouse kitchen and drafted an audacious political platform. In essence, the call to arms urged farmers simply to by-pass the corporate agricultural system altogether by creating their own grain terminals, flour mills, insurers, and even banks.

Townley was a charismatic speaker. Farmers flocked to hear him speak and to contribute to his fledgling organization, the Non-Partisan League. To the delight of crowds, Townley shouted, "If you put a banker, a lawyer, and an industrialist in a barrel and roll it down a hill, you'll always have a son of a bitch on top."

He was also a brilliant organizer and within three years the Non-Partisan League had completed its conquest of North Dakota's state government, with NPL majorities in both houses of the legislature and an NPL loyalist in the governor's office. The League then proceeded to implement the platform of reorganizing the infrastructure of agriculture particularly finance, grain storage, and grain milling taking the joystick away from the corporate players and handing it over to new, citizen-owned institutions.

The ascendancy of the Non-Partisan League was relatively short, but the populist current continued to run strong in the state. Indeed, the most significant populist reform arrived via a 1932 ballot initiative in response to farm foreclosures, over a decade after the end of formal NPL rule. Once again, angry farmers, after examining their options, chose the most militant and far-reaching. Rather than passing laws to shield farms from corporate takeover, the 1932 initiative simply legislated corporations out of the picture entirely, making it illegal not just for banks to seize the land of bankrupted farmers, but for any corporation to hold any farmland whatsoever.

Take that, robber barons!

At that time, only one other state, Oklahoma, had dared to put an anti-corporate-farming statute on the books. Subsequently, seven other Midwestern states joined North Dakota to implement such laws.

Anti-corporate-farming laws are about more than merely the legal nature of land ownership, or the tax status of farms. They are, quite simply, laws that determine what sort of society will exist in a rural region.

Compare two fertile valleys: the Red River Valley of North Dakota and the Central Valley of California. In the former, one is rarely out of sight of the familiar clump of trees denoting the presence of a farmstead. In the latter, one can drive for mile after mile and literally not see a human habitation. One sees workers, but they generally are disenfranchised migrant laborers, denied any power in the local community.

In the 1940s, sociologist Walter Goldschmidt made the first attempt to actually quantify the difference between those two types of rural society. According to the Goldschmidt Hypothesis, rural areas settled with family farms fare better according to a host of socioeconomic indices than those where large corporate farms dominate.

But while Goldschmidt framed his theory in abstruse statistical terms, it doesn't take an expert to notice one thing: it's a lot easier to find a political conversation in the Red River Valley of North Dakota than in the Central Valley of California. Just walk down the main street of any small town, step into one of the ubiquitous cafes, and listen to the talk.

Of course, the farmers of the Red River Valley do not consider themselves radical—most decidedly not. But that very sense that it is utterly normal and mainstream for ordinary citizens to collectively decide not just key political matters but also key economic ones reflects just how deeply the values of populism permeate the state.

It's safe to say that most Americans, in defining the boundaries of "free speech," do not share the same sense of entitlement, especially with regard to the policies of "private" companies. As sociologist Karen Orren notes, the workplace has long been excluded both conceptually and legally from the reach of democracy. Instead, the explicitly hierarchical principles of the traditional English doctrine know as "master and servant law" have prevailed, superceding the Bill of Rights. Even as late as 1844, it remained legal in the United States for employers to beat their employees. Such beatings, of course, no longer characterize the American workplace. But the idea that employees should have any significant say over core matters of corporate policy remains as foreign as ever. In practical terms, as more and more of the economy becomes privatized, places where the boundaries of ordinary conversation can include anything political matters, economic matters, whatever become increasingly exceptional.

Perhaps if Todd Leake and his fellow farmers had not been so firmly rooted in a populist tradition, they would not have considered the introduction of GM wheat their personal business. Had they inherited a more passive mentality, they might have told themselves that, since Monsanto owned the genetic patents underlying Roundup-ready wheat, it was between Monsanto and its customers whether seed for that wheat were sold in the state.

In launching the anti-GM wheat campaign, Leake and the Dakota Resource Council deliberately sought to tie their cause to traditional populism, emphasizing that both the anti-GM struggle and the original populist revolt were essentially about the same thing: preventing outside corporations from controlling wheat, the core of North Dakota's livelihood. In choosing a location to announce their campaign, they picked the North Dakota Mill, the epicenter of the original farmer revolt and a potent reminder of populist victory.

In 1915, when A.C. Townley set out in his Model A to rabble-rouse across North Dakota, even he could scarcely have anticipated the ferocious speed with which farmers responded, en masse, to his campaign. In little more than half a year, Townley's fledgling organization was publishing a weekly newspaper with a greater circulation than any other in the state.

Similarly, when the anti-GM campaign rolled into Bismarck, the state capital, in late 2000, it had already collected an amazing momentum. Farmers packed the hearing rooms of legislative committees considering the issue. Very quickly, both houses of the state legislature considered and enacted a new law making it illegal for the corporate agents to arbitrarily enter and inspect farmers' fields. The new protective mechanism was named Nelson's Law after Duane Nelson, a farmer who had casually opened his fields to Monsanto for inspection, only to find himself up to his neck in patent-infringement litigation.

In a sense, Nelson's Law established the same set of protections for farmers vis-à-vis private corporations that U.S. citizens already take for granted, by virtue of the Fifth and Fourteenth Amendments, in dealings with the government: search warrant and due process rights. The law simply stated that a private company could not enter land to enforce a seed patent without prior permission, and that whenever samples were selected a third party must be present so that a sample could be placed in neutral hands.

As for the proposal for a ban on GE wheat until all lingering issues were resolved, here too the farmer-led juggernaut seemed unstoppable. Before the House agriculture committee, Leake and others testified on the need for the ban, and the mood among the legislators, three of whom had PhDs in agricultural sciences and the rest of whom were farmers themselves, was so overtly favorable that when the beleaguered Monsanto lobbyist rose to testify against the ban, the chairman of the committee jokingly handed him a bottle of whisky, commenting, "Jim, I think you're going to need this."

The committee voted 14-0 to support the ban, and the legislation easily passed the North Dakota House of Representatives before Monsanto managed to marshall its allies and block the ban in the state senate, aided by timely intervention of U.S. Agricultural Secretary Ann Veneman, a former Monsanto board member, and President George W. Bush, who met personally with members of the North Dakota state senate during a brief visit to Fargo. In the wake of that pressure, the ban on GE wheat was watered down to a study of the issue.

It seemed to many that agribusiness had won the day. The populist impulse appeared to have fallen short; worse, it appeared that the efforts of Leake and company had served merely to provoke Monsanto toward even greater exertions to promote genetic engineering. The company began flying legislators on special "fact finding" junkets, working its vast network of grain marketing organizations, seed and herbicide dealers, research contracts, public relations firms, and pro-agribusiness farm organizations such as the Farm Bureau.

Of course, the anti-GM activists responded as best they could. In between the other demands of farming life, they crisscrossed the state, speaking to as many farmers as would listen.

By all the conventional ways that political resources are measured, Monsanto had the advantage, and yet in the one arena that really mattered, those same small-town cafes where the political conversation never ends, the anti-

GE advocates sensed they were winning. During the election cycle following the defeat of the GE wheat ban, three pro-GE legislators targeted by GE opponents were ousted, including the State Senate's leading GE advocate, Terry Wanzek, who was defeated by the vociferously anti-Monsanto representative April Fairfield. At the agricultural committee hearing that had voted unanimously against Monsanto, Fairfield had made it clear where her sympathies lay: "Clearly, before today, Monsanto and their lackeys have been running the agenda. I am inspired by how farmers and others broke the back of that agenda and sent Monsanto crawling back to St. Louis."

Such overt hostility toward Monsanto did not bode well for Roundup-ready wheat. Nor did the increasingly militant tone that opponents were assuming. Rather than devolving into arguments over the marketability of GE wheat overseas, the issue became increasingly expressed in the anti-corporate language of populism. As one farmer, Steve Pollestad, expressed it, North Dakotans had a choice. They could put the future of wheat "in the hands of people who are accountable to the citizens of North Dakota. Or, we could let Monsanto decide. And maybe we also could get Enron to run our utilities and Arthur Anderson to keep the books."

Of course, Monsanto has been no stranger to controversy, including across-the-board rejection of its genetically engineered food products throughout Europe and Japan. But until the campaign against GE wheat, the company had never faced stiff opposition from American farmers themselves. Quite simply, if farmers themselves turned against GE wheat, then all of Monsanto's political success in blocking legislative bans would be rendered meaningless. With roughly 47 percent of the U.S. acreage for hard spring wheat located in North Dakota, acceptance of Roundup-ready spring wheat by that state was absolutely crucial.

On May 10, 2004, Monsanto issued a curt press release announcing the withdrawal of all its pending regulatory applications for Roundup-ready wheat and the shifting of research priorities to other crops. The main factor in the decision, the company noted obliquely, was "a lack of widespread wheat industry alignment."

By then, North Dakota farmers had already joined forces with a wide network of activists across the United States as well as internationally. One North Dakota farmer, Tom Wiley, traveled to Europe, Australia, and even Qatar to spread the message of revolt. In Poland he told a receptive audience, "You fought hard for your independence. Don't give up your freedom to the biotech corporations. Saving seed is a basic human right."

Outside North Dakota, the anti-GM revolt was also spreading. Two more states, South Dakota and Indiana, followed North Dakota's lead in enacting laws protecting farmers from intrusive inspections. And in three California counties citizens used the initiative process to pass local moratoriums on GE crops.

Meanwhile, Todd Leake turned his attention to making the right of seed saving, the right to "brown bag," into something that would be afforded formal protection even in international law.

The notion that human freedoms should encompass such economic rights in addition to political rights such as speech is not new. As early as 1933, it was eloquently expressed by Franklin Roosevelt, then running as a candidate for President in the depths of the Great Depression. "As I see it," Roosevelt told his audience, "the task of government ... is to assist the development of an economic declaration of rights." During his last term in office, Roosevelt developed the idea further, proposing a "second Bill of Rights" that would address issues of economic fairness and security. Following Franklin Roosevelt's death, Eleanor Roosevelt served as chair of the United Nations commission that drafted the Universal Declaration of Human Rights. Adopted in 1948, that document blends "first generation" political rights with "second generation" economic rights.

From 1994 to 2001, civic society groups from around the world met with government officials under the aegis of the United Nations' Food and Agriculture Organization to work out international protections for seed. The International Treaty on Plant Genetic Resources for Food and Agriculture, more commonly known as the Law of the Seed, is the outgrowth of this campaign.

The treaty, which went into force in 2004, embodies a great deal of unresolved tension between the newly emerging patent rights on genetic material, which have appeared on the U.S. scene since 1980, and the concept of Farmers Rights, including the right to save seed. In the final document, the articulation of Farmers Rights is forceful, but the enforcement mechanism is absent, making the treaty more a starting point than an ending one. Still, as the history of human rights shows, the clear articulation of a right in international law tends to endow a legitimacy that over time may acquire the force of law.

Within the United States, the fight over GE seed is just one manifestation of a new outbreak in populist politics, often taking place in supposedly conservative rural areas. Whereas Todd Leake and other North Dakota activists took inspiration from that state's particularly strong history of militancy, activists elsewhere have sought more deliberately to rediscover and formalize the lessons of populism. Some, like the Pennsylvania-based Community Environmental Legal Defense Fund (CELDF) and Montana-based Reclaim Democracy, have condensed these lessons into two- or three-day seminars. In Reclaim Democracy's "From Here to Democracy" classes, executive director Jeff Milchen stresses the importance of local activists stepping outside normal regulatory channels and taking issue with the underlying preconceptions that prop up corporate authority. Echoing Milchen, CELDF's Thomas Linzey urges activists in weekend "Democracy School" sessions to reject the "single issue" model of activism and instead mount direct challenges to corporate legal rights. In describing the virtues of the approach, Milchen and Linzey sound strikingly similar to A.C. Townley and other rabble-rousers of the World War I era. Both emphasize that, given the overwhelming cultural dominance of corporate power, any political strategy that hopes to effect real change must act as much at the level of culture and mentality as at the level of more tangible legal gain.

For several years, anti-corporate activists across the country have paid close attention to CELDF's implementation of populist politics, which has focused on local governing bodies, especially township governments. Perhaps the best example of CELDF's work has involved helping township governments block out-of-state sewage companies and hog farms. Rather than work through the normal state regulatory channels, which appear more effective at dissipating opposition than at stopping polluters, scores of townships working with CELDF have passed bold initiatives that deny corporations the protection of constitutional rights. In addition, borrowing a page from the North Dakota populists, CELDF has worked with Pennsylvania counties to pass anti-corporate farming laws as a means of blocking industrial sewage and industrial hog farming projects. Most recently, CELDF has helped two Pennsylvania townships establish new "home rule" constitutions, take advantage of a feature of the state's constitution enabling local jurisdictions to exercise basic powers if they choose to do so.

To some legal observers, the anti-corporate assertions of Pennsylvania's counties and townships seem foolhardy, since an entire body of judicial opinion has grown up in support of corporate prerogatives. But that, according to Richard Grossman, a historian on anti-corporate struggles who frequently advises CELDF on strategy, that is precisely the point. "Inevitably," says Grossman, "the corporate attorneys are drawn into a situation where they tell citizens: 'You have no right to do what you're doing.' But when corporations say that to regular Americans, it's fighting words. Now they're really mobilized."

Of course, having been mobilized to fight corporate power at the level of basic rights, most Americans may be startled by just how profoundly the system has come to be rigged against them. Consider, for starters, the whole slew of constitutional rights garnered by corporations since 1886, including the Fourteenth, Fourth, Fifth, Sixth, Seventh, and most crucially First Amendment (i.e. political) rights. Add to that the considerable powers won by corporations in the past decade via multilateral treaties like NAFTA and the WTO, which provide corporate tacticians a means to trump national environmental, labor, and safety standards. Next add a whole series of pro-corporate adjustments in little-remarked aspects of common law such as the increasingly restrictive limits on punitive damages in tort suits, the increasingly pro-corporate interpretation by the courts of the Commerce Clause, and the increasingly pro-corporate uses of eminent domain. Going further, add a broad array of legislatively-conferred advantages for corporations, from lucrative tax code depreciation schedules to blanket liability exemptions for entire industries to gutted environmental laws. Throw in the ongoing rise of the corporate apparatus of media, lobbying network, and public relations, backed by the triumph of the pro-Big Biz faction within both major political parties. And if that weren't enough, add the fact that most significant "countervailing power" against the corporate juggernaut, America's labor unions, appear every year to decay deeper into ineffectiveness and disunity.

All those aspects of corporate hegemony add up to an overwhelming advantage for the corporate side in almost any political dual. Along with that preponderance of formal power comes a sense of inevitability, of acceptability, of legitimacy that all too often proves overwhelming.

Yet however improbably, the populist streak in American politics continues to resurrect itself. As demonstrated in the skirmishes over Roundup-ready wheat, a corporation can appear to prevail in the formal halls of power and yet die a "death of a thousand cuts" in the court of public opinion. And while corporate power often rests on dusty precedents accumulated over history, populist movements seem astonishingly adept at building upon their own historical accomplishments. In North Dakota and across the Northern Plains, the spirit of populism continues to evolve not just in the history books but through grassroots political organizations working at every level from township government to multilateral treaty-making. Of these, the most remarkable example is the Western Organization of Resource Councils (WORC), a regional umbrella coordinating the work of scores of local grassroots groups.

The germ of WORC was the Montana strip-mining boom of the early 1970s, which produced a unique coalition of environmentalists and cattle ranchers that succeeded in enacting a series of upgrades to Montana's environmental laws. From their successes in fighting strip-mining, WORC's methods of organizing quickly spread to five neighboring states, where member organizations over the years have successfully confronted a host of rural issues, from livestock policy to hardrock mining. Tactically, WORC likewise maintains a breadth of flexibility, sometimes focusing on the minute details of regulations, other times seizing upon basic Constitutional issues. Regarding which tactics are most suitable in the building of a populist movement, program director John Smillie notes dryly, "In a knife fight, anything goes."

Whatever their tactical inclinations, activists agree across the board that the flexing of the populist muscle produces effects far beyond any single issue, creating a sense of empowerment that is the core of all successful movements. Moreover, the ramifications of any particular populist mobilization tend to emanate in all directions. In North Dakota, for example, the atmosphere surrounding genetic engineering technology has changed notably in the wake of the GE wheat uprising. For example, when the bio-pharmaceutical company Agrigen approached the North Dakota State University agriculture department seeking flax germ plasm for GE research, NDSU's leadership promptly rejected the initiative, an about-face from the pro-GE leanings that had previously characterized that institution.

Of course, the real effect of any movement, the way it changes the sense of individuals and groups as to what is "normal" and what is "possible," can never be precisely measured. To Todd Leake, the victory over Monsanto had everything to do such intangibles. "In state where the motto is, 'If you can't say anything nice…,' this is the real story," he said. "How farmers caught on, wised up, and stuck up for themselves."

A.C. Townley, the founder of the Non-Partisan League, would certainly agree. Himself a failed farmer, Townley must have known both the depths of demoralization and the triumphant sense of renewed possibility delivered by the populist uprising. At a League rally in Glen Ullin, North Dakota, when a heckler asked Townley what the Non-Partisan League had ever done for him, Townley retorted, "It gave you the courage to stand up and ask that question."

Chapter 3

"GO HOME, RED STATE REBELS!"

By Roxanne Dunbar-Ortiz

"The Empire... is a bread and butter question. If you want to avoid civil war, you must become imperialists."
—Cecil B. Rhodes, 1895

ONE THING ABOUT A red state person is you don't care to stand out too much. You like to pretend you are a rugged individual, but you crave being regarded as "normal" by your friends, family, community. "Normal" is a collective definition that everyone appears to understand from an early age. So, when you become rebellious or weird or queer, you leave for one of the big cities along large bodies of water on the edges of red statedness, and probably never return, at least not to live. Both your family and your community prefer it that way, because you aren't there to embarrass, puncture balloons, or get in trouble with various authorities. That's how red states stay red. There's no multiplier effect of rebellion.

But that means that red state rebels are everywhere. They rarely identify themselves as such. When asked where they are from they will mumble "the Midwest," or "the southwest," "California" (not specifying that they are Okie descendants from the Central Valley, a red state within a blue state). I always probe to find out from where exactly. Being from Oklahoma and having outed myself in print (*Red Dirt: Growing Up Okie*), and having lived in San Francisco for many years, I'm usually looking for stray Okies, but am glad to find a Carolinian or Tennessean, Scots-Irish descended possible distant relatives, or a recovering Southern Baptist like myself (or other Protestant fundamentalist) from anywhere. I love meeting the ones who have become left wing political radicals, artists, anti-militarists, anti-imperialists, feminists and pro-feminists, Marxists. Many others leave red states by way of joining the military, with few of them becoming radicals although they might acquire tattoos and smoke dope, which wouldn't be looked upon favorably back home.

When you study an electoral map of the United States, you find that the hardcore red states (not including the mixed ones designated as "purple") comprise the former member-states of the Confederacy, along with the border states of Oklahoma, Arkansas, Missouri, Kentucky, Ohio, Indiana, and West Virginia, and all the western states except for California, Oregon, Washington, and New Mexico. The populations of the red western states are mostly descendants of migrants from the southeast and southwest. The congressional districts within the red states that are populated mainly by Blacks, Latinos, or Native Americans are blue enclaves, and the university towns and urban centers/suburbs fade from red as well.

So, let's face it, red staters boil down to rednecks, hillbillies, Okies, crackers, overwhelmingly Southern Baptist or Pentecostal Protestant, descendants of early settlers, mostly dating back to colonial times. Many, if not most, are of Scots-Irish descent, descendents of old frontier settlers. The idea that the United States is a "nation of immigrants" is a convenient myth developed as a response to the 1960s movements against colonialism, neocolonialism, and white supremacy. The ruling class and its brain trust offered multiculturalism, diversity, and affirmative action in response to demands for decolonization, justice, reparations, social equality, an end of imperialism, and the rewriting of history—not to be "inclusive"—but to be accurate. What emerged to replace the liberal melting pot idea and the nationalist triumphal interpretation of the "greatest country on earth and in history," was the "nation of immigrants" story.

By the 1980s, the "waves of immigrants" story even included the indigenous peoples who were so brutally displaced and murdered by settlers and armies, accepting the flawed "Bering Straits" theory of indigenous immigration some 12,000 years ago. Even at that time, the date was known to be wrong; there was evidence of indigenous presence in the Americas as far back as 50,000 years ago, and probably much longer, and entrance by many means across the Pacific and the Atlantic—perhaps, as Vine Deloria Jr. put it, footsteps by indigenous Americans to other continents will one day be acknowledged. But, the new official history texts claimed, the indigenous peoples were the "first immigrants." They were followed, it was said, by immigrants from England and Africans, then by Irish, and then by Chinese, Eastern and Southern Europeans, Russians, Japanese, and Mexicans. There were some objections from African Americans to referring to enslaved Africans hauled across the ocean in chains as "immigrants," but that has not deterred the "nation of immigrants" chorus.

Misrepresenting the process of European colonization of North America, making everyone an immigrant, serves to preserve the "official story" of a mostly benign and benevolent USA, and to mask the fact that the pre-U.S. independence settlers, were, well, settlers, colonial setters, just as they were in Africa and India, or the Spanish in Central and South America. The United States was founded as a settler state, and an imperialistic one from its inception ("manifest destiny," of course). The settlers were English, Welsh, Scots, Scots-Irish, and German, not including the huge number of Africans who were unwillingly hauled over in chains. Another group of Europeans who arrived in the colonies also were not settlers or immigrants: the poor, indentured, convicted, criminalized, kidnapped from the working class (vagabonds and unemployed artificers), as Peter Linebaugh puts it, many of who opted to join indigenous communities. Most of those who are today characterized as "crackers," "rednecks," and "white trash" are their descendants. Many of them, once freed from indenture, headed for the frontier to live off the indigenous communities and finally stealing their land, replacing them, but only to lose it as they became trapped in the market economy.

Only beginning in the 1840s, with the influx of millions of Irish Catholics pushed out of Ireland by British policies, did what might be called "immigration" begin. The Irish were imported cheap labor, not settlers. They were followed by the influx of other workers from Scandinavia, Eastern and Southern Europe, always more Irish, plus Chinese and Japanese, although Asian immigration was soon barred. Immigration laws were not even enacted until 1875 when the U.S. Supreme Court declared the regulation of immigration a federal responsibility. The Immigration Service was established in 1891.

Buried beneath the tons of propaganda that passes for U.S. History—from the landing of the English "pilgrims" and "Puritans" (cults of fanatic Protestant Christian fundamentalists) to James Fennimore Cooper's phenomenally popular *Last of the Mohicans* claiming "natural rights" to take not only the indigenous peoples territories but also those territories claimed by other states—is the fact that the founding of the United States was a subdivision of the Anglo empire, with the U.S. becoming a parallel empire to Great Britain. From day one, as was specified in the Northwest Ordinance that preceded the U.S. Constitution, the new republic for empire (as Jefferson called the U.S.) envisioned the future shape of what is now the lower-48 states of the U.S. They drew up rough maps, specifying the first territory to conquer as the "Northwest Territory," ergo the title of the ordinance. That territory was the Ohio Valley and the Great Lakes region, which was filled with indigenous farming communities.

Once the conquest of the "Northwest Territory" was accomplished through a combination of genocidal military campaigns and bringing in European settlers from the east, and the indigenous peoples moved south and north for protection into other indigenous territories, the republic for empire annexed Spanish Florida where runaway enslaved Africans and remnants of the indigenous communities that had escaped the Ohio carnage fought back during three major wars (Seminole wars) over two decades. In 1828, President Andrew Jackson (who had been a general leading the Seminole wars) pushed through the Indian Removal Act to force all the agricultural indigenous nations of the Southeast, from Georgia to the Mississippi River, to transfer to Oklahoma territory that had been gained through the "Louisiana Purchase" from France.

Anglo settlers seized the indigenous agricultural lands for plantation agriculture worked by enslaved Africans in the Southeastern region. Many moved on into the Mexican province of Texas—then came the U.S. military invasion of Mexico in 1846, seizing Mexico City and forcing Mexico to give up its northern half through the 1848 Treaty of Guadalupe Hidalgo. California, Arizona, New Mexico, Colorado, Utah, Texas were then opened to "legal" Anglo settlement, also legalizing those who had already settled illegally, and in Texas by force. The indigenous and the poor Mexican communities in the seized territory, such as the Apache, Navajo, and Comanche, resisted colonization, as they had resisted the Spanish empire, often by force of arms, for the next 40 years. The small class of Hispanic elites welcomed and collaborated with U.S. occupation.

Is the term "immigrants" the appropriate designation for the indigenous peoples of North America? No.

Is the term "immigrants" the appropriate designation for enslaved Africans? No.

Is the term "immigrants" the appropriate designation for Mexicans who migrate for work to the United States? No. They are migrant workers crossing a border created by U.S. military force. Many crossing that border today are also from Central America, from the small countries that were ravaged by U.S. military intervention in the 1980s and who also have the right to make demands on the United States.

Finally, is the term "immigrants" the appropriate designation for the original Anglo and Scots-Irish settlers? No.

These people, particularly those that made up a virtual civilian army squatting on indigenous lands outside the British, then U.S. boundaries, carry the national origin story upon which U.S. nationalism is based, and they are ideologues and literalists, both with the Bible and the U.S. origin story. It's a package passed down through the generations, wars refreshing the story, its purity, washed in blood. These are the Jefferson/Jackson people. It's no accident the electoral college was established so that urbanites would never be allowed to dominate the state; they may have their enclaves in the big cities and on university campuses. No accident that the blue-blooded, WASP ruling class Bush family moved to Texas in order to come to open political power. The Democratic Party, founded by the ultimate redneck, Andrew Jackson, was destroyed when its favorite son, LBJ, signed the Civil Rights Act of 1964. The Republican "Southern strategy" was implemented successfully. Thomas Frank, author of *What's the Matter with Kansas?*, is dead wrong; these people know exactly what their interests are, and it may not reside in the Republican Party, but it surely isn't the Democratic Party. Most of them just don't vote, but the Republican Party has been able to galvanize a strong constituency from that base by hooking up with the fundamentalist churches and the ideology of white settler supremacy.

To understand the red state constituency, and the great potential of red state rebels, it's essential that we abolish the mythical grid through which we are brainwashed to view the founding and development of the United States. Few red state rebels have done this. Woody Guthrie came close, but in singing "this land is your land; this land is my land…" he fulfilled the ideals of his namesake, Woodrow Wilson, the ultimate Scots-Irish old settler, and imperialist. We have to acknowledge that the U.S. is a settler-state, not a nation of immigrants, and it's an empire, not a nation-state. Canada, Australia, New Zealand, and the Latin American states are similarly constituted, but none of them dominate the world or even come close, although the character of white supremacy in those societies is similar.

Settler states with minority descendants of settlers, such as Guatemala, Bolivia, Ecuador, South Africa, can seize majority rule, not that all have, but no such possibility exists for the indigenous in settler-states in which the majority are immigrants who are just trying to be a part of the settler state and be accepted as "real Americans." With decolonization, European settlers either left the newly liberated states in Africa, Asia, the Caribbean, and the Pacific or stayed on under majority rule. The U.S. has had some thorny issues explaining hanging on to its overseas colonies acquired in the early 20th century—Puerto Rico, Guam, Marshall Island, Samoa, Philippines—while it illegally created states of Hawaii and Alaska. No one, except Native Americans, questioned the U.S. continental holdings, proving that genocide is an effective political instrument. Left, right, and center have in common an allergy to delving into the effects of the U.S. being a settler-state and simply find the descendants of the gnarly old setters repugnant. If there were no surviving descendants of the indigenous peoples, no surviving descendants of old settlers, no surviving descendants of Mexicans in the northern half of Mexico appropriated by the U.S., no surviving descendants of enslaved Africans, perhaps this history would be less important, but that's even hard to figure. Had genocide, assimilation, and segregation been wholly successful, it would be an even more perverse social order and more dangerous to the survival of humanity than it is.

Christian Protestant fundamentalism is not the core issue as I once thought. If so, atheism or liberal religion would work, but it doesn't, because the true religion is Americanism. And the debate between the Democratic and Republican camps concerns interpretations of Americanism. Rebels have been relatively ineffective in changing the course of U.S. history precisely because they haven't challenged "Americanism" and haven't acknowledged their true history. Some have tried to replace "Americanism" for a time with "internationalism" or fellow traveling with various socialist states or by rationalism, but without comprehending the myth and its power, in fact accepting it as a given, nothing works. After all, rationalism by definition does not consider anything other than the present reality and certainly not emotions, passions, love, hate, identity, all of which make up any nationalism, which is what "Americanism" is. Even when Protestant fundamental missionaries go evangelizing among the dark and poor overseas, they carry the message of Americanism. Some have inferred that they form fronts for the CIA, and they do in a sense, but not with pay or prior arrangement, just a common goal of promoting Americanism.

Sometimes, I think I may be the only leftist, Marxist, feminist, anti-imperialist, anti-racist in the United States who was raised as a Protestant Christian fundamentalist. I remained an evangelizing true believer of the Southern Baptist faith (the largest Christian denomination in the U.S.) in rural Oklahoma until I was 19 years old. My dream growing up was to be a missionary. Leftist accounts or opinions about such individuals and groups strike me as being correct in expressing alarm, but also based on acute ignorance combined with hatred for the lower classes, particularly poor and working-class whites, particularly in the South. Most such self-appointed "experts" steer away from dealing with Protestant fundamentalism among Latinos (the fastest growing market) and African Americans (a majority) and focus on poor whites, the last bigotry that is tolerated by most of the left.

Although there are at least two high-profile WASP "born agains" from the blueblood Eastern ruling class—George W. Bush and Pat Robertson—they are atypical; most Protestant fundamentalists grow up in the poorer segment of the working class, often rural, as I did. The proto-fascist right wing (now mainstream ruling class) has been able to capture and promote for their own ends a mass movement that took off in the Reagan administration but had been brewing since the 1950s when Protestant fundamentalism and patriotism merged under the banner of anti-communism. Politicized fundamentalism was born in the vortex of Cold-War anti-communism and in opposition to school integration that followed the *Brown v. Board of Education* Supreme Court decision of 1954. It took three more decades for political fundamentalism to begin achieving national electoral hegemony, fired by a new cause, ostensibly women's right to have abortions that was legalized nationally with the *Roe v. Wade* Supreme Court decision in 1973. Ostensibly, because the right wing backlash was much larger than abortion and went to the heart of the ancient socio-political-cultural acceptance of patriarchy by both men and women, which, as a result of the mass women's movement in the preceding years, was shattered. Gay liberation picked up steam during the same period. Less than a decade later, the right wing brought Ronald Reagan to the presidency, although the anti-women's rights movement had scored victories under born-again Jimmy Carter's administration.

The right wing, hiding under the cover of anti-communism and coded white supremacy (crime, welfare, pre-marital pregnancy), continued under the guise of "protecting the family." But, behind those masks were and are interests that favor the military-industrial ruling class, which pushes for the end of social spending, leaving the state as a vehicle solely for the benefit of capitalism and the war machine. Everything is to be privatized, with the imagined nuclear family as the self-sustaining core of the social order.

The Democratic Party is simply incapable of challenging organized fundamentalism and the transformed Republican Party. Many liberals and a good number of leftists seek to restore the New-Deal-to-War-on-Poverty stance of government, but the policies of that era were driven by the organized working class in the first instance and the Civil Rights Movement in the second; those government policies were stopgaps to prevent the overthrow of capitalism. Now it is obvious that they did not go to the root causes of oppression and exploitation, and it is doubtful that the reform strategies of the past can be re-enacted today or in the future.

What concerns me is not so much that the ruling class has come to this strategy of populist fascism with politicized Christian fundamentalism as its mass base—after all, capitalism is a corrupt and unworkable (for the many) system—as that so many of those who are committed to social justice, even to a future socialist society, have written off the poor and the working class that they perceive to make up the "mass movement" of this project. Instead of working to unmask the agenda of the ruling class, many liberal and left activists are trying to figure out how to offer religion lite and avoid the issues of abortion, gay liberation, and other "social" issues. One thing I know about Protestant Christian fundamentalists from having been one, however, is that it cannot be substituted with "spirituality" or liberalism.

Christian fundamentalism/evangelism is a precariously balanced house of cards that dwells in the mind of an individual. Remove one card, and down it comes. It is a self-contained system. Just ask any of us red state rebels who got away. Once the belief system is accepted, no rational argument can penetrate the mind of the converted. The system rests on quite simple assumptions: you have heard the word of god personally calling you; you have been "born again" or "saved"; you recognize that Jesus is the true son of god who died for your sins; the Bible is literally the truth, the word of god. You do not have to be baptized to be a "born again," but it is recommended, and it must be immersion at an age of reasoning, not sprinkling babies (Catholic) or adults (Methodist, etc.). To be a member of a Southern Baptist church (or some other fundamentalist church), you must be baptized by immersion. When I "went forward" to be "saved" at age 13, I took the preacher literally when he said I didn't have to be baptized, and because I was asthmatic and terrified of being without breath, I said I would prefer not to be baptized. For two years, the preacher, his wife, my mother, the deacons, and nearly every member of the church visited me to try to talk to me about being baptized, and I finally caved. It was two years, everyone else in my age group had been baptized—an embarrassing and terrifying experience. Nor are preachers necessary, theoretically. The "saved" are said to have a "personal relationship with Christ" and can interpret the Bible for themselves without interlopers. But why would anyone choose to do that when the preachers and revivals are so exciting? And in rural areas and small towns, colorful fundamentalist preachers are the best shows around.

When I hear Jim Wallis (God's Peoples) call himself an evangelical, I have to laugh. I know what he means: Christianity inherently is evangelical, but he is no fundamentalist. Wallis tries to convince his ignorant, liberal, secular audience that his kind of "evangelism" can challenge the "bad" kind. Not a chance. I wish it were so. I tried to make the transfer when I was nineteen years old. I fell in love with a fellow Oklahoman my age who was an atheist. Fortunately, for me, he did everything he could to free me of my fundamentalism, which took about six months. He had read the Bible (he was raised Christian in a liberal family) and could argue me down mostly using arguments from science, particularly evolution and astronomy. Scientific knowledge became more majestic to me than the Book of Revelation and the Rapture. It is no wonder that fundamentalists insist purging evolution from the schools. The *Chronicle of Higher Education* reported in 2006 that forty percent of biology teachers in the public schools avoid teaching evolution, not all because of their beliefs, rather to avoid harassment from fundamentalist groups and parents.

I didn't immediately become an atheist, however; I still believed in a human-like creator god. I joined the Presbyterian church and was married in that church. The services were so boring and reserved that I left it after a year, and tried the Lutherans. I joined a small congregation in Oklahoma City that held services in German. I loved the Martin Luther hymns in German, which—in

English—were also favorites in the Baptist church, but I was the only attendee under sixty years old. Later, my husband and I moved to San Francisco, and I enrolled at San Francisco State College, where I joined the Unitarian church. There was no talk of Christ or God, but I found it boring also, a waste of a Sunday morning when I could be reading. I had the good fortune to take a historical geology course from an evangelical atheist, who convinced me that a creator god was something I no longer believed in. Then, I found Marxism in my second year at San Francisco State—at last, a set of fundamental beliefs I could be inspired by and excited about. Nothing less than an equally fiery passion can replace fundamentalism in the mind of one seasoned by its flames.

However, it's important to acknowledge that war, marketed as national defense (we are surrounded by enemies), has been a means for the ruling classes to solidify national unity and consensus since the founding of the United States, even during the New Deal era and its aftermath into the 1960s. Since the defeat in Vietnam, that has not been so easy.

It's odd how white northern volunteers in the Southern Civil Rights struggles of the early 1960s had no problem tolerating the Protestant fundamentalism of Blacks, but today those vets, as well as new generations of leftists and liberals find Protestant fundamentalism among poor and working class white to be repulsive. It's a class thing. The liberal elites consider Blacks the other, while whites are reflections of their own shaky superiority. As Rep. Charlie Rangel said, when he asked his opinion of President George W. Bush, "He proves that white supremacy is a lie."

The descendants of the old settlers don't have a tangible economic interest in their sense of lordship, as protectors of the founding myths, nor are they explained entirely by white supremacy, which is one school of thought. They are deeply ideological and moralistic in their concern.

Many of my leftist friends look to a demographic solution, where the old settlers swamped with immigrants, something the oligarchy have attempted for over a century. This scenario complements the fear mongering about the possible disappearance of Euroamericans due to Mexican immigration touted by right wing racists. But, if Americanism as the ruling ideology is the issue, why wouldn't future generations of immigrants adopt or bow to it as have past immigrants? I think the solution lies elsewhere. I think it resides in those people who represent the origin story, particularly the young among the red state rebels, not all of whom are leaving these days. The solution lies in rebellion.

No one likes to be taken for a fool, not least rednecks. Here, the old adage, "the truth will make you free," still resonates.

The first book I wrote, in 1974, was a history of land tenure in New Mexico. The book was published in a new and updated edition in 2007. In researching, revising, and writing new text for it, I returned to the land question in the United States. And land remains on my mind, what in the Marxist tradition is called the agrarian question, as the crux of the issue of the red state phenomena. Marx and Engels saw little revolutionary potential in agrarian communities; only when farmers were deprived of the land and forced into proletarian dependency and alienation could they become revolutionary and smash capitalism. But, with 20th century decolonization movements in Asia, Africa, and Latin America, the agrarian question became unavoidable, so Maoism took up the banner of agrarian revolution. Unfortunately, with the discrediting of Maoism during the past three decades, the agrarian question has nearly disappeared in our thinking about revolution and social transformation. Yet, for the majority of humanity that still lives off the land as farmers or agricultural workers, it remains the only question. The anarchist tradition is much closer to the land, but these issues are hardly discussed in U.S. anarchist circles.

The part of North America seized by British, then U.S. settlers, 1607–1850, was made up of indigenous farmers. And from first settlement to the 1930s, it remained principally agrarian. European settlers, mainly from England, Scotland, and Ireland, were overwhelmingly farmers, peasants, from generations of the same. They came to North America looking for land to farm. With the support of the British colonial institutions, and later the United States government and military, these settlers appropriated land from the indigenous farmers, a kind of original sin that has seldom been acknowledged. Poor Anglo farmers without slaves, the great majority of settler farmers, could not compete on the market with the enslaved African labor enjoyed by plantation operators. But they could raise their own food and feed their families and even have some surplus to sell or barter. And in working the land, they came to love the land.

With the 1846–48 United States war against Mexico, the northern half of Mexico became the U.S. Southwest, populated by both indigenous and Mexican farmers, who were descendants of Spanish settlers, mixed with Indians. Following the Civil War and emancipation, Africans were freed from enslavement, and some received reparations in land taken from plantation owners or in new territories that had been seized. Africans had been farmers in Africa when they were enslaved, and they had worked the land in North American in bondage.

By 1880, a little over fifty percent of the U.S. population was farming, but the proportion declined to seventeen percent in 1940, dwindling to about two percent by the year 2000. What happened to those who would have become farmers? Were they no longer needed? Growing food remained and will remain a necessity, but large corporations took over the land and displaced individual farmers. Patriotism—in the form of allegiance to a distant government, with its flag and other symbols, with its wars in distant lands—has filled the black hole left by the loss of land and a way of life they craved, however harsh. For would anyone choose to endure the hardships of farming, if it were not for irrepressible love? Yes, farm laborers (as well as enslaved Africans) were forced to plant and pick crops for corporate planters in earlier times and have been compelled to do so for huge agribusiness concerns since their rise, but they too came (and still come) from peasant cultures and would prefer to farm their own land if they could. The settlers came for land—those Scots-Irish, Germans, Japanese, and so many other peasants from faraway places where their land had been seized or their commons enclosed. Armies assisted in pushing indigenous farmers off the land they farmed or where they followed the game, so that settler peasants could own a piece of land, only to lose it through intentional government policies, supposedly to create "efficiency."

What happens to a society when it literally loses its roots in the earth? We take for granted that some of us are born to music or mechanics or mathematics, to the word or the brush and canvas. May there not be those whose heart is in the earth, in tending it, in planting, growing, and harvesting? Indeed for the Pueblo Indians and Hopi of New Mexico and Arizona, corn is the center of their religion. What becomes of those so born and their progeny? They become throwaway people, no longer needed. Yet, we still need to eat the fruit of the earth, or for that matter, the bounty of the sea—I expect the same applies to fishing communities. Why do we as a society choose to replace ten thousand farmers with an absentee corporation? It isn't more productive, but even if it were, is it moral to destroy the lives of so many that want only to farm?

Not only have U.S. government policies destroyed subsistence farming in North America; now they are trying to destroy it in distant lands with their "free trade" agreements—the World Trade Organization, the North American

Free Trade Association, the Central America Free Trade Agreement, and the Free Trade Area of the Americas. Mexico changed its constitution to do away with the *ejido*, the land reform measure from the Mexican Revolution in the early 1900s, driving millions of farmers off the land and to the U.S. border to cross illegally for jobs. China is doing away with the collective farms that have been so successful in feeding its vast population, most of whom were starving before the Chinese Revolution. French and Japanese protection of small farmers has been challenged in trade courts by the United States.

My father was a born farmer in Oklahoma, but he never owned his own land. For years, he rented farms or sharecropped. When he could no longer do that because the medium-sized farmers who employed him went under and were replaced by corporations, something in him died. He moved to Oklahoma City and worked as a roofer. The second half of his life—he died at age 93—was painful. His tragedy is ours as a society. This is not to say that everyone, or even many, would want to return to farming the land, and I am one who would not, even if I could. But, two percent of the population still working the land is far too few to provide the balance a society requires. Farmers fought long and hard to stay on the land. The Muskogees and the Cherokees and the other Algonquin farmers of the eastern half of North America fought to keep their land, and lost. The Pueblo Indians fought and still fight to farm. The settler farmers who took indigenous lands fought to farm throughout the nineteenth century and even through the 1930s, finally crushed by the Great Depression and drought—Dust Bowl days. That was the excuse. Actually, New Deal policies were themselves designed to end subsistence farming. Farmers could have survived with government assistance, but the New Deal allowed banks to foreclose and destroyed surplus food production to maintain high prices, while people were starving. The government could have bought and distributed the food they destroyed ("dumped in the ocean," my father used to say). So much for the free market—free only with government intervention on the side of the corporations and finance capital. Those Dust Bowl refugees were put to work picking cotton and fruit for agribusiness in California, the Pacific Northwest, and Arizona, until the war industry grew, and they went to work in defense plants.

Think of all of those angry ex-farmers and wannabe farmers making bombs and fighter planes. Whole new generations followed in that nasty work, a good many others serving in the military, now transformed into a business, not a civic duty. They get to drop the bombs and man the guns on the tanks that the others manufacture. Subsistence farmers like peace—not war that takes away their young sons, and now daughters. Getting rid of them, reducing them to a tiny minority, has made military recruitment and passive acceptance of war much easier than during World War I, when farmers rose up in rebellion, as did workers, against a "war for big business," which all modern wars are. Why would we be surprised by increased violence (requiring more jails and cops than schools and teachers)? Why are we surprised that blind patriotism and a promise of heaven after death, even Apocalypse, as scripted in the Book of Revelation, would replace love of the land and of all living things? And consider all that land given to agribusiness, drying up the aquifers, poisoning the air and soil with nitrates from fertilizers, spraying pesticides, and now spreading genetically modified plants and cloned cows and hogs.

Embracing the agrarian question changes our perspective on historical issues, such as our understanding of settler-colonialism as the basis of forming capitalism in the United States, as the basis for genocide. It also allows us to consider, for instance, the so-called immigration issue, which is, after all, an agrarian question. Mexican and Central American farmers are being pushed off the land, many continuing work in agriculture here, but most are being pushed into sweatshops or hog-killing factories. They are migrant workers, not immigrants, and they would rather be able to survive on the land in Mexico. Surely, the most critical crime against humanity was the commodification of land, which forms the core of capitalism. Let's think about the land, learn to love it, understand that it is sacred because it is sustenance. Let us, the red state rebels, take up the agrarian question.

Chapter 4

TURNING OFF THE OGALLALA SPIGOT: TOWARD A NEW WAY TO FARM ON THE GREAT PLAINS

By Julene Bair

IT IS NO MYSTERY why Great Plains farmers irrigate. My farming father and grandfathers struggled against the weather odds in our dry western end of Kansas their whole lives. It seldom rained enough, and each year they took a gut-wrenching gamble planting their wheat.

In the late 1960s, technology came to the rescue. My father put in his first irrigation well. With well water, he could engineer his own rainfall and also grow more lucrative crops such as corn and soybeans. When his old heart finally failed him 30 years after he began irrigating, he owned five wells.

Our farm's original well happens to be among those monitored by the Kansas Geological Survey. I visited the agency's Web site recently and was as dismayed by a graph there as I had been watching my father's failing vital signs on the hospital monitor. Both tracked the approach of death—with one significant difference. My father died naturally at the end of a normal human lifespan. We are killing much of the Ogallala Aquifer, draining water that took thousands of years to accumulate. Without this waste, the water would sustain life for many generations to come.

During his evolution from dryland to irrigated farming, my father became part of a system that can't be sustained, because it depends on burning nonrenewable energy to pump nonrenewable water from this ancient aquifer, which stretches from South Dakota to Texas. Most of this energy and water goes into producing corn that is then fed to cattle.

To grow corn, farmers plowed up more of their grass.

"How else could we feed the world?" my father would say when I lamented the loss.

But he could have fed the world more healthfully and less wastefully if he had skipped the corn and shipped beef directly from his grass to the table. Compared with grain-fattened feedlot beef, grass-fed beef is much lower in artery-clogging saturated fat and contains more omega-3 fatty acids, which are thought to aid cardiovascular health. When we eat meat from grass-fed animals, we profit from their ability to convert protein from a self-renewing resource, the grasses that grew here in the first place.

I used to accuse my father of being environmentally insensitive. He knew that the aquifer was finite and allowed that "they will have to stop us eventually"—they being the government.

"Until they do, though," he said, "I got mine!"

He loved to infuriate me with that response. I especially hated that the federal farm program underwrote the waste by offering price supports for corn.

But as one of my father's profiteering heirs, now I too am part of the entrenched and inefficient system. Turning off the spigots would reduce the flow of cash land rent into my pocket by two-thirds.

That prospect troubles me. But not as much as other numbers. There are more than 880 irrigation wells in our county. Out of our five alone we have pumped more than 6 billion gallons of water. That's enough to keep the 5,000 people of Goodland, the town nearest our farm, in water for more than 10 years. An aquarium covering a football field would need walls over 2.5 miles high to hold that much water.

Our farm recently signed up for a government conservation program that is helping us cut our water use by 50 percent. But even at this rate we are wasting water.

The time has come for "them" to stop us—all of us. Instead of price supports for corn, Plains farmers need help switching back to dryland crops or grass-fed livestock. Among the dryland crops may be seed sources of oil that could be turned into biodiesel, reducing our nation's dependence on fossil fuels.

I would vote for any legislator who pushes to end irrigation out of the Ogallala. I believe that I am not the only farmer or farm heir who would. We grew up on this land drinking this water, and know its real value can't be measured monetarily. We will rally behind genuine leaders who will argue their own consciences and awaken ours.

Chapter 5

"WE'RE GONNA BE HEROES": BURNING RAINBOW FARM

By Dean Kuipers

REAL ESTATE KING TOM Crosslin should have been a hero in the evangelical Christian stronghold of the red portion of western Michigan— he was a Republican who voted for both Bushes, a self-made rich man who drove a Rolls Royce and a red Ford F-350 and a Jaguar, a philanthropist, a bedrock libertarian who believed in freedom of religion and privacy above all else. Church groups even set up tents at his nationally famous hemp festivals, where bands played for days on his sprawling Rainbow Farm and advocates pushed for the legalization of marijuana. But then the county prosecutor took his son, and threatened to take his land, and Crosslin and his gay lover went to war against their government.

AUGUST 31, 2001

"I can't believe they haven't killed you boys already."
—Merle Haggard, first meeting Tom Crosslin and Rollie Rohm
on Rainbow Farm, July 2000.

Rainbow Farm campground was empty on the Friday morning Tom Crosslin burned the place to the ground. Two teenage lovers named Omar Alham and Vanessa Hunckler had been the last to leave, taking down their tent two days before, but that red morning they were flying toward it again, fishtailing down the dirt road that was starting to washboard because nobody had paid to grade it that summer, dust billowing in a monster ecru cloud behind. Tom hadn't really told them why they had to leave, he'd said only "stuff's happening," but they'd taken that as enough of a statement from a place that had been a living statement for years. Omar had been crashing at the farm on and off since the 4th of July, along with a lot of other people, and Nessa—she shortened it to Nessa—had just returned to it in a kind of pilgrimage.

Tom's eviction had been direct, but in his eyes they saw a glimmer of the generosity and hope that had caused people to gather on his property for years, and that had brought them back one more time. So Omar's big car bounced through the swamp bottoms of southwestern Michigan at 80 mph and Nessa clung to the door, the baby-blue 1987 Mercury Grand Marquis barely hitting its top range as he took the back way to the farm, Fox to Quaker to Kirk Lake Road, where there were never any cops. Orange caution tape wrapped around the car sizzled and fried at speed, and the front bumper rattled where it hung by duct tape, the noise sending pigs bolting up from their feeders and putting chickens on the wing. The campers at Rainbow Farm had called the car the Hempulance because Omar flung it along the county roads like an emergency vehicle, driving fast as a point of pride and carrying the weed, arriving just in time with the antidote to ordinary blues. Now it seemed like it was Rainbow Farm that needed saving.

On any other Labor Day weekend, as many as 5000 people would have been pouring through the Rainbow Farm gates for Roach Roast, their annual fall camp out where Tommy Chong or Merle Haggard or Big Brother and the Holding Co. would play on the big stage and the best-known hemp advocates in the country would preach the legalization of marijuana. It had been that way since 1995, when Tom Crosslin and his lover Rollie Rohm had begun hosting festivals there.

Now they were in some kind of trouble, and Omar and Nessa weren't too certain of the technicalities. Tom and Rollie had been busted for growing some pot in May, and they were in a big feud with the county prosecutor. The Memorial Day festival had been canceled but the Labor Day blowout had still been a go until a few days earlier, when suddenly Tom shut the gates and started talking about how he and Rollie were going to be heroes.

It was only 8 a.m. when he slid to a stop in front of the campground store in a spray of dust and gravel.

Tom was sitting on a picnic table in front of the farm's coffee shop, under a wooden sign that read The Joint, burning a fattie and drinking coffee with

Rollie in the shade of the building's long porch. This was the morning ritual, and the men shared the ease of having been together for 11 years. But both were also dressed in camouflage fatigue shirts and pants, still a little cardboard-stiff, and new boots. The look didn't suit them. Tom was 46 and normally wore jeans, running shoes, and a T-shirt with a windbreaker. Sometimes he'd choose a tie-dye when Rainbow Farm festivals were on. Longhaired, skinny Rollie was younger than Tom, only 28, and still looked like a kid. He was partial to T-shirts and Levis and baggie genie pants.

Tom didn't smile. The summer had run him down, his weight had dropped from about 230 on a medium frame to 210 or so, but his face was still round and his eyes kept up their friendly droop at the corners. His thin brown hair was clean but lay flat on his skull. Tom made an impression as a large, softly charismatic man with his fast talk and pale blue eyes, but he was quiet now. He was hungover. Rollie seemed similarly preoccupied.

Jimmy Lee "Jimbo" Collett sat with them too. A powerfully-built man of 40, he worked at the farm and lived some of the time in a travel trailer on the back side of the big campstore. He shaved his head to accentuate his muscular bulk and had a little black goatee, and was also wearing camo. Omar and Nessa were his friends, and in a moment of quiet inspiration he'd given the Hempulance its name.

"They knew we were coming back that morning," Vanessa told me later. The night before, the two had been partying at the farm and Tom had promised Omar he could have two cans of dayglo paint, pink and green, that had been used to paint the farm's 1932 Farmall tractor. The psychedelic tractor had become an icon, a symbol of Rainbow Farm, especially after farmhand Travis Hopkins had appeared that summer on the cover of the regional paper, the *South Bend Tribune*, perched atop a tractor and giving a defiant, raised-fist salute.

"We had no idea what they were gonna do," Nessa said. "We didn't even know that they was supposed to be going to court that day. But there was something in the air."

Even then, the two 18-year-olds wondered why anything had to change. The place looked the same. From the gravel parking lot where they stood talking, the building that held The Joint and the big camp store and the shower rooms stretched away to the north. To the west, gravel paths and two-tracks led back through acres of grass campsites to the 10-acre festival field, a kind of natural bowl where a covered wooden stage poked off the top of a hill. To the south, directly across the parking lot, was a large, comfortable two-story farmhouse where Tom and Rollie lived. Sided in light green and trimmed out in cream with a gray-green roof, the house grabbed mention as having been beautifully redone. Behind the house to the southwest was a seven-acre marsh, part of which was dug out as a pond.

Chickens were burring low in the henhouse in the backyard. Red-winged blackbirds set up their electric whirring on the pond. Omar and Vanessa swung at early-morning deerflies. The place smelled and sounded right, but something dark had opened up in its heart, a presence that made the two teenagers nervous. They didn't understand who was coming to take this all away, but Tom kept saying, "All they're gonna get is ashes."

For a couple days they had watched Tom turn festival guests away from the campground, saying, "The farm is over," and "They've messed with us too long, and we just can't do it anymore. You guys are gonna have to go home." The people who showed up were travelers and Rainbow Family crusties and union workers, libertarian fomenters and conspiracists and blue-collar weekenders, academics and spontaneous dancers, all looking for space and amplified music. They came to remote Cass County, Michigan, from across the state line in Elkhart, Indiana, or from big trees Oregon or big horizons Oklahoma or the big 'burbs from Florida to Quebec. Almost everyone who came to the festivals was looking to smoke grass and promote legalization. But this time they had to just burn one and split. Tom let them take a free T-shirt or a pack of Rainbow Farm rolling papers or any sodas that might be left in the store, then closed the gate behind them.

Nikki Lester, who had managed the camp store, stopped by the day before and left with a "bad feeling." One of Tom's best friends from the village of Vandalia, Dwight Vowell, Sr., had been there that same day with a truck and Tom had told him to take everything of any value out of the store—groceries and camping supplies and the espresso machine and the hot case for the nacho cheese dip, plus the glass cases that held the extensive headshop and all the Tommy Chong bongs, pipes, urine test kits and Rainbow Farm lighters and Frisbees that were left. Travis Hopkins said he knew that "shit was coming down." The farm's former manager Doug Leinbach, who had known Tom for 30 years and over that span had been his most trusted friend, was there on Wednesday afternoon and said Tom was "desperate." He wasn't acting right.

"Just like if you back a wild animal up into a corner, you're going to see them react differently than when they're free to roam about the land that they're used to," said Doug.

Tom thrived on conflict and brinksmanship, so no one knew for sure where any of this was leading. The state was going to prosecute him and Rollie, and Rollie's 12-year-old son, Robert, who had grown up on Rainbow Farm, was in foster care. Tom had lots of lawyers and had survived many legal battles on his properties in the past. He'd worked for eight years outfitting Rainbow Farm with stages, a store, equipment and staff. He'd spent hundreds of thousands of dollars, and now he'd stripped it all away in a week.

Omar noticed the flags on the flagpole had changed since the night before. There had always been an American flag, a rainbow flag that symbolized gay unity, and a small white flag bearing a red cross to recognize medical marijuana. Now the American flag flew upside down, a universal symbol of distress.

Omar and Nessa got the paint, but stayed less than 15 minutes. "Tom wouldn't let us stay," Omar said. "They were puffing a bowl, and I was like, 'Hey, I want to stay and smoke one more bowl.' He was like, 'No, you can't. You gotta go.'"

"'But,' Tom said, 'watch the news tonight,'" added Nessa.

They were all crying, except for Rollie, who wasn't one much for tears.

"Tom didn't say what he was gonna do," added Omar. "They kept saying they were gonna be heroes. Tom didn't say it first. Jimbo was crazy, I bet he said it first. Rollie wasn't saying a lot besides, 'It's time for this to end.'"

Omar honked and spun the tires of the Hempulance as he gunned the car out of the gate. He looked in his rear-view mirror. "They were standing there and Tom gave me a Nixon, you know what I mean? Two victory signs; two peace signs."

***

Tom Crosslin embraced the country life. He had raised hogs and turkeys and cows and painted a cartoon pig on his mailbox. He had trucked extra produce from his big gardens to soup kitchens. Like a farmer, he was in the habit of rising at dawn, always the first up, making strong coffee to go with a little green bud from the tupperware dish they kept in the kitchen. Most of the stash was Mexican that summer; he and Rollie had to cut back. They couldn't afford the hydroponic smoke they called "lawyer bud" anymore unless a friend gave them some, which was the only charity Tom Crosslin would abide. He'd caffeinate and marinate, then walk the two-track that circled his 54-acre farm with a gentle Rottweiler dog named Thai Stick, making notes on improvements.

Building improvements were his money business. During the summer of 2001, he still owned seven of the many properties he'd purchased in the area, most of them in the nearby village of Vandalia and 30 miles away in Elkhart. Over the years, there had been so many properties, even his bookkeeper lost count, but one court survey indicated there had been at least 52 at one point and maybe as many as 80 overall—rental units, single-family houses, commercial spaces—a good number of which he'd sold off in order to build Rainbow Farm.

Around noon that Friday, he scuffed through the wet grass with Thai Stick, his pockets filled with matches and lighters. He was a man who lived large, a man with a thousand friends, and a man who knew the power of symbolism and large gestures.

He stopped at a newish, double-wide modular building set up on cinder blocks beside a line of walnut and cherry trees. This was the farm's production office, where entertainment coordinator Derrik DeCraene had kept sound equipment and hour upon hour of tape—all the speakers, all the bands, the whole recent history of a place that become the center of the marijuana movement in Michigan.

Far off, a dog barked on Black Street and Thai Stick turned her head. Over the cornfields to the west, a black cloud of starlings formed and reformed, jerking through the air. The morning heat raised up the hovering insects, a kind of suspended tonnage in mosquitos, deerflies, gnats and no-see-ums waiting to add their chitins to the earth.

Tom opened the door to the production office. It was packed with bales of dry straw. He nudged the dog out of the way and ignited the golden hay. Once it caught, it went up with a sickening thud, like a body hitting a wood floor. As the flames licked out the windows and consumed the building, he calmed the dog and walked toward the pump house in the field. That would be the next to go.

***

It is indicative of how the situation had decayed at Rainbow Farm that when Buggy Brown saw the smoke from the fire, he did not call the fire department.

He had originally moved to Vandalia to be part of the farm's activism, and in the last few days he had been afraid of something like this. He also made a point of not taking the roads when he drove over there that morning, because he knew someone coming down Pemberton Road might get shot. Instead, he took the dirt lanes between cornfields and entered through a farm gate off the back of the property.

Buggy and his co-worker Richard Deans were milking cows at the farm of Ann File, the matriarch of a prominent local family whose several connected hog farms butted up against Rainbow Farm to the southwest. Neither Buggy nor Richard were employees at Rainbow Farm, but the venue's pro-pot campaign was one of the reasons both of them worked nearby. Buggy was 34 and his girlfriend was Nikki Lester, who worked in the camp store. Richard, whose nickname was Rainbow Richie, was a gay teenager and he considered Tom and Rollie to be role models.

"When I got back there, the only thing I saw was Rollie at the house," said Buggy. Rollie told Buggy that Tom was "unavailable." Rollie was also carrying a new Ruger mini-14 assault rifle with a 30-round clip full of .223 ammunition. "At that point, it was the band VIP trailer that was on fire, and I went up to Rollie. And he said 'It was time,' and that I needed to leave. Rollie was always a mellow individual. And his temperament and personality did not change at all, anytime, during any of this. I asked him if we had time for one more bowl. I went and got my bowl and we shared that a little bit, and I gave him a hug and I left. I went back out the back way."

Rainbow Richie was scared. When Buggy came to get the pipe, he said not to get out of the van, and that suited Richie just fine. He wanted to tell Rollie he loved him, but he didn't know what the hell was going on. As a gay kid who felt misunderstood at home, he was afraid to lose the two men who made him feel safe and accepted.

Seeing Rollie with a gun confirmed Buggy's fears. Rollie was slight and emotionally fragile, not given to a lot of dialogue. Nor was he in the habit of carrying guns around the farm; in fact, weapons had always been forbidden there. But he had one then, a strange new accessory in a summer that had seen his sporty, easygoing demeanor turn profoundly sad and monolithic.

Buggy had only lived in the area about 15 months, but like hundreds of people in the community, the farm was at the center of his life. It was a private farm but a public refuge, with an espresso machine, two pool tables, a jukebox and what Tom liked to call "the best coin laundry in the county." Other than a bar, there was not a single other place to hang out in the area. The farm was a licensed campground, so anyone who cared to could grab a patch of grass and pitch a tent.

With its nationally-advertised hemp festivals and voter registration drives, Rainbow Farm had also become the center for cannabis activism in the state of Michigan. The farm and its employees were founding sponsors of the Personal Responsibility Amendment, an initiative that was close to having enough signatures to get on the ballot in 2002 and behind which the movement to legalize pot in Michigan had surged to new prominence.

This was something Buggy believed in, and he didn't want to see all that work fouled up with guns. When he got back to the File's, Buggy called Sheriff Joe Underwood, a big, even-tempered African-American man widely respected in the community. They had never talked before. Buggy told the Sheriff not to send anyone out to Rainbow Farm, that the fire would burn itself out safely. He told them the men were armed.

He kept this phone call a secret for many months, for fear that others in the community would think him a traitor. But others had made this same phone call.

Scott Teter was the Prosecuting Attorney for Cass County. At 1:30 p.m. on August 31, Grover Thomas Crosslin and Roland Eugene Rohm were due in county court for a hearing with Teter where it would be decided whether or not they'd have their bail bonds revoked on the drug charges from their May bust. They were scheduled to meet with their lawyer at 12:30. They'd never turn up.

***

County Prosecutor Scott Teter sat in his tiny, windowless office that morning in the Cass County courthouse cobbling together the paperwork that would put Tom Crosslin and Rollie Rohm back in jail to await trial. He had more than enough cause to revoke their bond, but for months the news traveling through the briars said that Tom and Rollie weren't coming out. What that would mean was anybody's guess. A protest? A massive occupation led by the Michigan Militia? Whatever it was, Teter could only assume that the last days of Rainbow Farm would be something potentially bad or humiliating for him and his office. Just about everything Crosslin did turned out that way.

Rollie's biological son Robert had celebrated his recent birthday in foster care. Prosecutor Teter and county Probate Judge Sue Dobrich had ordered the county Family Independence Agency to remove Robert from his middle-school classroom on the day the farm had been raided in May. This was questionable and far from routine: marijuana cases were not regularly found to meet state criteria for "abuse and neglect." In his absence, the mood on the farm grew dark and explosive.

As far as Teter was concerned, he'd given them enough rope. They were supposed to be staying off the weed as one of the provisions of bail and Tom hadn't even tried. And even though Rollie had been attending the drug treatment meetings mandated by the Family Independence Agency as a condition for getting his son Robert back, he was still using. Teter might have even let that go, but Tom and Rollie had attempted to have a pathetic little impromptu hemp festival in August, at which about two-dozen people drank beer and smoked up. Two of them were narcs.

Teter had also made a big play that week, a heavy-handed move to lock up the situation at Rainbow Farm. He had filed to seize Tom Crosslin's farm under state drug asset forfeiture laws. These civil statutes allowed law enforcement to seize any property used in a drug offense—land, houses, farm equipment, cars, including all the stuff in them—and were originally written to cripple the big-money operations of organized crime. But in the early 1980s, President Ronald Reagan unleashed a feeding frenzy by letting federal, state, and local law enforcement agencies keep the profits from seized goods. By the mid-'90s, it had turned into a billion-dollar annual racket nationwide. Fighting these seizures required posting huge bonds, and the civil proceedings were so stacked against the defendants the property was almost impossible to recover. Most of those subject to forfeiture simply walked away from their property, even if they beat their criminal case—or even, as was the case 80 percent of the time, they weren't even charged with a crime—simply because reclaiming it was too expensive.

Teter had only to get a judge to sign the forfeiture order and Rainbow Farm would cease to exist, even if Tom and Rollie walked free. He had been threatening to do it for four years but hadn't had a shred of usable evidence. That day, he was going to get it done.

Teter knew Tom's lawyer, Dori Leo, a former prosecutor herself from Kalamazoo County. Her firm, Vlachos & Vlachos, could mount a substantial fight. He also knew that Tom could sell properties to pay for his defense and that he wouldn't go down without a slug-fest in court. Teter had gained the upper hand by filing for the forfeiture months before it was expected.

In his opinion, the rural county's worst problems were child abuse and drinking and drugs, and here were these hillbillies Tom and Rollie promoting marijuana, a Schedule I narcotic under the U.S Controlled Substances Act. Worse, the pair had at least some contact with the Michigan Militia.

Future Michigan Governor Jennifer Granholm, the state attorney general then and a Democrat, had her eye on Rainbow Farm, too. Teter had asked for her help to bring state resources to bear on the place, like state police roadblocks during the festivals and undercover narcs from the SWET—the SouthWest Enforcement Team, or "Dope Team." He had organized a task force devoted to shutting down Rainbow Farm. That task force included Teter, Granholm, Sheriff Joe Underwood and some of his staff, agents of the FBI and the U.S. Bureau of Alcohol, Tobacco and Firearms and the federal Drug Enforcement Administration, Michigan State Police and county prosecutors from around the state. Teter had played a leadership role on the drug issue and he felt like he had to deliver.

The civil forfeiture suit sat like a bomb on his tiny desk. All he had to do was get Tom and Rollie in front of county Judge Mike Dodge without incident.

But he wasn't that lucky. When the phone rang, it was Joe Underwood telling him that Rainbow Farm was burning.

***

Tom held his own identical Ruger Mini-14 by the stock, watching for desecrators, for defilers, for the first flashes of paperwork waved by an army of clerks coming to take his farm away. Nothing moved. All three men predicted that the cops would put a spotter on the highest spot on the property, the hill directly south of the house. Festival-goers had labeled the hill with a little wooden sign that read "Mount This." The farm's own Peace Police had put a camp up there during shows for the same reason—it provided a view of Pemberton Road in both directions and overlooked the house.

Rollie and Jimbo stood in the house watching the TV news. Fire trucks and squad cars amassed at a roadblock where Pemberton met Black Street a mile away. Jim was nervous about whether or not he should stay. He had a wife and two kids living in Cassopolis and he'd already been in a string of trouble in his life. Thai Stick paced and would not settle.

Worry tended to drive Rollie into resolute silence, but Tom was the exact opposite; he was coming out of his skin. One thing he did not abide well was waiting. He was prone to driving, driving and talking, lighting out in his tired 1976 Rolls Royce or "Big Red," his Ford F-350 diesel crew cab 4X4 pickup with the cap on the back. He'd take any errand just for the drive, going the long way down back roads, seeking out tractors holding "For Sale" signs, stopping at estate sales and asking the people gathered there what else they'd heard about, where the action was. That's the way Tom preferred to do business: face-to-face, having fun.

Tom snatched up the Ruger and called to the dog. He stopped in the doorway and made sure there was a round in the chamber, then stepped out to take a look around. The pump house and a series of small wooden cabins were burning, too. Choking black smoke poured like a funnel cloud into the gloaming noon. But just beyond the smoke, the sun lay warm as ever on his pond and high bank of woods.

Growing up in Elkhart and the flatlands of Indiana, this feral, glacier-scarred bit of Michigan wilderness was full of possibilities to Tom. On the map it's a green zone, a staggered cluster of ranger-station colors indicating state game areas—mostly sprawling swamps and protected hardwood breaks. On it's intermittent high prairie, agriculture is king, but everywhere else it's camp country, a place of homespun resorts and pine cabins and weedy lakes where city girls got out of their clothes and into bikinis. There was a time for Tom when it was all about those girls, but it had always been about the boys who chased them, too. People like himself vacationed here, working-class people, lots of them with heavy accents from Kentucky and Tennessee and southern Indiana. Though Michigan is a heavily populated state, the 8th highest in the nation, Cass is dotted mostly with farms and tiny crossroads towns built around gas stations and generic ciggies. The county sits in the southwest corner of the state, just beyond the heavy industrial zone of Gary, Indiana and the megalopolis of Chicago, a longtime resort area set with small-time RV parks and lake cottages where snowmobiles and jet-skis could be run, white-tailed deer could be killed or guns shot regardless, and bibles could be cracked in relative seclusion.

The names of the dozen or so camps and retreats held the promise of Native American fantasy and hot nights in musty pine bunkhouses: Wakeshma, Tamarack, Tannadoonah, Sun Chi Win. But, increasingly, the turn of the place was toward bible camps. The biggest camp in the county was Friedenwald, a sprawling complex founded by the Mennonite Church in 1951 on remote Shavehead Lake, named after the fierce Potowatomi leader who burned the village of Chicago. The 2000 census found only 51,104 residents in Cass County, but in the summers the population could easily double with the influx of the lake resort crowd.

Rainbow Farm offered something different, a place for people who wanted a vacation where they could freak freely. Tom had always said about it: "This is a place about alternative lifestyles. Being gay is just one of 'em. Smoking pot is just one of 'em. There's a bunch more, and this is a place where people can be free."

This is what separated Tom Crosslin's progressive beliefs from the communitarianism that has come to represent American political life on both the right and the left. He didn't believe in sacrificing some rights, like the right to smoke weed, just for the good of the community. His property rights were an absolute. On this point he would not compromise, and when people were on his property they could do as they pleased. People had to learn to live like adults who could be trusted with their freedoms, no matter how uncomfortable.

But the state—and Teter—had a more limited view of his rights. Juddering in the ground under his boots, he could feel the heavy knocking of an approaching helicopter.

***

The helicopter's urgent drumming came closer as Tom walked away from his burning pump house. Embers rained down on the grass amidst the RV sites.

Teter wouldn't get his buildings, wouldn't sell them to finance more of his SWET narcs, but Tom's whole identity was wrapped up in them, too. What was left grew more hollow as it burnt, a shell. Every moment he had less and less to lose.

Before he got to taking down the camp store, he'd go take one quick look from the top of Mount This. He kicked down the main gravel drive and up through the grass, past the house where Jim and Rollie sat, and across the back lawn. Down a two-track into the trees was a depot crowded with blue recycling barrels in a hollow alongside the road. A line of blaze orange "No trespassing" signs were visible in the woods, marching up the steep hill. Tom was sweating in his full camo by the time he reached the top. About ten yards into the dense undergrowth was a rock fire pit where his festival security used to camp. He could hear radios crackle and bark far off, but nothing moved. Tom stood in the keening hush of leaf rustle and treefrog drill and whippoor-will moan and watched the emptiness of the road. He knew every creeping grapevine on this spot, every flowering dogwood lurching sideways for a slice of sun shot through the dark canopy.

Suddenly, the helicopter slapped across the treetops overhead, a blue and yellow four-passenger that felt like it was only a few feet from the leaves. He jumped as it whapped into a banked turn over the store, obviously there to look at the farm. He shook off the electric shudder of adrenaline and tried to focus on the chopper. It could be cops. It looked like cops. He stopped where he stood and watched it, fingers tightening around the Ruger. It was the high-est spot on the farm, and he'd always had a special feeling about it. It was the exact spot on which he would die.

Chapter 6

CRITICIZE CHENEY, GO TO JAIL

By John Blair

FEBRUARY, 2002

TONIGHT I WAS ARRESTED for nothing more than exercising my rights as a citizen in what I thought was a free country. Dick Cheney came to my town to stump for one of the Environmental Dirty Dozen, Indiana 8th District Congressman John Hostettler.

I had made up a sign that stated, "CHENEY-19th Century Energy Man." The event was held at the convention center across the street from Evansville's government center. I walked down the street with my sign in hand to a location that I thought would at least be visible to the people entering the $100 to $1000 event.

As I stood across the street from the people who were entering the event, I was approached by a plain clothes policeman. The cop confronted me saying that protesters were not allowed in that area. I asked why since it was clear that everyone but protesters were allowed in the area in which I was standing. In fact, the whole incident took place as the public employees who worked at the government complex walked by without being accosted by the police at all.

It was clear that I was singled out only because I had a sign.

In the course of our conversation, several other cops surrounded the scene, more out of curiosity than anything else. I even surprised myself with my calm demeanor but I will admit to asking several questions concerning the 1st Amendment and why others were allowed in the area and I was not.

The main cop informed me that if I did not go more than a block away to the area he apparently had just arbitrarily decided was to be used by protesters, that I would be arrested. I complied and started to walk away. When I turned to ask if it was OK to go to the parking lot where hundreds of people were gathered, either leaving work or arriving to attend the event, he instructed his uniformed men to arrest me.

The cops failed to read me my rights. They even talked among themselves what the charge should be. Finally they decided to write it up as "disorderly conduct."

An 87-year-old man who was standing there with me observed the whole thing and told the local media how shocked he was about what happened. I was shocked too. I was not in the least belligerent, although I did ask questions of the officer who ordered my arrest.

What I was arrested for was exercising my rights, not necessarily to protest since I had done none of that. No, this was a preemptive arrest to assure that no one going to the event would see any protesters let alone hear any protests.

I have learned a lot about civil liberties in my years as a photojournalist and as an environmental activist. I also understand the need for security, especially for people like the Veep. However, I was singled out simply because I was carrying a sign that showed my disdain for Cheney. That is something that certainly falls within the realm of rights our country's founders fought to attain.

If you can be confronted by a cop simply because you are carrying a sign, then it won't be long before you will be subject to arrest for writing a letter to the editor or speaking out about injustice. If I had been in an area that was cordoned off or otherwise secured, there may have been reason to tell me to leave. Indeed I may have been legally subject to arrest. But none of the people passing by were confronted by any authority. They did not have a sign stating their views. They were not exercising their free speech rights.

Frankly, I felt as if this must be akin to the silence that was mandated by the Taliban towards Afghani women. Events such as this will certainly quell the prospect of protest of all official actions. I fear that we have become just what Osama Bin Laden wanted us to be when he ordered the attacks on 9/11.

I am going to plead, "NOT GUILTY" when I am required to go to Court. I will never say anything more accurate in my life.

DAY TWO

It was difficult sleeping last night. I stayed awake questioning whether this was all worthwhile. I awoke early to make my court appearance on a disorderly conduct charge. I got to court to find that the prosecutor had decided that my charges should be increased to a Class A Misdemeanor called Resisting Law Enforcement instead of the lesser charge. So now I am facing what could be a year in prison for my political crime of carrying a sign to a political event. Some people have suggested that I was marked before I even got there. I do not believe that to be the case, but it is true that I am a very outspoken member of this rather compliant and docile community here in southern Indiana. It has also been said that I am courageous for what happened last night. I would beg to differ since I had no intention of getting arrested and took no pride in being forced to be a spectacle in my home town.

I had some great advice on the possibility of bringing a Civil Rights action in Federal Court. I will consider that path. However, I am trying to remain focused on what is turning out to be the battle of my life with Peabody Energy and their plans to build two 1500 MW power plants—one in Illinois and one in Kentucky. The one in KY is in the comment period until February 28. The comment period was supposed to end tomorrow. Am I ever glad it was extended since I have not been able to focus on that at all today.

Today has been a mixture of elation and depression as people have called and written their support. In fact, I arrived at my office after court to find my flag at half staff and a Kleenex anonymously attached to my door. Very metaphoric.

Also on the positive front, a friendly attorney, representing another client showed up in court and offered me his services *pro bono* for my defense. I accepted. Then, too, a local TV station has decided to do an in-depth (at least for TV) analysis of the things that I am involved in from the numerous environmental fights to winning the Pulitzer for News Photography. No doubt that will be an ego boost, but...

It does not in anyway make up for the trampling my civil liberties took last night. In court this morning, the Prosecutor tried to imply that I was being removed from the scene because I was some sort of threat to Cheney. I guess the pen is mightier than the sword.

In the affidavit, signed by the arresting officer, it was stated that the boss cop told me to leave or get arrested "at least five times." In fact, I was told that only once and I then complied. But, of course, they had to make something up in hopes that I would come into court this morning and bow to their injustice.

I am not sure how to counter the lie in the affidavit since my only witness is an 87-year-old man with hearing problems.

That is what has been depressing today. When the cops lie, what is anyone to do to defend themselves.

POST SCRIPT

It is hard to believe that more than three years has passed since I was arrested for merely carrying a sign which said "Cheney-10th Century Energy Man" outside a political rally featuring our vice president. But that was 2/6/02.

In any case, the dubious charges against me were dropped a couple of weeks after that and I sued the City of Evansville and several of their policemen for violating my civil rights using arguments under both the 1st and 4th Amendments of the Constitution.

Later Federal Judge Larry McKinney issued his decision and backed me up on three of the four counts that were being litigated. Actually, he kind of spanked the officers and the City for arresting me with "no probable cause" and their establishment of an overly large "no protest" zone.

Of course, I am delighted in the decision and look forward in the negotiations that I will have in determining the monetary punishment that will be paid by the City. I can assure everyone who receives this note that while I will not be greedy, I will make sure the monetary award is sufficient to cause enough pain to assure they will not do this sort of thing again.

I was exceptionally well represented by the Indiana Civil Liberties Union and their dedicated civil rights attorney Kenneth Falk. It is really great to know that such an organization exists and is there for us when we need them.

Last, I hope that my case serves to inspire others across the country to stand up to the assault on our civil rights that is occurring in our country today. George Bush likes to speak about liberation of Iraqis and Afghans but has consistently pursued a policy of attacking the rights of citizens in the US.

The only way we can remain free is to make sure that each of us exercises our freedom each and every day, every hour. Freedom is like a muscle, if it is not exercised, it will atrophy. We must never let that happen.

Thanks for all the support that has been given me over the last three years. It has been very helpful in staying the course.

Chapter 7

KENTUCKY AT WAR

By Bob Moser

CAROL TRAINER COULD HARDLY process what was happening. To her, a 60-year-old grandmother and Vietnam veteran, of all people. On Memorial Day, of all times. Arrested for protesting the war at, of all places, Abbey Road on the River, an annual five-day Beatles tribute that had adopted a fortieth-anniversary Summer of Love theme for 2007.

Forty years ago, when the Louisville native married Air Force officer Harold Trainer, Carol wouldn't have gone near anything associated with the Summer of Love. "I wasn't an activist; just the opposite, in fact." But since 2002, when the Trainers—he retired from twenty-three years in the Force, she from eleven years as a Northwest Airlines flight attendant—found that they couldn't keep quiet about the catastrophe that was poised to unfold in Iraq, they've been unlikely stalwarts in one of the country's feistiest grassroots antiwar movements.

At the Abbey Road Festival, Carol had joined cohorts from the Louisville Peace Action Community (LPAC), passing out "End the War" pamphlets to incoming patrons—many of them young folks duded up for the occasion in flowers, beads and peace signs. Early that afternoon, she'd decided to join the fun inside, have a couple of beers and dance along to the music she'd missed in the '60s. After spotting a couple of youngsters holding up peace-symbol signs, she figured it would be OK to walk around with her bright blue End the War! sign. The festival's producer gave her explicit permission to do so. After all, it was perfectly in tune with the spirit of a festival whose grand finale would be a musical production called "Hell No, We Won't Go."

Trainer didn't make it that far. As she was dancing and singing along to the strains of psychedelic nostalgia, holding her sign off to the side of the main festival stage, an oversized sheriff's deputy came stalking toward her. "He comes up to me and says, 'Drop your sign,'" Trainer recalls. "I said, 'Why?' He said, 'I told you to drop your sign.' He grabbed it out of my hand when I didn't drop it. That kind of started me. I thought, What's going on here? I kept asking why and he wouldn't tell me." The only explanation Trainer received, after her arrest, was that offended patrons had complained that she was harassing them and ruining their fun. She says that while dozens of people thanked her for the message, she had been confronted by four patrons, including one veteran "who said, 'This is Memorial Day—we're here to enjoy ourselves.' I said, 'When do the people in Iraq get to enjoy themselves?'" Crying and struggling with the deputy, she tried appealing to Mayor Jerry Abramson, who was watching the show nearby, but he "just stared and glared at me and didn't say a word." The deputy and a Metro Police officer dragged her off forcefully in handcuffs. "I did not go quietly," Trainer acknowledges, and she ended up charged not only with disorderly conduct at the festival but also with resisting arrest and assaulting an officer. (Two of the charges were ultimately dropped; on the advice of LPAC's attorney, she agreed to do forty hours of community service for the resisting-arrest charge without admitting guilt.)

"You don't think that this could happen in the United States, you know," says Trainer. "One thing that irritates me is when some military people come up and say, 'I'm over there so you can do this. So you have the right.' And I'll say, now, after this, 'No, I don't have the right.'"

While protesting the war has alienated the Trainers from many of their old military buddies—"They tend to think we've left the reservation," says Harold—they've become fast friends with "peace people" they once despised. "They've really accepted us very well as partners in the peace effort," Harold says, "even though we're military." While LPAC, a spinoff of Louisville's large and active Fellowship of Reconciliation, includes its fair share of hardcore pacifists, the group—like so many other peace efforts around the country—has flung its tent wide open. "When Harold and Carol joined us," says longtime activist Judy Munro-Leighton, "it elevated our credibility about one million percent. When people came up to us at the state fair, or wherever we were demonstrating, and said, 'Yeah, what the hell do you know about it?

You've never fought in a war,' we could point to Carol and Harold and say, 'They have.'"

Carol Trainer's twelve hours in jail kicked off the most raucous summer yet for Kentucky's antiwar movement—a vibrant microcosm of the coalition of peace activists, military veterans and families, blue-collar hard hats and college professors, old and young and (mostly) middle-aged, who have been spurred to action by the bloodbath in Iraq.

LPAC has been a force since the buildup to the war, bringing out hundreds to loudly protest George W. Bush's six speeches in Louisville since 2001, holding regular street-corner demonstrations, marking every Iraq anniversary and landmark death count with in-your-face panache. They've chartered a plane to fly over the Kentucky Derby flashing an End the War banner. They've commemorated Iraq milestones with displays of empty shoes, empty shirts and—in 2007—4,000 white flags along the Ohio River. They've read the names of Iraqi and American dead from the county courthouse steps. And they've been particularly creative when it comes to getting under the skin of Kentucky's pro-war politicians.

When Louisville's Republican Congresswoman, stubborn Bush supporter Anne Northup, refused to meet with her antiwar constituents, LPAC posted "Missing" posters around the city with smiling images of Northup, labeling her a "lapdog" who "answers to Bush." They staked out her home for seventy-three straight Sundays with "a variety of signs you can't even imagine," says Munro-Leighton, until Northup finally consented to a meeting. "We had a cardboard Bush with a bubble to show he was speaking, and we changed the message weekly to 'I Love Ann,' or 'My War's Going Great!' or 'I Sold the Country.' On the first anniversary of the war, we made her a cake out of black cardboard and put it on her car. 'Happy Anniversary!'"

Tarred by her unflagging support for Bush and the war, Northup lost her 2006 bid for a sixth term to Louisville's John Yarmuth, an antiwar Democrat. With Northup dispatched, Kentucky's peace brigade laid plans to fry a far bigger fish in 2008: Senate minority leader Mitch McConnell, Bush's powerful Iraq War ally.

As summer—and McConnell's recess vacation—approached, two new sets of nontraditional allies materialized to help LPAC bird-dog the senator, who makes his home in Louisville with his wife, Labor Secretary Elaine Chao. Matt Gunterman, a 30-year-old rural Kentucky native and Yale University graduate student, launched the DitchMitch blog earlier in the year, bringing together a varied band of bloggers from around the state on a composite site with a common goal. And in June, two young native Kentuckians and a Navy veteran opened an Iraq Summer headquarters in Louisville, part of a national campaign by Americans Against Escalation in Iraq (AAEI) to target key members of Congress with a homegrown antiwar message before they returned to Washington to resume the war debate.

By mid-August McConnell was sending out fundraising letters complaining about being harassed by "the '60s antiwar movement on steroids." But as the Republican kingmaker well knew, the reality was something altogether different from that old stereotype—and considerably more formidable.

Jim Pence is a 68-year-old, Salem-smoking, pickup-driving, self-proclaimed hillbilly from economically devastated Hardin County, retired after thirty-five years in the factory at the American Synthetic Rubber Corporation. Politically inactive until 2004, when Bush's re-election and the war in Iraq spurred him to "vow to fight with every ounce of my strength from then on," Pence now makes some of the freshest, funniest antiwar and political videos anywhere—and as a result, he's become the unlikely heart and soul of Kentucky's DitchMitch campaign.

Linking from his own Hillbilly Report website to DitchMitch and You-Tube, Pence puts up snappy vignettes on subjects ranging from Kentucky's annual bipartisan political hoedown at Fancy Farm—where McConnell made a hasty exit this year after being jeered by protesters carrying signs showing him as Bush's hand puppet—to a fanciful take on Bush and Condoleezza Rice's relationship, set to the tune of Frank Sinatra's "The Way You Look Tonight," to a hard-hitting series of exposés of liquor-industry fundraising by Ron Lewis, the holy-rolling Congressman from Pence's district. "I don't know, I just disappear into them," Pence says on a dog-day August morning, navigating Louisville traffic en route to the Iraq Summer office. "I stay up some nights till 4 and 5 in the morning, editing these things."

DitchMitch creator Gunterman, whose postgraduate goal is to fire up an Internet-based "Ruralution," connecting grassroots progressives from rural America to spur political action, sees Pence as a prime example of the passion and wit that generally go untapped by Democrats and urban progressives. "There's no one like Jim in the entire United States," says Gunterman. "Not with his age and his ornery attitude. He is very much a hillbilly, and he's rein-vigorated the term."

In his three years of crisscrossing Kentucky to publicize its antiwar and progressive insurgencies, Pence has also stirred up the state's traditionally tim-id left-wingers. "When I first went out with my camcorder, I'd go up to people at peace rallies and ask them, 'Would you like to say something to Mitch?' and they'd just go, 'Uhhh...' Or even if they would say anything, they'd say, 'But I don't want my picture taken.' I just kept saying, 'The newspaper's not even going to cover this, and if TV does, it'll be for ten seconds. Whereas this video's going up on YouTube tomorrow.'" As Pence kept filming and posting his increasingly popular videos, the activists opened up and embraced this new mechanism for showing that, yes, the military stronghold of Kentucky has a vigorous antiwar effort. "People are stepping out more than they would a few years ago," Pence says. "Now I can't get them to stop talking when they see that camera. People know me now, and for the most part they trust me—whether or not they should!"

While Pence and DitchMitch have inspirited Kentucky activists, they've also pushed the state's more established media to take notice of the progressive groundswell. "DitchMitch gives us the power to hold the media accountable in Kentucky for the first time," says 24-year-old Shawn Dixon, a native of rural western Kentucky who's just started his first year at NYU law school. In 2004, when Dixon was working as deputy policy and communications direc-tor for Democrat Daniel Mongiardo's uphill Senate challenge to Republican Jim Bunning, he spent much of the campaign in a state of frustration over Kentucky newspapers' assumption that the incumbent would cruise to victory. "There was no recognition that this would be a competitive election and that this guy was beatable until about a month before the election, when it became impossible to ignore." Bunning wobbled back to Washington with a slender 23,000-vote victory, but this time around, with LPAC continually raising eye-brows and DitchMitch helping to popularize the anti-McConnell movement, "the media don't have a choice," Dixon says. On the same day in late July that Louisville's *Courier-Journal* ran a column about McConnell's dip in popular-ity (below 50 percent approval), the *Herald-Leader* in Lexington ran a story, sixteen months before the election, titled "McConnell Vulnerable."

That's music to Pence's ears. "It's not just what he's done to perpetuate this war," says the high-tech hillbilly. "It's what he hasn't done for Kentuckians, with all his power, on healthcare and so many other issues that really matter to folks at their kitchen tables. We're trying to cut through the kind of moral-values crap that McConnell's been using for twenty-five years to get himself elected. We're doing what we can to show the emperors without their clothes. And show that the folks who don't like Mitch, and can't stand this war, are just regular people like me who finally woke up and spoke up."

The Friday before the "Take a Stand" town-hall meeting that would culminate Louisville's Iraq Summer, Desert Storm veteran Brian Smith spent the first day of his most unusual summer vacation yet, volunteering round-the-clock for the antiwar effort. Smith has been working with Iraq Summer since June, when its three paid staffers hit the ground in Louisville. "I've been in charge of making coffee, making smart-ass remarks and doing guerrilla ops," Smith says. The previous night, that meant joining Louisville natives and Iraq Summer organizers Aniello Alioto and Sara Choate in planting fifty bright red Support the Troops/End the War signs outside a fundraiser where McConnell was speaking on behalf of scandal-plagued Republican Governor Ernie Fletcher.

"We want to be where he is," Smith says. For two long, hot, parched months, that's where Iraq Summer, combining forces with LPAC and other peace groups around the state, has been. They've bird-dogged McConnell's fundraisers. They've organized a stream of rallies and vigils outside McConnell's home. And they've drawn in a new batch of blue-collar and military folks like Smith, who still pinches himself when he looks in the mirror and sees an antiwar protester looking back.

"Initially I supported the war," he says, "more because I felt it was a duty to support the troops because I knew what they were going to be going through. When I saw antiwar protesters here at first, they gave me a little bit of a rise, because I felt that they didn't really understand the issues and would be proven wrong." He laughs. "Now I'm spending all my spare time working with them." Abu Ghraib was a breaking point for Smith. "My only defense of the war to that point had been, 'Well, at least we're the good guys.' After that, I had nothing left. But what really activated me was the surge. I thought after the 2006 elections things would change, but they just steamrollered right over us. So I went from there to the peace rally in Washington in January." A group he met there, Veterans for Peace, later connected him with Iraq Summer. "I would never have believed, a year ago, that I'd be doing anything like this," Smith says.

Nor, for different reasons, did Alioto, who'd been teaching diplomacy and national security classes to youth leaders in Washington, DC, when AAEI's national field director, Kate Snyder, called to ask if he'd return to Kentucky to dog McConnell. "I said no. I didn't want to go work for some peacenik, 'Let's end the war and sing songs' kind of campaign. But she said, 'This is a pro-military, pro-veteran campaign. It's not antiwar; it's anti-reckless war.' Then my ears pricked up."

Alioto found even more grassroots anger back home than he'd imagined. When Iraq Summer canvassed McConnell's neighborhood, "87 percent of the people who answered their doors took an End the War yard sign. I like numbers," he says, chuckling. But Alioto has also found that "there's still a lot of organizations, and a lot of individuals, that are scared to get involved. We get a lot of back door help. The hardest part is letting people know that we're not the traditional antiwar movement."

The nontraditional nature of the movement is on vivid display August 28 at the Take a Stand rally. A crowd of nearly 800 packs a Bellarmine University auditorium to hear not only from the expected cast of politicians, including Congressman Yarmuth, but also grassroots warriors like Smith, who leads the Pledge of Allegiance wearing several days' worth of stubble along with his old Army infantry jacket. There's 85-year-old Jean Edwards, a legendary local peace-and-justice activist, and her 15-year-old granddaughter, who asks the question, What would Gandhi do? There's a liberal white Presbyterian minister who went to Mississippi in 1964, during Freedom Summer, followed by an African-American minister who surveys the room and declares, "We are the people that can end this war. It has always been and will always be us—the good people, the common people, the regular people. It will always be incumbent upon us, when we have had enough." There's Bill Londrigan, the state's AFL-CIO chief, echoing that theme: "This is a war of elites fought by the working people of this Commonwealth and this country." And there's Lieut. Col. Andrew Horne, who's pondering an antiwar challenge to McConnell in '08, pacing the stage talking about why he chose to lead his National Guard unit into Iraq—and why he subsequently turned into a national Vote-Vets spokesman against the war. Horne leads a refrain that will be echoed during the evening's culminating event, a candlelight march to the senator's home: "Hey Mitch, can you hear us? We are the people!"

The marchers are mostly solemn and orderly, sticking to the sidewalks under pink-streaked evening skies as they wind up busy Bardstown Road to the accompaniment of honking horns, then down through McConnell's leafy old neighborhood. Informed that "We're going to McConnell's," one neighbor, standing on his lawn to view the procession, urges the folks: "Blow him up!" A few doors down, a white-haired senior citizen in a blue scooped-neck T-shirt hangs over his side porch bellowing a different opinion: "Damned idiots—you're helping kill 'em!" His plump face is scarlet with fury.

On the sidewalk in front of McConnell's nondescript two-story brick condo waits a thin line of counter-protesters, most of them portly, scruffy, tattooed bikers who have parked their hogs in formation across the way. Some hold signs reading Peace Through Strength and Stand Strong Mitch, while others aim cameras at the protesters in a vain attempt at intimidation. It's impossible not to notice the irony: how much more "mainstream" the war protesters, a mostly middle-class khakis-and-polo-shirt crowd, look than the ragtag defenders of Corporate America's favorite member of Congress. Across the street, the only sign of possible life in the condo is a yellow light glowing through the upstairs window shades. (McConnell's spokesperson will later say that the senator was in Lexington that night, helming another fundraiser.) When McConnell's defenders finally rumble off, Smith shakes his unruly head of black curls and grins. "They got no staying power," he snorts. "All huff, no tough."

To say the least, it has not been an exemplary summer break for Mitch McConnell. The Larry Craig scandal was one thing. He's also taking flak from conservative Kentuckians for supporting Bush-style immigration reform. More disturbing has been the floundering campaign of Governor Fletcher, a former right-wing Congressman handpicked by McConnell to run for governor in 2003. Plagued by a criminal investigation into preferential hiring for state offices, Fletcher has been spectacularly unpopular throughout most of his term.

Worst of all, though, is this nagging band of peace protesters. Will they be a temporary phenomenon, drifting apart after the war finally sputters to a halt? Or could this strange confluence of urban liberals, independent-minded hillbillies and populist bloggers turn into the Republicans' worst nightmare:

a left-leaning version of the silent majority that's propelled the likes of Mc-
Connell into office for the past few decades? Clearly feeling the pressure,
McConnell has tried to dip a toe in the new reality while clinging to the
tried-and-true. While he wildly claimed on CNN in July that Kentuckians
"overwhelmingly" support his backing of Bush and the war, the senator has
nuanced his rhetoric, making vague promises of "changes" in September after
the much-ballyhooed surge winds down. Despite that halfhearted concession,
he hasn't been allowed a moment's peace.

And sure enough, even on the blazing hot morning after Take a Stand
(which also attracted hundreds to Lexington and Newport rallies), some sixty
protesters and fans carrying I "heart" Mitch signs are waiting for McConnell's
gun-metal SUV to pull up at Boone Tavern, a colonial inn that graces the tiny
eastern Kentucky college town of Berea.

"I think the war is wrong," says Lisa Myers of Lexington. "We're spending all this money that we could be using for healthcare, for education—for
positive things. This war is costing us $9 billion a month, and we have poor
people, lots of them."

Meanwhile, Jim Pence is busy coaxing local protesters to speak their minds
into his camera. "I'm Laura Mangus, from Berea, Kentucky," says a somber-
faced woman holding a long rectangular sign reading, How Much More Misery and Death Per Gallon? "I'm here today on behalf of my son, who came
back from Iraq very, very wounded. When you have a son that calls you at 2:30
in the morning wanting to blow his brains out because of what he saw and
experienced in Iraq, you darn well better know I'm going to be here to let my
senator know what I think about this."

"I had twenty-eight years of military service," an elderly fellow in a lawn
chair, antiwar sign propped up in his lap, tells the Hillbilly. "I think this war
is absolutely stupid." "Hi there," says a wise old face, peering into Pence's
camera. "My name is Sister Nan and I oppose war in general, and this war in
particular."

Around noon, the protesters cluster around the front of Boone Tavern,
chanting, "Enjoy Your Lunch, End the War!" in the direction of the room
where McConnell is holding forth. With an air of determined calm, McConnell's senior Kentucky staffer, Larry Cox, materializes. "Mitch knows your
position," he says. "There's no way he can ignore the sentiment here. Things
are changing now. There is very likely to be a change in direction." Why won't

McConnell come out? various voices grumble. "Would the senator come out to address just one question?" "No," says Cox. "Would the senator come out if we promise not to ask any questions?" another protester suggests. "No."

After Cox escapes back into the fundraiser, accompanied by a stirring chant of "End the War!" the protesters trickle around to the back entrance, where McConnell's SUV sits idling. Martha Wilkie of Lexington, holding a sign with Thou Shall Not Kill on one side and Blessed Be the Peacemakers on the other, waits by the door alongside a gaggle of McConnell's admirers. She carries the scriptural sign, she says, because "people who support the war are all so into the Bible. But they disregard what's actually in the Bible." And speaking of disregarding, she says, "What in the world is McConnell scared of? Why won't he just come out and talk to people?"

The question lingers in the still, hot air for another half-hour. And then, in a flash, McConnell's ride goes ripping down the driveway and swerves around to a side door. Head down, the most powerful man in Kentucky skitters down a flight of steps and ducks inside the vehicle while his constituents come rushing around the corner, watching the back of their senator's SUV as it speeds him away, snug in the air-conditioned comfort of his increasingly fragile cocoon.

Chapter 8

THE U.S. VS. CHARITY RYERSON: YOUNG AND RADICAL

By Steven Higgs

FIVE DAYS BEFORE CHARITY Ryerson surrendered herself to the minimum security Federal Prison Camp at Pekin, Ill., she spoke nonchalantly about the six months she would serve for cutting a padlock during a protest at the School of the Americas. Curled up on the couch in *The Bloomington Alternative* office, Ryerson was unapologetic about her crime, and seemingly unphased about her time.

"Personally, I'm going to put this on my resume," she said. "I'm not going to decide that I want to join corporate America and have this thing erased. It's part of my lifelong commitment to activism. ...

"There's a girl who just got out of the jail I'm going to. I got a letter from her, and she said I'd probably have to work in the welding shop. I'll be carrying around metal. I'll be the tool girl for a month or something. It sounds really boring."

As her first month as federal prisoner #91335-020 drew to a close, 21-year-old Ryerson was no less sanguine when she wrote the *Alternative* in mid-August: "It's not quite as easy here as I'd hoped, but I'm almost through my first month. I'll certainly come out unscathed."

Unscathed, perhaps, but not unaffected—and apparently not undeterred in her mission as a social justice activist. Ryerson's note was accompanied by a stack of material she had already gathered on "mandatory minimums." She promised to send information on the "prison industrial complex."

Included in the information packet were articles on the crushing impacts that federal mandatory minimum sentencing guidelines in drug cases have on the lives of people like fellow Pekin inmate Diana Webb.

A former attorney from Kansas City, Mo., with no criminal record, Webb is serving 150 months in prison for Conspiracy to Manufacture Methamphetamine, even though no drugs were ever produced, and her three co-defendants initially provided sworn testimony that she was not involved.

Webb's co-defendants included a man who never did a single minute of jail time for forcing his way into her house and beating her with a baseball bat and a tire iron. He and his colleagues received reduced sentences of 46 to 60 months in prison in the drug conspiracy case after they changed their stories to help prosecutors convict Webb.

"This gives a little background on one of the appalling cases in here," Ryerson wrote. "Since she was an attorney, she has the best documentation of her case, but I don't think that this is isolated."

"Anyway, tons of women here with tons they want to say but nobody hears them. Congress ignores them because they're felons and can't vote. The media pay little attention. They feel very isolated and don't know how to get their stories out. It's strange how trapped one can feel in a prison with no fence."

**

In some ways, Charity Ryerson's prison term is the fulfillment of a career goal. The Indianapolis native turned Bloomington activist has been committing acts of civil disobedience for a variety of social justice issues since she was 19.

While attending school on a full scholarship at Loyola University, Ryerson was the eighth member of the "Loyola 7," who were arrested while protesting economic justice issues at Nike Town in the Chicago loop. "It was supposed to be the Loyola 8," she said. "I just sat there, and they arrested everyone around me. They wouldn't arrest me."

Ryerson had twice before joined the thousands of protesters who, since 1990, have annually converged on the U.S. Army's School of the Americas at Fort Benning, Ga., aka the School of the Assassins. The SOA is a U.S. government-sponsored terrorist training camp for military thugs from Latin America and other Third World countries. Its alumni include former Panamanian strongman Manuel Noriega and the 1989 killers of six Jesuit priests in El Salvador. The protest is held on Nov. 17, the anniversary of the Salvadoran slayings.

"This was my third year going down," Ryerson said of the 2002 SOA protest. "I had crossed the line before, but there were too may people that year, so I didn't get arrested. They just bused me off and dropped me off."

Led by New England priest and SOA Watch founder Father Ray Bourgeois, the SOA protests have grown steadily and raised awareness about the U.S government's complicity in human rights violations worldwide. Last year's drew more than 7,000 protesters, 96 of whom were arrested, including seven nuns and 10 minors.

Ryerson said that after 9/11, the U.S. Department of Defense, which had assumed control over the SOA and renamed it the Western Hemisphere Institute for Security Cooperation, erected a fence to keep the protesters from entering the base.

"They put up this stupid little fence that sort of goes down to this creek," Ryerson explained, "and all the nuns go down and wade through the creek to get around, and it's kind of a pain if you're old and all that. So we decided to cut this lock on this little pedestrian gate, to sort of push the envelope."

Logistically, cutting the bolt made it easier for elderly protesters to enter the base, Ryerson said, and it may have prompted more people to do so.

"But also, it sort of radicalized the movement a little bit," she said. "The SOA movement isn't really radical. It's very religious and sort of spiritual. It's a lot of prayer and singing. The actual civil disobedience is a funeral procession. It's really very Catholic. What we wanted to do was to push the envelope and make it a little more radical."

The other half of the "we" Ryerson referred to was her partner Jeremy John, a 22-year-old Bloomington activist who brought the bolt cutters and busted the lock and is likewise serving six months in federal prison in Terre Haute.

The 86 adults who were arrested were prosecuted for Class B and C misdemeanors of trespassing. Ryerson and John were also charged with trespassing and destruction of federal property, an A misdemeanor.

***

Charity Ryerson may be only 21-years-old, but she has a solid grasp of the role that nonviolent civil disobedience has played throughout American history. She cites a litany of examples, from the Boston Tea Party to the Civil Rights movement of the mid-20th Century.

"People act like this sort of radical action is something new or something atrocious," she said. "Well, that's not true. It's been happening and happening and happening throughout history. And it's been a really important part of history. A lot of people think that the civil rights movement would have gone through just fine had no one pushed the envelope."

Indeed, Ryerson sees radical action through creative, nonviolent civil disobedience as a legitimate, necessary component of the 21st Century global struggle for social, environmental and economic justice. And, based on her first-person observation of repression in the Mexican state of Chiapas and her experience as a student organizer against the World Bank, Ryerson argues the times demand it.

"I don't know what else to do," she said. "When I think about the stuff that I know we have been doing for so long with our foreign policy, and what we've been doing in Latin America, what we've been doing in Southeast Asia with our sweat shops and with Free Trade, and with Plan Colombia and the Drug War, and obviously I can go on and on and on forever."

As she prepared to become one of the statistics, Ryerson also pointed out that the United States has the highest per capita incarceration rate in the world. And more than half, 58 percent, are imprisoned for nonviolent crimes—like Diana Webb.

"That's way above and beyond Russia and other places that have high percentages in prison," Ryerson said. "And so, we've got this huge clamp down by our government on the people, and I just feel like it's tightening and tightening and tightening. And if we can't finally wake up and see what we're doing to the rest of the world."

She cited the impact of the decision to "push the envelope" at last year's SOA Watch protest as an example of the power of civil disobedience.

"We've gotten a lot of media coverage for this. When I think of the number of people who know what the Western Hemisphere Institute for Security Cooperation is, just in Indiana, and consider that there were 86 people prosecuted from all over the country. ..."

"I would guess that because of the two of us, maybe 500 people—not including media coverage, the people that read the articles—know about it that didn't before. When your friend goes to jail, or a friend of your friend goes to jail, or your client's daughter goes to jail—it's like those links seem sort of insignificant, but they're not. They're actually huge."

"When I think about the effect that one stupid little padlock has had, I mean, it's ridiculous. That padlock cost 12 dollars, and look at the impact."

***

To keep her scholarship at Loyola, Ryerson would have to return to school upon her release from prison in January. Chicago in January, two weeks after classes started? Perhaps not, she says. "I'll probably just hang out down here."

She and John will be on probation for a year and will not be allowed to leave their hometowns without permission. But Ryerson does not see that as too inhibiting a factor in her work.

"Yeah, we're kind of at their mercy," she said. "So that's kind of irritating. But, at the same time, there are a lot of things to do without breaking the law. I've been very busy for the past two years being an activist, and I've never ... I guess I've broken the law a few times, but I haven't actually been caught."

And there's no lack of issues to work on, she says, "There's tons, and I'm sure I can easily go a year working my ass off without getting arrested and get good work done. Personally, I'm really drawn to the I-69 thing. When I get out, I'm really excited about that."

"So, at least for me, there's a bazillion issues. And radical action is almost, I mean, it's urgent, it's necessary, it needs to be happening more."

Chapter 9

SHOWING CONVICTION AT ECHO 9

By Bill Quigley

THE ECHO 9 LAUNCHING facility for the intercontinental nuclear missile Minuteman III is about 100 miles northwest of Bismarck, North Dakota. Endless fields of sunflowers and mown hay dazzle those who travel there.

The fenced off site at first appears innocent. Until you get close you cannot see the sign that says deadly force is authorized against trespassers. A 40 ton nuclear missile lies coiled beneath the surface of a bland concrete bunker. Echo 9 is but 50 feet from a gravel road. This one Minuteman III missile has over 20 times the destructive power of the bomb dropped on Hiroshima.

After you realize what a launching facility looks like, you can see that the pastoral countryside is full of nuclear weapon silos. One nuclear weapon launching site lies just across the road from a big country farmhouse, another just down from a camp for teens. There are 150 other such nuclear launching facilities in North Dakota alone.

Sunflowers, farmhouses, teen camps and nuclear weapons, who would have thought the power to destroy the world many times over could fit in so well? The people of this state will not need to turn on CNN to know when the nuclear holocaust arrives.

On the morning of June 20, 2006, three people dressed as clowns arrived at Echo 9. The clowns broke the lock off the fence and put up peace banners and posters. One said: "Swords into plowshares—Spears into pruning hooks." Then they poured some of their own blood and hammered on the nuclear launching facility.

Fr. Carl Kabat, 72, along with Greg Boertje-Obed, 52, and Michael Walli, 57, were the people dressed as clowns. Carl Kabat is a catholic priest. Greg is an ex-military officer, married and the father of an 11-year-old daughter. Mike is a Vietnam vet who has worked with the homeless for decades. Greg and Carl are members of the Loaves and Fishes Community in Duluth. The three are called the Weapons of Mass Destruction Here Plowshares.

They placed a copy of the Declaration of Independence, the US Constitution, international legal condemnations of nuclear weapons, bibles, rosaries, bread, wine, and a picture of Greg's daughter on the top of the missile silo.

Then they waited until the air force security forces came and arrested them.

They were charged with felony damage to government property and were kept in North Dakota jails until their trial in September.

In their trial they planned to argue to the jury that because the Minuteman III is a weapon of mass destruction it is illegal under international law. They hoped to share with the jury testimony from the Mayor of Hiroshima about the effects of nuclear weapons. They asked to have Professor Francis Boyle testify about the illegality of nuclear weapons. And they planned to introduce the 1996 advisory opinion of the International Court of Justice outlawing nuclear weapons.

They hoped to put on evidence that warheads launched from the Minuteman III missile silo can reach any destination within 6000 miles in 35 minutes. The nuclear bomb launched from a Minuteman silo produces uncontrollable radiation, massive heat and a blast capable of vaporizing and leveling everything within miles. Outside the immediate area of the blast, wide-spread heat, firestorms and neutron and gamma rays are intended to kill, severely wound and poison every living thing and cause long-term damage to the environment.

But the judge ruled the jury was not permitted to hear this evidence.

The night before the trial, the peace community of North Dakota, along with friends and supporters from across the US, shared a Festival of Hope potluck supper, songs, prayers and calls for peace at a local Unitarian church. The North Dakota peace community was very supportive. Even the federal prosecutor and an air force investigator joined the festival after being invited to attend by Carl, Greg and Mike. They too were welcomed by the community.

On the day of the trial, the judge asked people about their backgrounds and their opinions about nuclear weapons. Those who expressed any skepticism about the use of nuclear weapons were struck from serving on the jury by the government. Likewise, a Baptist missionary with a dove on her collar and all the Catholics were excluded.

Fr. Carl Kabat represented himself in the trial and gave his own opening statement. Dressed in a rumpled roman collar, black jeans and white tennis shoes, it was apparent he came right out of jail to the courtroom.

Fr. Kabat told the jury that he had been a priest for 47 years and spent three years in the Philippines and several more in Brazil where he witnessed poverty and hunger on a scale unimaginable to the US. After that, he said, he was ruined to life in the United States. He could not allow 40,000 children a day to die from malnourishment while our country built and maintained thousands of nuclear weapons.

Carl admitted that he had spent over sixteen years in prison for protesting against nuclear weapons. He told the jury that he understood that because he was 72 he might die in jail in punishment for this protest. "I don't know if I am doing the right thing or not, I am only doing the best I can. If anyone can think of anything better to do to stop this insanity then, by all means, do it! It is up to all of us to do something to stop this madness!"

He said they dressed up as clowns as "fools for Christ," and because "court jesters were often the only ones who could tell the truth to the king and not be killed for it!" We realize most people do not care about nuclear weapons. "To them we are nutballs," he said. "We are doing the best we can to stand up against these evils. My feeling is do what you can do about injustice, then sing and dance!"

Fr. Carl pointed out in some detail that nuclear weapons violated international laws. "Now I am not a lawyer," he kept saying, "but I know the International Court of Justice has ruled these are illegal." He asked the jury "Why do you think it is it illegal for North Korea or Iran to have nuclear weapons when we have thousands? I don't want anyone to have them.

"The weapon at Echo 9 can kill the entire population of New York City— just that one missile and we have thousands of them! This is insane! Polls say that 87% of the people in the US want us to get rid of nuclear weapons—let's do it! People may think we're nuts for dressing up as clowns and risking jail to get rid of these weapons, but it is these weapons that are actually insane!"

Greg Boertje-Obed spoke briefly to the jury about growing up in the Midwest and the south. He was dressed in rumpled pants and a t-shirt decorated with the symbol of a local Native American tribe. He told them that he was married and the father of a young daughter. He admitted he basically did not know anything about nuclear weapons or civil rights. He joined ROTC to be able to attend college and was made an officer. His military group discussed nuclear war and one made a powerful case for first-strike. All the time he was a churchgoer. In graduate school he started awakening to the contrast between the religious values he found in church and the actions and priorities around him. Greg told the jurors of his journey into resistance as he realized that nuclear weapons were both illegal and immoral.

Michael was described to the jury as one of 14 children who grew up in the Midwest. He joined the Army and spent two tours in Vietnam. After a religious conversion, he began a life of voluntary poverty and assisting the homeless and sick.

The prosecutor called an FBI agent who told the jury all about the events of June 20, 2006. He described the defendants as polite at all times. The prosecution projected huge photos of the three dressed as clowns, pictures of the Echo 9 launching facility, and pictures of the items left behind on the wall of the courtroom.

Fr. Carl asked the FBI agent if he had found a statement that the three left on site. The judge allowed Carl to read the statement into the record at this time. Carl put on his reading glasses and in a loud voice read to the courtroom:

"Please pardon the fracture of the good order. When we were children we thought as children and spoke as children. But now we are adults and there comes a time when we must speak out and say that the good order is not so good, and never really was. We know that throughout history there have been innumerable war crimes. Two of the most terrible war crimes occurred on August 6th and 9th, 1945. On August 6th, 1945, the United States dropped an atomic bomb on the city of Hiroshima, Japan, killing more than 100,000 people (including U.S. prisoners of war). Three days later the U.S. dropped an atomic bomb on the city of Nagasaki, Japan, killing more than 50,000 people. Use of these weapons of mass destruction on civilian populations were abominable crimes against humanity.

"The U.S. has never repented of these atrocities. On the contrary, the U.S. has deepened and expanded its commitment to nuclear weapons. The U.S. built a large nuclear-industrial complex which has caused the deaths of many workers and has resulted in killing many more people by nuclear testing. Our country built thousands of nuclear weapons and has dispersed weapons-grade uranium to 43 nations. Each Minuteman III missile carries a bomb that is 27 times more powerful than those dropped on the Japanese people. The building of these weapons signifies that our hearts have assented to mass murder. Currently the U.S. is seeking to research a new class of smaller nuclear weapons demonstrating its desire to find new uses for weapons of mass destruction."

The prosecution then called a succession of young Air Force folks, who served as security for the Minuteman missiles in the silos in this area, to briefly describe the arrest and detention of Carl, Greg and Mike. Each one said the clowns were cooperative, non-violent and peaceful.

At the conclusion of the first soldier's testimony, Fr. Kabat asked him, "Do you know what was in the ground at Echo-9?" The flustered airman said, "No, sir, I do not." "You don't know what is in the ground there?" Fr. Kabat asked again incredulously. "No sir," repeated the helicopter airman. The courtroom was stunned.

For the next half hour, every one of the rest of the young Air Force people called as witnesses by the government either said they did not know what was in the ground, or refused to answer Fr. Carl, saying "that is not my area of expertise, sir."

Not one single soldier acknowledged that they were guarding nuclear weapons!

The final prosecution witness was a Lieutenant Colonel who said the damage to the site was over $15,000 because a spin dial lock on a hatch was damaged and had to be exchanged for another.

The Lt. Colonel, after initially refusing to do so, admitted that a Minuteman III missile was in the silo but that the Department of Defense would not allow him to say anything more.

After the prosecution rested, the judge ushered the jury out of the room. Then the three were allowed to introduce into the record the evidence of the International Court of Justice decision about the illegality of nuclear weapons, the testimony of the mayor of Hiroshima, and two statements by Professor Boyle about international law and its condemnation of nuclear weapons. The judge was asked to dismiss the case because of this evidence. When the judge declined, Greg told him that he was making a mistake. The judge responded that in light of all the other federal cases he had reviewed he was not making a mistake. "But in the judgment of history, you are," Greg responded. The judge noted Greg's objection for the record and re-started the trial.

With all the rest of their evidence excluded, the three defendants tried in their own words to tell the jury about how international law condemned nuclear weapons, what kind of damage the weapons caused, and how the very existence of nuclear weapons was robbing the poor of the world of much needed resources.

Fr. Carl choked up several times talking to the jury when he described the extent of hunger and starvation he had witnessed. "Nuclear weapons," he said softly, "and hungry children, are the two greatest evils in our world."

Michael told the jury how he joined the army at the suggestion of a family member and ended up spending years in Vietnam. While there he heard about the death of Martin Luther King, Jr., described on the base as "an agitator." He described his later work with the poor and how it was consistent with his peace work. He concluded by correcting the record. "These young military people testified that after we arrived at Echo 9 it became a crime scene. But in truth, Echo 9 was a crime scene long before we ever got there. Nuclear weapons are war crimes that are designed to kill innocent civilians. They are outlawed by international law and by God's law. This was a crime scene long before we got there, and is still a crime scene today."

Greg showed the jury the picture of his daughter. "I brought this to Echo 9 as a symbol of why we again and again try to disarm nuclear weapons. We do this for the children."

With the evidence finished, it was time for the jury to decide. The judge would give instructions to the jury about how to decide the case.

The defense asked for two instructions about justice, one from the preamble to the US Constitution another from Judge Learned Hand—both were denied by the judge. Defendants asked that the jury be read the First Amendment—denied. International law? Denied. Nuremberg Principles? Denied. The US statute defining war crimes? Denied. The US statute defining genocide? Denied.

The judge then went forward and instructed the jury to disregard anything about nuclear weapons, international law, and the good motives of the defendants. The effect of these instructions was to treat the actions of the defendants the same as if they had poured blood and hammered on a Volkswagen—pure property damage.

Limited like this, the jury came back with felony guilty verdicts for all three defendants. As they filed out, Fr. Carl called out to them, "Thank you brothers and sisters!"

One of the jurors told people afterwards that many on the jury learned a lot in the trial and were sympathetic to the defense, but "the judge's instructions left us no option but to find them guilty." As she walked away, the juror waved to supporters and yelled "Peace!"

The local paper reported one lawyer concluding that, despite their convictions, "History will have different judgment on their actions."

The three remain in jail. They are in good spirits and at peace in the justice of their convictions. Greg pointed out that juries in Europe were allowed to learn about international law when evaluating the actions of peace protestors. "Why do English, Scottish, and Irish juries get to know about international law, but not US juries? Why do our judges keep our juries deaf and blind to the law of the world?"

Mike noted "The ungodly will always say Let our might be our norm of justice.'"

Fr. Carl, who feels "fantastic—as usual," said, "One with God is a majority, and some day the will of the majority will triumph!"

For their convictions, they face sentences of up to 10 years in prison and fines of up to $250,000 each.

PART TWO: MOUNTAINFOLK

Chapter 10

BIG SKY REBELS: MONTANA'S PROMISE OF CHANGE

By Joshua Frank

YOU CAN GO HOME again, but it might break your heart or turn your stomach. Even if your home is Montana. Perhaps especially here, where there is so much to lose.

No, Montana is not what it used to be. Corporate behemoths have taken over small family-owned farms, and public forests have been squandered and sold to the highest bidder. Poverty and racism run rampant. Native Americans are being corralled onto even tighter plots of land. But while things seem disheartening, voices of hope continue rumbling across the Big Sky Country.

With Montana, like so many other "lost cause" states, not fitting neatly into the Blue State/Red State dichotomy, even Thomas Frank would be baffled. Don't get me wrong: this is still Republican country. Oversized SUV bumpers flaunt "W" stickers, and almost every Ford truck touts a yellow "Support Our Troops" magnet. There is no question that these flag-waving Montanans overwhelmingly voted for Bush in 2004.

Having grown up on the eastern side of the continental divide in Billings—Montana's largest city with a population exceeding 90,000—I know this area well. Dubbed America's drug stricken "Crank Capitol" by *Time* in the late 1990s, Billings is nestled beneath the shadows of 500-foot sandstone cliffs. The snowcapped Rockies are due west. The mighty Yellowstone River cuts through the town's south end. It's searing hot in the summer and bitter cold in winter. A forty-minute drive to the southeast will bring you to the impoverished and desolate Crow Agency Indian reservation, which houses the memorial for the Battle of the Little Big Horn where General George A. Custer met his much-deserved fate. This land has a bloody ubiquitous history, the aura of which can be troubling for those familiar with its past.

Much has changed since I left Billings some years ago. An insipid Mormon temple has been erected on the outskirts of town near a glitzy country club. Wal-Mart, Home Depot, Barnes and Noble, Starbucks, dozens of tasteless eateries, and countless cookie-cutter homes have relentlessly extended the city's boundaries. Once unique, Billings now resembles most any place you would find in these sprawling Xeroxed States of America.

Teenagers fill their weekends with beer, sex and cheap booze, remnants of which pepper the roads off the beaten path. Things are not much different for the slightly older crowd. You are just more likely to find these Generation Xers frequenting the local bars and passing joints back and forth in their pick-up trucks. Who can blame them? This is the rhythm of the new American dream, the anthem for surviving cultural homogeneity: do what you must to escape the mundane. Take two and pass.

A cursory glance probably wouldn't reveal so much as a chirp of dissent in these parts. That is, of course, if you aren't referring to the right-wing militiamen that have made Montana famous in the 1990s. But I am not talking about the tax averting Freemen, who stockpiled weapons and took on the Feds, or the chemically inclined Ted Kaczynski's fetish for sending loaded love letters. I'm talking about a populist backlash that is fast gaining speed on these remote country roads.

WELCOME TO MONTANA

Some things, like the volatile weather that can turn from rain to snow in minutes, rarely change out here. But there are aspects of life in Montana that the public can help determine. The Red State marker that the politicos and pundits have given to places like this is not etched in stone.

Just a few decades ago things on the Montana prairie changed, but sadly it was for the worse. Before the rightwing takeover of the state legislature in the late 1970s, this place was actually thriving with progressive politics. Take Democratic Senator Lee Metcalf, who was a staunch wilderness supporter during his tenure in D.C. and would likely be considered an eco-terrorist by today's standards. On the heels of the great conservationist Bob Marshall,

Metcalf became a relentless advocate for the wild, where he attempted to make Marshall's public forest vision a reality. He stood up against timber barons, big oil, and land developers, rarely backing down. He cherished Montana for its ecological beauty, wildlife and serenity.

The truth is Montana has a long history of going against the traditional grain. Perhaps it was the populist farmer instinct that permeates this culture. Along with electing Metcalf, voters also sent liberal Democrat Mike Mansfield to Congress and the Senate nine consecutive times. Sen. Mansfield's most enduring accomplishment came when he engineered the passage of the Civil Rights Act of 1964 during his tenure as Senate Majority Leader. Using Senator Hubert Humphrey as his floor manager, Mansfield quietly rounded up the necessary votes and broke the Southern filibuster, which cleared the way for the passage of the monumental legislation. Although both Mansfield and Metcalf had plenty of glaring flaws, there is no question that they, compared to today's corporate Democrats, were remarkable.

Of course, we can't talk about progressive politics in Montana without mentioning Janette Rankin, whom in 1916 became the first woman ever elected to Congress. A social worker by trade, Rankin was a tireless defender of the underclass. She was also one of the first representatives to speak out against child labor practices in the early 20th century. But it was her opposition to war that led her to her most exceptional accomplishment: just four days after taking office, Rankin voted against U.S. entry into World War I. Violating Congressional procedure, she spoke out during roll call prior to casting her vote and declared, "I want to stand by my country, but I cannot vote for war!"

During the rest of her term, Rankin fought for many political reforms, including civil liberties, women's suffrage, birth control, child welfare, and equal pay among sexes. She was ahead of her time on nearly every issue. Sadly, however, Rankin's vote against World War I sealed her political fate. Later, after much harassment back home for her war resistance, she was gerrymandered out of her Montana district. When she ran for a Senate seat, she was overwhelmingly defeated.

Like so many states, an electoral map does not do justice to what has actually taken place on the ground politically or historically. In fact, in 1992 Montana's electoral points went to Bill Clinton as Ross Perot captured a quarter of the votes. And the contradictions are not much different in the so-called Blue States, where right-wingers run rampant and dominate state and local governments. One need look no further than Schwarzenegger's reign in California or Bloomberg's grip in New York City, not to mention the conservative Democrats who rule the roost in the Interior West. We'd all do well to abandon such divisive and inaccurate Red/Blue labels, and unite behind common causes. Indeed some Montanans are.

***

Today, a fair portion of the population is pissed. And rightfully so. Montanans have suffered far too long under the boot of the conservative majority. Many years have passed since Metcalf and Rankin were in office. Most recently it was the cavalier Governor Marc Racicot, now a rising star within the Republican establishment, who used Montana as a stepping-stone for his own political trajectory. After Racicot left office in 2000, the state was faced with the putrid stench of Judy Martz, a frightful Republican corpse of a governor who bragged that she was the "lap dog of industry." Martz was the personification of John Sayles' Dicky Pilager character in *Silver City*, an unsightly puppet for corporate interests and damn proud of it.

Ol' Judy earned herself quite a rap sheet after her election in 2000. She shielded timber companies from litigation and supported deregulation as Montanans saw their electricity bills skyrocket. Much to the dismay of her voting base, she undermined public schools. Gouged taxpayers. Destabilized local business owners. Angered small farmers. Martz was a political train wreck, and Montana reacted accordingly. By the summer of 2004 her approval rating had sunk to a meager 30 percent, an all-time low. Without a wince of shame Martz opted not to run for reelection. A sensible decision—surely the wisest of her brief political tenure.

Sick and tired of Republican rule, many Montanans voted to replace Martz with Democrat Brian Schweitzer—a wealthy cattleman who has operated ranches across the state. A naturally gifted orator, Schweitzer had almost defeated entrenched US Senator Conrad Burns, a popular Republican stooge who had ties to lobbyist Jack Abramoff, back in 2000. And Montanans love Schweitzer because, like an honest cowboy, he shoots it straight.

"If I stay in Washington for more than 72 hours I have to bathe myself in the same stuff I use when my dog gets into a fight with a skunk," he said after a visit out to D.C. a few years ago.

Running on a split ticket in 2004, Schweitzer picked moderate Republican State Senator John Bohlinger to be his running mate. Bohlinger was a pragmatic choice, as it is well known that John is just a donkey in elephant attire, bow tie and all. He simply swapped parties when he chose to run for state congress in a conservative Billings district in 1992. Bohlinger knew his constituents would vote Republican out of habit and a penchant for hating Democrats.

John Bohlinger was right and the Schweitzer camp capitalized on their collective ignorance under the banner of "bipartisanship." But Montana's neo-populism isn't about party loyalty. Instead it seethes with a true disgust for big government. A fair majority of Montanans don't trust their elected officials—state or federal—and the higher up on the ladder you go, the more pessimistic things they'll have to say about our broken system and the fools that run the show.

In 1999, when Schweitzer drove a batch of old-timers across the border into Canada to see how much cheaper pharmaceuticals were there, he made his mark with senior citizens. As Schweitzer explained in a radio address shortly after he was elected, "The purpose of those trips was to demonstrate the hypocrisy of Congress' trade policies. They passed NAFTA, told us that it would be great for the consumers of the United States. We'd be able to have products and consumer products cross the border from Canada and Mexico, and the United States freely, and that we would find greater choice. And we have NAFTA and we're supposed to have free choice for everything but medicine."

Not bad for a post-Clinton Democrat. Since his January 2005 inauguration, Schweitzer has been vocal in his opposition to the Bush agenda. He even called for the return of Montana's guard troops from Iraq so they could help battle wildfires, which raged in the summer of 2005. Schweitzer is not buying the Republican's call to privatize Social Security either. "Today we're talking about Social Security, something that might happen 20, 30, 40 years from now," he said after a recent meeting in D.C. when U.S. governors spent an afternoon with the President, "But guess what's really happening? ... We're cutting Medicaid. We're cutting programs in the heartland."

But don't get too excited; Schweitzer is no radical. He is cautious and pragmatic. He opposes gay marriage (though I'm told this is the case only because Bohlinger would have declined to be his running mate had he come out in favor of gay marriage) and wants to expand Montana's private prison system, one of the state's only growth industries. As the *New York Times* asserts, "Schweitzer veers right on many economic and social issues: he … favors the death penalty and preaches about lowering taxes and balancing budgets."

Schweitzer's win wasn't the only interesting development in the state since the turn of the century. Montanans also voted in favor of medical marijuana. Despite what liberals claim, these Red Staters may have some common sense after all. And compared to a "liberal" Blue state like Oregon, where citizens nixed a medical marijuana initiative in 2004, Montana sure as hell seems like they are on the cusp of change.

***

Brian Schweitzer was just the beginning of the political change happening here. Montana's newest U.S. Senator is not exactly the type of Democrat you'd see backslapping New York City fat cats on their way into an elaborate fundraiser for Hillary Clinton. In fact, Jon Tester, who was elected to the Senate in 2006, isn't your typical Democrat. He's almost not a Democrat at all. In fact Tester ran his campaign against Senator Conrad Burns on just that platform. He was tired of the scandals and dishonesty that engulf our national politics and professed that the polluted Beltway could use a little Montana house cleanin'. Voters agreed, and Burns was defeated in one of the tightest races in state history.

An organic farmer by trade, Tester, a former state legislator, ran his family's homestead just outside Big Sandy in northern Montana, where the winter chills can chatter your teeth as early as mid-September. Sporting a Marine drill sergeant buzz cut, Tester is essentially an NRA approved populist with libertarian tendencies who vowed he'd redeploy troops from Iraq as well as repeal the PATRIOT Act. And although nobody would consider Tester an anti-globalization activist, his position on international trade is more in line with the protesters who shut down Seattle in 1999 than with the Democratic Leadership Council.

On a "Meet the Press" broadcast shortly before he took office, Tester even addressed the most evaded issue in national politics: poverty. "There's no more middle class," he asserted to Tim Russert, "the working poor aren't even being addressed. Those are the people who brought us here [to Congress] and they need to be empowered. It's time to show them attention ... We have to use policy to help that situation."

In a debate in September 2006, Conrad Burns attempted to paint Tester as wimpish on terror. "We cannot afford another 9/11," Burns chided. "I can tell you that right now, he [Tester] wants to weaken the PATRIOT Act." To which Tester bravely countered, "Let me be clear. I don't want to weaken the PATRIOT Act. I want to get rid of it."

Tester built his campaign from the ground up, shunning support from nationally known Democrats like John Kerry and Hillary Clinton, as he knew they'd rub Montanans the wrong way. Instead, the nearly 300 pound farmer who lost three fingers in a meat grinding accident as a child, drove around the state so he could chat face-to-face with his potential constituents.

Fortunately for Tester, he's used to bucking the system. His first foray with the Washington Consensus came in 1998 when he ran for the Montana legislature because he was outraged over the huge energy hikes that had resulted from the state's deregulation of the power industry. And he's been speaking out against policies that pit working folks against the corporate class ever since. Tester even occasionally touts renewable energies and a livable minimum wage.

Still, like Montana's current governor, Tester isn't an ideal politician, if there is such a thing. While he may remain strong on some issues, he is weak on many issues of social justice, such as the death penalty and gay rights. Nevertheless, Tester's campaign and personal appeal may serve as a winning blueprint for left-leaning populists out here in the Interior West. Indeed Brian Schweitzer used the exact formula to become governor two years earlier.

Yet, Jon Tester's win wasn't even the biggest triumph for the state. The largest political victory for Montana came when voters overwhelmingly shot down a mining initiative in 2000 that would have returned the dreadful and polluting open-pit cyanide heap-leach mining to Montana's hills. Big mining companies put up millions to raise support for the bill, but Montanans didn't bite. Environmentalists and the public won outright.

Open-pit cyanide heap-leach gold mines have long-polluted water and left environmental destruction in their wake. Montana is used to it. Throughout the state these vast toxic pits have poisoned streams and drinking water, killed off wild trout, desecrated the landscape and created environmental catastrophes that have cost taxpayers millions to clean up.

Still, the greatest change in Montana isn't happening in the electoral arena. It is taking place on the ground where a plethora of movements, from environmental causes to anti-corporate organic farming, are coming to a head. Election Day hoopla is only a shadow of the real activism going on. These agitators know that ultimate victory requires enduring many, many losses and years of protest before cultural changes are reflected in policy and ultimately, their daily lives.

There is a dreadful attitude still lingering out in Blue America where folks put the majority of their energy into electoral politics, anticipating that change can only happen within the confines of the voting booth. And it's a downer. No doubt "blue" is an apt color to describe the dejected mood that still paints our coastal states even with the Democrats in power. Fortunately, progressives, libertarians, anarchists, and others out here in Montana, although a tiny minority, have rolled up their sleeves and continued their work. Elections are never deterrents. They have stayed the course, never abandoning their issues, and are slowly winning as a result.

Maybe liberal Blue Staters will realize this isn't "fly-over country" after all, and borrow a page from these Red State dummies.

Chapter 11

SOMETHING ABOUT BUTTE

By Jeffrey St. Clair

BUTTE, MONTANA ISN'T A mining town. It's a mined town.

The core of the city is hollow, tunneled out. Beneath the shattered surface of the Hill, there are more than 10,000 miles of underground passages and thousands of shafts, glory holes descending deep into the bedrock. Every now and then, holes will open in the crust of the earth, swallowing sidewalks, garages and dogs.

Houses, black as ravens, are sunk into mine waste heaps and slag piles, the exhumed geological guts of the billion dollar hill, once coveted and swiped by America's dark lord, John D. Rockefeller, during the end game in the War of the Copper Kings. People still live in the hovels.

Gallows frames prick up through the town like quills on a porcupine. Once, these steel derricks cranked the miners down into the depths in hoist cages, now they resemble the frightful gibbets that haunt the backgrounds of Bruegel's paintings from the years of the Black Death. Many that went down never came up. The tunnels of Butte are also a catacomb, holding the bones of more than 2,500 miners.

In the 1880s, Butte was the biggest and wildest town between Denver and San Francisco. It boasted 75,000 people and the most opulent opera house west of Manhattan. There were whorehouses and banks, theaters and bars, French restaurants and the Columbia Gardens, one of the world's fanciest amusement parks.

It's the place where Cary Nation's sobriety campaign came to a crushing end, when the madame of Butte's leading brothel pummeled the puritanical crusader to the floor of the bar, as hundreds cheered, beer steins raised high.

The mine barons didn't live in Butte, where the day mansions were stained black by the smoke of the smelters, but up in Helena, which once harbored more millionaires per capita than any other city in the nation.
Those days are gone.

Today, Montana has a crop of millionaires, but they've made their money in Hollywood, Atlanta, or New York City and now hide out, like the James Gang, in large compound-like ranches, sprawling over mountains and trout streams. Otherwise, Montana's economy is on the rocks, beleaguered by chronic high unemployment and wages as depressed as you'd find in rural Mississippi.

And Butte leads the way. Fewer than 30,000 people live here now and the number erodes every year. There's only intermittent mining being done now and few miners remain, mainly old-timers, many of whom wear oxygen masks along with their cowboy hats.

Butte has gone from being the richest hill on earth to the world's most expensive reclamation project and the nation's biggest Superfund site. The only good paying jobs in town these days go to the supervisors of those charged with cleaning up the mess and to the medical technicians who routinely test the blood of Butte's children for arsenic and lead.

The Superfund designation doesn't end in Butte. It extends down the entire 130 mile long course of Silver Bow Creek to Milltown Dam at the confluence with the Clark Fork River outside Missoula. Silver Bow Creek: that's what the Butte Chamber of Commerce handouts call it. But that's not how it's known to the locals. They call it Shit Creek, for its sulphurous stench and sluggish orangish-brown water. For decades, this stream served as little more than an industrial colon for the fetid effluent of Butte's mines. It is a dead river and a deadly one, too.

The Milltown Dam holds back six million cubic tons of toxic sludge: cadmium, arsenic, copper, lead, manganese, zinc. It continues to pile up year after year. No one knows what to do with it, though some local wits have suggested trucking it to ARCO's headquarters in downtown Los Angeles.

On the east side, the town of Butte comes to an abrupt end. The Berkeley Pit yawns across nearly a square mile of terrain. The gaping pit is filling inexorably with waters so acidic that they can't sustain life of any kind.

Over it all presides the Madonna of Rockies, a 100-foot tall statute perched on Continental Divide that glows at night like a slab of radium. Her arms are outstretched in piteous benediction of the hellish wasteland below. The locals call her Our Lady of the Tailings. She was erected in 1985 by a group of miners in hopes that the boom time would return.

It hasn't.

Not to fear. The town fathers have a plan to recharge Butte's flatlined fortunes. They want to turn Butte into a tourist haven, a kind of toxic wonderland. After all, they figure, people can't help looking at traffic crack-ups, the bloodier the better. Why wouldn't they throng to the nation's most poisoned city?

Perhaps they could call it Poisonville National Park. Poisonville. That's the name Dashiell Hammett, America's hardboiled Dante, gave to Butte in *Red Harvest*, his strange nocturnal novel of political corruption and corporate filth. "The city wasn't pretty," writes Hammett on the opening page of *Red Harvest*. "Most of its builders had gone in for gaudiness. Maybe they had been successful at first. Since then the smelters whose brick stacks struck up tall against a gloomy mountain to the south had yellow-smudged everything into uniform dinginess. The result was an ugly city of forty thousand people, set in an ugly notch between two ugly mountains that had been all dirtied up by mining. Spread over this was grimy sky that looked as if it had come out of the smelters' stacks."

That was written in 1929. The skies are clearer now that the smelters are shut down. But the town looks much the same. Only there's less of it.

There's a precedent, of sorts, and it's close at hand. Down the road 23 miles to the west is the town of Anaconda, once the biggest and foulest smelter complex in the world. The ore from the Butte mines was taken by the Company's railroad to Anaconda where it was chunked into the giant blast furnaces and melted down to commercial copper. The waste rock was piled in mammoth dumps. The smelters belched out their lethal smoke 24 hours a day, seven days a week, for decades. The smelter fallout turned the daytime sky dark and coated the land with poison in a radius of fifty miles or more.

Now, all that's left is a single dark smelter stack 534-feet tall and the sinister heaps of poison rubble, Montana's version of the tower of Isengard in Tolkien's *Lord of the Rings*. Today the stack and the hill it sits on are within a state park. But the ground is so polluted the public isn't permitted entry. It's a roadside photo-op, like the cooling towers of Three Mile Island.

But the big draw in Anaconda these days is the world class $8 million golf course, designed for ARCO by Jack Nicklaus and built on toxic mine wastes. The sand traps are black ash, culled from the burnt slag swept out of the smelters' ovens. It gives a whole new meaning to sand hazard.

"Odd as it sounds, those dumps are historic resources," says Mark Reavis, a Montana architect who is pushing the scheme to make Butte a national park. "The preservation community here is worried we're going to lose, bury and cover-up all signs of mining. Butte should be a monument to a societal decision: the quest for minerals. I'm trying to preserve. They're trying to clean up."

This mad scheme appealed to Bush's haughty Interior Secretary Gale Norton, for whom slag heaps seemed to exude an almost aphrodisiacal allure. The Bushites were desperate to jettison the troublesome notion of corporate liability for Superfund cleanups entirely. If they can do it in Butte under the banner of historic preservation so much the better.

***

On this fall day, fierce winds slam down off the spine of the Rockies, whipping the tailings into metallic dust devils that swirl down the streets, blowing by the great, decaying mansions of the mine bosses, the banks and the bordello museum, the courthouse and zinc bars, coating cars and people in a powder the texture of crushed bone.

My friend Larry Tuttle and I walk into a bar to get out of the toxic wind. Tuttle runs a green group called Citizens for Environmental Equity. It's a small outfit, but they carry a big stick and they like to whack big companies. Indeed, Tuttle may be the mining industry's biggest pain in the ass. He's seen it all, from the poison ruins of Summitville to the huge gash in the Little Rockies made by the Zortmann-Landusky mine. But even Tuttle seems awed by the Butte's 150 years of self-abuse. And he's been here before.

"You can't believe it until you see it," he says. "Then when you do, you feel as if you can't trust your eyes. It's the smell that makes it real."

On the wall of the bar is a ratty poster from a few summers back promoting Evel Week, a festival celebrating the exploits of Butte's most famous native son, the daredevil Evel Knievel. I'm sorry I missed it. Out waitress tells us that Joan Jett and the Blackhearts kicked ass on the final night, "as fireworks lit up the sky like bombs over Baghdad." Jett's brand of leather-metal seems perfectly geared to the sensibilities of Butte. This isn't a town for rodeos, but machines. Heavy ones.

"Evel cares about this place," the waitress tells us. "That's a lot more than you can say about the bosses at ARCO or those people at EPA. They don't give a fuck."

It strikes me that Evel Knievel is the perfect hero for the post-industrial West. His body is as broken as his hometown. Knievel's doomed aspiration led to him attempt to jump his jet-cycle across the maw of the Snake River Canyon. It was the perverse denouement of a bizarre career. Each Knievel event was an audacious flirtation with suicide, each one grander than the next. Meaning the odds of death were greater. In Knievel's world, the motorcycle jump replaced the public hanging as a spectacle.

We drain our beers and head west down Park Street, past the shuttered storefronts and EPA projects to decontaminate the front lawns of row after row of houses, many of them empty. The road takes us to Montana Tech, once the great mining school of this company town. The school gets a cut from the proceeds of almost every mining and logging operation in the state of Montana, a financial incentive to keep churning out students to work as unquestioning zombies for the very industries that are laying waste to the West.

Our destination wasn't the college, but the sedulously advertised World Mining Museum located on a backlot of the campus. The museum turned out to be little more than an enclosure of mining detritus—a gallows frame, hoist cage, rail cars, sheave wheels, dick shovels—with a few utterly unapologetic interpretive displays.

At the entrance to the Montana Tech campus is a bronze statue of Marcus Daly, the financial trickster who transformed Butte from a roughneck mining camp into the biggest boom town in the Rockies. The bronze is by America's most gifted sculptor, Augustus Saint-Gaudens. You get the idea Daly wouldn't have had it any other way. He saw himself as the Cosimo de Medici of Butte and Saint-Gaudens as his Cellini. Saint-Gaudens, it seems, had other ideas. His Daly is hardly a triumphal figure. The statue, erected two years after the robberbaron's death, depicts a porcine and blustery tycoon. It reminds me of Melville's *Confidence Man,* a smirking demon cackling up at the Madonna of the Rockies.

Butte got its start in 1864 when gold was discovered along Silver Bow Creek. But Butte wasn't destined to be a gold rush town. The real money was in a cheaper mineral that ranked second only to iron as the most important metal of the industrial revolution: copper. And in 1876 Daly laid his hands on one of the purest veins of copper in the world, the Alice Claim on Butte's hill. "The world doesn't know it yet," the squat Irishman boasted. "But I have its richest mine."

Daly headed back to San Francisco where he rustled up an impressive retinue of California gold rush millionaires as financial backers for his scheme to develop the Butte copper mines, including George Hearst, Lloyd Tevis and James Haggin. Haggin was dark-skinned and reportedly of Turkish descent. When Daly's arch-rival, William Clark, publicly smeared Haggin as "a nigger," it launched a decade-long feud that became the first shot in the famous War of the Copper Kings.

Of course, time and circumstances heal all wounds among industrial magnates and eventually Daly and Clark patched things up in the name of politics and profit. Clark went on to become a US senator from Montana, where he shepherded the interests of the mining conglomerates and became a favorite target of ridicule for Mark Twain. "He is said to have bought legislatures and judges as other men buy food and raiment," Twain wrote of Clark. "By his example he has so excused and so sweetened corruption that in Montana it no longer has an offensive smell. His history is known to everybody; he is as rotten a human being as can be found anywhere under the flag; he is a shame to the American nation, and no one has helped to send him to the Senate who did not know that his proper place was the penitentiary, with a ball and chain on his legs. To my mind he is the most disgusting creature that the republic has produced since Tweed's time."

Daly's company took it's name from one of the nearby mines, which supposedly derived from Horace Greeley's ridiculously optimistic assessment in the early days of the Civil War that Gen. McClellan's troops would encircle and squeeze the life out of Robert E. Lee's forces "like a giant Anaconda." It may not have been an apt description of McClellan's rather timid performance, but it did come to serve as the perfect totem for the nature of Daly's company.

Daly soon bought up or squeezed out nearly every other claim in town. Eventually, Anaconda's mines would yield up 20 billion tons of copper, fully a third of all the copper used by the US from the 1870s through the 1950s. Before the final frenzy, Anaconda's mines would generate more than $20 billion worth of copper.

Daly pumped the profits back into his operations. He built the town of Anaconda to smelter the Butte ore and it became an industrial complex to rival the steel mills of Gary. It wasn't just mineral claims Anaconda acquired. The Company owned more than a million acres of timber land, hundreds of sawmills, railroads, banks, and the rights to most of the water in western Montana. During its heyday, Anaconda would employ two-thirds of the workers in the entire state. And, naturally, it owned politicians, judges and every newspaper in Montana except one, the *Great Falls Tribune*.

By the 1890s, Anaconda was a true behemoth, a regional monopoly that few dared to tangle with. Its soaring profits soon captured the attention of the big daddy of trusts, Standard Oil, which made haste to acquire Anaconda in 1899. The people of Butte were warned that the travesties of Daly's reign would seem benign compared to what awaited them under the iron fist of Henry Rogers and Standard Oil. In a prophetic speech on the steps of the Butte courthouse, Augustus Heinz, the last independent operator in town, told 10,000 angry mine workers: "These people are my enemies: fierce, bitter, implacable. But they are your enemies, too. If they crush me today, they will crush you tomorrow. They will cut your wages and raise the tariff in the company store on every bite you eat and every rag you wear. They will force you to live in Standard Oil houses while you live, and they will bury you in Standard Oil coffins when you die."

Heinz was in the midst of a fraught battle with Anaconda over ownership of a particularly rich vein of copper that zigzagged through the Hill in a maze-like pattern. Anaconda took Heinz to court to seek sole possession of the vein. When the Company's handpicked judge refused to resolve the dispute in its favor, Anaconda shut down its operations, threw 6,500 miners out on the streets, and held the town hostage until it got its way. Heinz was defeated and Anaconda seized complete control of Butte. Then it turned its sights on destroying the only force that stood in its way: Butte's labor unions.

The extractive industries of the West-the logging camps and mines-were as brutal on workers as they were on the land. In Butte alone, more than 2,500 miners lost their lives in the tunnels and glory holes. Another 250,000 were injured, many seriously. Others got sick from foul water and cancerous air. A health survey of 1,000 miners in 1914 found that at least 400 of them suffered from chronic respiratory diseases. The maimed and ill were forced to work until they dropped, then they were discarded like human mine tailings.

Thus it's not surprising that Butte, the nation's biggest mining colony with some of the most wretched working conditions imaginable, became one of the birthing places of the American labor movement. In 1878, Marcus Daly tried to slash wages at his mines from a miserly $3.50 a day to $3. More than 400 miners walked off their jobs and paraded through town behind a brass band in protest. Then they formed the first union in town, the Butte Workingmen's Union. Daly got the point.

Soon there was only one mine that operated as a non-union shop, the Bluebird Claim. On June 13, 1887, union members marched to the mine and took the Bluebird miners to the Orphean Hall to forcibly induct them into the union. They told the befuddled mine boss they were there to: "gently intimate to the men that the shutting down of the mine would be in accordance with the eternal fitness of things."

A few years later, Butte's workers played the key role in forming the Western Mining Union. The Butte Miner's Union became Local Number One. By 1900, more than 18,000 laborers in Butte belonged to various trade unions: waitresses and bartenders, typesetters and sawmill workers, blacksmiths and brewers, teamsters and theatrical employees, hackmen and newsboys.

By and large, Daly got along with the workers and their unions. He'd worked as a laborer in the gold and silver mines in California and, to some degree, sympathized with the plight of the miners. He was also practical. Daly wanted to increase productivity as fast as possible and would do almost anything to avert a strike or a slow down.

This state of affairs changed immediately after Standard Oil absorbed Anaconda. Standard Oil had no tolerance for labor unions and set out to destroy the miners' unions of Butte. They hired Pinkerton agents to infiltrate the unions, finger the lead organizers, and sabotage the unions from the inside. The Pinkerton men developed a blacklist of union leaders that Anaconda used to summarily fire 500 workers, saying they were Socialists. Workers were required to sign the equivalent of loyalty oaths, identifying their political and union affiliations. Miners deemed radicals and agitators weren't called to work.

In the meantime, although the price of copper had soared from 8 cents a pound in 1878 to 20 cents a pound in 1914, Anaconda's wage-scale had remained the same: a flat $3.50 a day. This prompted a strike and violent counter-attack in 1914 that culminated in the dynamiting of the Miner's Union Hall. A few weeks later, Anaconda refused to recognize the legitimacy of the Western Federation of Miners.

But the union organizers kept at it, largely in the person of the IWW's Frank Little, a mesmerizing speaker who was running the IWW's Free-Speech campaign in Butte—the model for the Free Speech Movement in Berkeley. Little lashed out against the wretched working conditions that led to the Granite Mountain catastrophe, where 168 miners died agonizing deaths in the Speculator Mine. He also urged miners to reject the draft and refuse the call to fight in World War I, a message that appealed strongly to the Irish, Germans and Serbs who made up the bulk of Butte's mine workers.

Soon the Company had had enough. In the early morning hours on August 1, 1917, Little was rousted from his bed in a boarding house by Anaconda goons. They tied him to a rope behind their truck and dragged him down the main road in Butte. Then they lynched him from a railroad trestle. More than 7,000 people came to his memorial service.

But the Anaconda had won the day. The state of Montana bowed to their murderous masters at Anaconda HQ and officially banned the IWW and then enacted the Sedition Act that outlawed "disloyal, profane and scurrilous" writings and speeches of any kind-made by working people naturally.

Future labor uprisings would be crushed for Anaconda with the help of the National Guard and the US Army. From 1917 through 1921, Butte was an occupied town. The US Army captain sent to police Butte was none other than Omar Bradley, later a five-star general and commander of US Forces in Europe during World War II, who arrived in Butte with the Army's Company F in January of 1918. During his time in Butte, Bradley's troops crushed two strikes, seized the two union halls, and arrested more than 100 striking workers, charging them with sedition—Posse Comitatus Act be damned.

"When my men are ordered to do a thing, I believe they will do it," Bradley said after the raids. "We got orders to quell a riot and had no alternative but to quell it. I am glad nobody got seriously hurt, but I would rather have seen a lot of people hurt than to feel that my boys had let me down."

Thus Anaconda now gave marching orders to the US Army operating on domestic soil. Sixty years later, the Company, now a global giant, would call on Henry Kissinger and the CIA to protect its interests in Chile, where the government of Salvador Allende had nationalized Anaconda's copper mines. Allende fell and Pinochet's dictatorship, loyal to big copper, took its place, installing a 25-year-long reign of terror. This time around thousands of people got maimed, tortured and killed.

***

To get the best view the Berkeley Pit, you must enter a tunnel that could double as a runway for one of Evel Knievel's mad jumps. You emerge into a void: before you is a hole in the earth a mile and a half wide and more than 2,000 feet deep. The flesh-toned terraced slopes look like a ziggurat in the making. This is the Mammoth Cave of quarries.

A man next to us is leading a tour. He tells a group of retirees that as big as it is the Berkeley Pit isn't the largest open pit mine on earth. That honor belongs to the Kennecott mine south of Salt Lake City.

"Yes," Tuttle interjects. "But the Kennecott mine wasn't allowed to fill with water. Not yet, anyway."

The Berkeley Pit is filled with 17 billion gallons of acidic water and it's growing every day. From the viewing platform, it looks like Montana's evil version of Crater Lake.

By 1955, Butte had become the most relentlessly mined patch of land on the planet. But the richest veins of copper were beginning to run out. Anaconda, driven by the remorseless logic of efficiency, made a crucial decision to switch from mining the underground tunnels to excavating a giant open pit. It was a move that slashed jobs and trashed an already mangled landscape.

There was a minor obstacle. Half of Uptown Butte stood on the site Anaconda wanted to dig up. These city blocks included old mansions, the Columbia Gardens amusement park, the opera house where Twain spoke and Caruso sang, and the Irish community of Dublin Gulch, where miners once pelted J.P. Morgan himself with rotten tomatoes. It was yet another of Anaconda's hostage-taking schemes: allow us to gobble up your town or we'll shut down and move our operations to Arizona or Chile. The town fathers relented, of course, as they had always done. So did labor, even though it meant fewer jobs and lower pay.

So a new age was inaugurated in Butte: the era of open pit mining and chemical processing. New technologies and bigger machines allowed Anaconda to simply gnaw up the bedrock, pulverize it and strip out the metals in a chemical wash, leaving behind toxic waste heaps taller than any hill in Indiana. This noxious method would soon spread across the West. As so often before, Butte served as a working laboratory for some of the mining industry's most fatal ideas.

How long does it take to excavate a hole this big? About 20 years of 24 hour a day blasting. By the 1970s, the giant pit was pretty much played out. The price of copper had plunged. Newly enacted environmental laws began to nag at the company. Anaconda tried one last blackmail scheme in 1974, saying that to continue operations it would have to consume the rest of downtown Butte. The town's politicians got behind Anaconda's scheme to blow up the old core of the city, in a kind of civic suicide pact. But wiser heads urged caution and Anaconda lost interest. They shut down operations at the pit later that year.

In 1977, Anaconda sold off its operation to ARCO. The deal must surely go down as one of the most lame-brained acquisitions in American history. ARCO claimed that it felt too tied down to oil and gas operations and wanted to diversify into minerals. That rationale might sound compelling in a prospectus, but investors must have shook their heads at the decision to acquire an ailing mine that hadn't turned a profit in years. Perhaps they were looking for tax write-offs.

What they got was something quite different. In 1982, Butte was declared the nation's biggest Superfund site and ARCO was named the responsible party, on the hook for financing the clean-up of Anaconda's toxic playpen. Of course, the mess could never be cleaned-up, but the bill for what locals call the "suck, muck and truck" operation could tally in the hundreds of millions of dollars.

Then ARCO committed one of the great environmental crimes of our time. The company turned off the pumps that kept the tunnels of Butte from flooding with water. The internal plumbing of Butte had been permanently wrecked by the thousands of miles of underground tunnels that had pierced through the water table. When the pumps were shut off, the water poured through the tunnels, leaching a periodic chart of poisons out of the earth. This poisonous brew soon drained into the Berkeley pit. The waters flow there at the rate of more than five million gallons a day. Every day. Forever.

The waters of the Berkley pit permit no life to exist within them. It is a lake of sulfuric acid, powerful enough to dissolve metal. The cobalt-colored waters lure migratory birds down from the flyway to and from Canada. It's a lethal pit stop, since only a sip of these metallic waters is enough to kill. Over the years, thousands of geese, ducks and swans have perished here. In 1996 there was a mass poisoning, when nearly 400 snow geese died in the pit's lethal waters. Autopsies showed that the birds burned to death from the inside out—for the snow geese one taste of that water was like downing a pint of Drano.

In fifteen years or so, the poisonous waters of the pit will have risen to a level that will cause it to spill into the local aquifer, wiping out springs, wells and creeks. ARCO has belatedly begun construction of a pumping station near the pit at Horseshoe Bend, but there's no guarantee that it will work. Or that if it works, it will work in time to save the aquifer.

Meanwhile, ARCO continued to play political games with the clean up. The governor of Montana at the time was Judy Martz, a slaphappy Republican who used to run the Butte garbage company. ARCO financed her political career, but not without the stench of scandal. In 1999, when Martz was lieutenant governor, she and her husband bought 80 acres of land from ARCO along Silver Bow Creek. They paid only $300 an acre for the property, less than half the going rate for similar parcels in Butte. Martz chose not to publicly disclose the transaction, even though at the time the state was involved in litigation against ARCO over the cleanup of the very same Silver Bow Creek.

Martz is a kook, but she's ARCO's kind of nutcase. In her campaign for governor Martz proudly vowed to be "a lapdog of industry." And she's kept her word, going so far as to call the wildfires that scorched the West in 2002 "acts of environmental terrorism." Where is Mark Twain when you really need him?

* * *

Yes, history does continue to repeat itself in Butte. But not for much longer. The town has nearly reached its geographical limit.

In 1984, soon after ARCO pulled the plug on operations at the Berkeley Pit, financier Dennis Washington opened a new deep pit mine a few hundred yards away. He paid ARCO $18 million for the land. Then he engineered tax breaks from the nearly bankrupt city and the state, won waivers of environmental liability, got subsidized power and other inducements. And in a final blow to Butte's historical identity, Washington's East Continental Pit mine operated as a non-union shop. The mighty Gibraltar of Labor had finally been mined to dust.

Naturally, Washington made a killing. Perhaps as much as a billion dollars on that $18 million investment. Then in 2000 his mine too suspended operations. Of course, there's no requirement to restore the land. So now an extra 2.5 million gallons of acidic water streams into the toxic pit. It's the oldest story in the West: privatize the profits, socialize the costs, the risks and the fallout. And then hightail it out of town.

Perhaps the idea of a park here isn't such a bad idea after all. But it should be a national battleground, like the bloody fields of Antietam or Little Big Horn-hallowed ground where both labor and the environment were laid low.

The headstone on the grave of the Wobblies' great martyr Frank Little reads: "Slain by capitalist interests." It's a fitting epitaph for Butte as well.

Chapter 12

THE ORIGINS OF THE WESTERN GREENS: A THIRD FORCE IN WESTERN POLITICS

By Jeffrey St. Clair

FOR THIRTY-FIVE YEARS THE Democratic Party has enjoyed a nearly unquestioned hegemony over environmental politics, even though the greatest gains for the Earth were made during the Nixon administration.

In fact, environmentalists, along with civil rights and pro-abortion groups, have long constituted the activist core of the party: they have been its most effective organizers, most faithful (and forgiving) voters and most aggressive fundraisers.

But out in the American West there are signs that this long-standing relationship is heading for a crack-up. In several key western states, New Mexico, Montana, and Arizona, where the lines of separation between Republicans and Democrats have blurred to indistinction, have been launching independent and third party campaigns with the premeditated intent of evicting Democrats from seats they have long held. Encrusted incumbents, they call them.

The reason: mounting anger at the Democratic Party's neglect and, in many instances, active subversion of pro-environmental policies, particularly regarding the forests and rivers on federal lands in the West.

The price of these independent campaigns may well be the election of more Republicans to federal and state offices. But this is an outcome that many greens are willing to accept as the down payment on building a new political movement—and as a just political punishment for past abuses.

"The Democrats now represent a far greater danger to the environment than Republicans," asserts Tim Hermach, director of the Native Forest Council in Eugene, Oregon. "Clinton and Gore damaged our cause more in eight years, than the Republicans did in twelve."

Similar sentiments course through the campfire conversations of environmental activists across the West, a region that has lacked a true environmental champion in the Congress since the defeat of Senator Frank Church in 1980.

Green activists aren't alone in their disgust with the two-party system. A poll in the *Los Angeles Times* disclosed that 54 percent of American voters support the rise of a third party. The support is strongest among liberals (64 percent) and Westerners (60 percent).

Ironically, it took the end of divided government and the election to the presidency of a politician who came of age during the ascendancy of environmentalism as political force to fuel a discontent that had been smoldering for years.

Most greens greeted the election of Bill Clinton and Al Gore with a queasy optimism. While the Clinton/Gore campaign placed environmental protection and public lands reform near the top of the agenda, Bill Clinton was something of a known quantity. His record as governor of Arkansas, fused with his neo-liberal rhetoric, suggested a governmental posture that would sacrifice environmental quality for political expediency or the appeasement of corporate backers.

Even so, the pro-environment themes, expertly deployed during the 1992 campaign by Al Gore, played well across the country, particularly in the West, where Clinton captured seven crucial states. The Western Strategy, which proved pivotal to Clinton's election, was decidedly green in tone. It appealed to the changing demographics of the New West: suburbanized, soft-tech, mobile and capitalizing on the environmental amenities, and not the extractable commodities, of the Western landscape.

Within months of taking office, the Clinton administration began to beat a hasty retreat from its commitment to environmental protection. In March 1993, at the first hint of opposition from old-style Democratic politicians in the West, the administration backed off of its already timid proposal to reform archaic mining, timber and livestock grazing policies. An agitated Jay Hair, the usually temperate director of the National Wildlife Federation, condemned the betrayal as a case of political "date rape."

This was swiftly followed by a seriously compromised plan for the management of the national forests in the Pacific Northwest, home of the Northern Spotted Owl and endangered stocks of Pacific salmon and steelhead trout. Many long-time forest activists viewed the Clinton plan, known as Option 9, as worse than proposals offered during the first Bush administration that were deemed illegal by federal courts. Scientists predicted that Option 9 would not stop the spotted owl's slide toward extinction. But Clinton, Gore and Bruce Babbitt pushed their plan forward, steamrolling their former allies in the big green groups, and in 1994 new timber sales in ancient forests were being offered for sale to timber companies for the first time in six years—a feat that had eluded Bush the Elder. These were Clinton-created clearcuts and his administration boasted proudly of them.

Further backsliding followed, including relaxed pesticide standards; weakened regulations for the Endangered Species Act; a plan for the Everglades tailored to meet the demands of the sugar barons and real estate moguls of South Florida; failure to take decisive action to protect Columbia River salmon due to opposition from Speaker of the House Tom Foley and the aluminum companies; and the political firing of Jim Baca from his position as director of the Bureau of Land Management for his determination to reform grazing practices on federal lands.

Most of these policy flip-flops were engineered at the behest of Western Democrats, whose prevailing political strategy could be summed up this way: ignore the environmentalists; distance yourself from their issues; they will vote for you regardless of what you do. This regressive behavior has been repeatedly reinforced by mainstream and corporate conservation organizations, who almost unilaterally endorse Democratic candidates, even those with stunted environmental records.

Thus, early into the Clinton administration, environmental activists found themselves in the position of the Christian right during the reign of Reagan and Bush the Father: all packed up, but nowhere to go. While some conservationists resigned themselves to another era of environmental mediocrity, others decided to make a decisive split from a party that incessantly talked environmental values, while doing the dirty work of the corporate polluters.

The first shot in this rebellion was fired in Montana in the spring of 1994 by an unlikely candidate at an equally unlikely, but extremely vulnerable, incumbent. Steve Kelly, an artist and hard-core environmental organizer from

Bozeman, launched an independent campaign against eight-term incumbent Pat Williams, a liberal Democrat, for Montana's sole congressional seat. Williams, who won his last election by the slimmest margin in the House, was majority whip and was viewed by the Clinton administration as a key player on health care and environmental matters.

Correctly fearing that any attrition of votes from the left might doom Williams, the Democrats desperately tried to knock Kelly off the ballot, a tactic they would later use against Ralph Nader. But Kelly fought them off. Even though Kelly was a political novice who had never before run for public office and was so cash-strapped that his campaign couldn't even print bumperstickers or yard signs, early polling showed that he had won the support of nearly 10 percent of Montana voters. This showing prompted the *Rothenberg Political Report*, viewed as something akin to Biblical prophecy by Beltway savants, to suggest that Kelly's campaign might tilt the Montana race toward the Republican challenger, Cy Jamison. Jamison, an ideological clone of James Watt, became notorious as Bush's Bureau of Land Management chief for his numerous attempts to eviscerate the Endangered Species Act, actions which incurred repeated reprimands from federal courts.

The national Democratic Party and Clinton took the threat to Williams' seat seriously. In an effort to redeem the congressman's reputation as true green, the Administration deployed Al Gore to Missoula for a public booster session. This was a risky mission for the Ozone Man, because the more tightly the White House was seen to embrace Williams, the more the congressman tended to squirm to the right of the administration. Shortly after Gore's pitstop in Montana, Williams told the *Seattle Times* that he believed the Clinton administration "was making the same mistakes in trying to protect the land under Bruce Babbitt that the Reagan administration made early on in trying to use up the land under James Watt. Both came at it ideologically and went too far." With progressive congressmen like this, Kelly asked, who misses the likes of Ron Marlenee?

Montana and Idaho contain more than 15 million acres of federally-owned wildlands, the last refuge of the grizzly bear, gray wolf and bull trout. This is the largest swath of unprotected wild forest land outside of Alaska, but much of it, indeed most of it, is threatened by clearcut logging, roadbuilding and gold mining. In 1989, Kelly co-founded the Alliance for the Wild Rockies, a hard-nosed environmental group based in Missoula that developed the

Northern Rockies Ecosystem Protection Act (NREPA), a visionary piece of legislation that would protect all of these wildlands as either federal wilderness areas or national parks. While NREPA, probably the last hope of keeping the grizzly from going extinct, steadily gained support in Congress, serious consideration of the bill's merits was obstructed by Williams, who used his leadership position in the House to deny hearings on NREPA and push forward his own bill, which would have opened 4 million acres of wildland in Montana alone to clearcutting by timber giants such as Plum Creek and Champion International.

Kelly's anger at the anti-environmental policies of Williams, Jamison and the Clinton administration spurred his decision to run for Congress. "The Clinton administration was retreating from its campaign pledges to protect our public lands and Pat Williams played a key role in pushing them in that direction," Kelly told me. "Williams repeatedly voted against mining reform, grazing reform and measures to end subsidies to multinational timber companies. Worst of all, from my point of view here in Bozeman, Williams sponsored anti-wilderness legislation that condemns 4 million acres in Montana to logging and mining. Cy Jaminson's record spoke for itself. He never pretended to be anything but what he was: a voice for pillage."

As it turned out, Kelly was far from a single issue candidate. He was pro-choice, anti-nuke, an advocate for campaign finance reform and a single-payer health care system. But the issue that drove him to make his decision to bolt from the Democratic Party was the party's environmental betrayals.

Polls in Montana showed that Kelly was on to something. A few weeks prior to the election, a poll conducted by Lee Newspapers (a statewide chain in Montana) showed that 32 percent of Montanans supported passage of NREPA, a bill Kelly helped to write. By contrast, only 14 percent of Montana voters backed Williams's timber-industry oriented bill.

He didn't shy away from being labeled a spoiler, either. "I ran to win," Kelly said. "But if Williams and I had both lost and Jamison had won, it would have been a victory for Montana wildlands. Jamison never would have wielded the kind of power that Williams did."

This kind of unrepentant attitude earned Kelly the enmity of many liberals and prompted a testy rebuke from *The Missoulian*, a long-time backer of Williams. The paper's editorial writers carped at Kelly for "waging an environmental jihad—a holy war in which anyone opposed to NREPA is an expendable infidel."

For his part, Pat Williams sniped that Kelly's campaign threatened to wreck "the carefully constructed coalition between labor and conservationists. It will be a generation before it comes back."

But the marriage of labor and greens was chimerical at best, made up of labor leaders who had sold out workers to maintain a cordial relationship with transnationals such as Plum Creek Timber and professional conservationists who have traded off millions of acres of wildlands to secure ready access to politicians.

"If these independent political campaigns cause some conservative Republicans to get elected, well at least we don't have to guess where they are on an issue," said Larry Tuttle, director of the Portland-based Center for Environmental Equity. "Frankly, when it comes to changing the incentives that lead to environmental destruction, evironmentalists often have more in common with the National Taxpayers Union than with many incumbent Democrats."

Tuttle, who formerly headed the Wilderness Society's office in Portland and ran for congress as a Democrat in 1986 and 1988, points to the fact that the Democrat-controlled Congress annually awards nearly a billion dollars worth of subsidies for logging, mining and grazing on public lands. These subsidies are a legacy of the progressive "job creation" policies from the Great Depression (and earlier), which have long since been captured and perverted by multinational corporations, such as Louisiana-Pacific, Chevron and Noranda Gold, that feed off the public lands and the federal treasury.

Kelly and other independent greens hope to forge a new kind of politics in the West, mining regional veins of anarchism, anti-authoritarianism and libertarianism. "I told people I was running to the right of Jamison on fiscal issues and to the left of Pat Williams on most social issues and the environment."

Meanwhile, down in New Mexico, the spirited uprising of El Partido Verde, which ran a slate of candidates for local, state and federal offices beginning in 1994, threatens to topple the Democrats' long-standing stranglehold on the state house and establish a permanent and powerful new presence on the political landscape across the Southwest.

"El Partido Verde is a coming together of various people's movements, which have been disenfranchised by the pro-business policies of the Democratic Party: environmentalists, Hispanics, Native Americans and social justice groups," Pat Wolff told me. Wolff is a Santa Fe environmentalist and animal rights organizer who ran as a green candidate for state land commissioner, a position once held by Jim Baca. She was the first woman to seek that office.

A kind of Southwest Rainbow Coalition, El Partido Verde is a potentially explosive mix that is being emulated across the West. Hispanics and Native Americans alone account for more than 50 percent of the population of New Mexico, who have long been treated as electoral chattel by the Democratic Party. The initial platform statement of El Partido Verde called for campaign finance reform, assistance for community-based businesses, property tax relief for homeowners and small farmers, single-payer health care and strong environmental protection standards. "This is what the Democratic Party should have been about all along," Roberto Mondragón told me.

Mondragón is a Hispanic radio commentator and publisher of bi-lingual books, who served two terms as the Lt. Governor of New Mexico in the 1970s and 1980s. He ran on the El Partido Verde ticket for governor, challenging three-term Democratic incumbent Bruce King, a multi-millionaire rancher with a dismal environmental record, which includes support for a large nuclear waste dump near Carlsbad. King also vetoed numerous bills attempting to reform grazing, logging and mining on state lands. In that first election cycle, the candidates in El Partido Verde garnered between 10 and 30 percent of the vote, despite running on a miniscule campaign budget. "Look out," said party chairman Abraham Gutmann of Taos. "We are the third force in Western politics."

The environmental establishment and other Democratic Party loyalists were not amused. They hissed that such defections only throw elections to right-wing conservatives, viciously hostile to all that the liberal elites hold dear. Jim Baca, for example, who narrowly lost a primary challenge to Bruce King, refused to support the candidacy of his friend Mondragón, saying such campaigns "balkanize the political process."

Of course, that's precisely the goal of many of the new crop of greens, who see the two-party system as corrupt and undemocratic duopoly controlled by financial elites, imperialists and corporations. It was past time for a break up.

In 1994, I wrote a profile of Steve Kelly's Montana campaign for the Sunday Outlook Section of the *Washington Post*. Two days later the Sierra Club, which has long engaged in an incestuous relationship with the national Democratic Party, lashed out, trashing Kelly and other Greens, in a sad attempt to salvage the pitiful campaigns of their pseudo-environmentalists bosses in Congress.

"Green Party candidates support radical environmental change, and in some cases that's good and necessary, but they have zero chance of winning," chirped Daniel Weiss, the Sierra Club's national political director. Weiss delivered this strange assessment shortly after announcing his organization's unequivocal support for Kelly's opponent, Pat Williams, despite the fact that the Montana congressman rated a mere 54 percent (out of 100) on the Sierra Club's own political scorecard. This is how the Beltway Green became the mavens of mediocrity.

More and more environmentalists, however, are ignoring the ultimatums of Gang Green. They have concluded that the demolition of the Democratic Party's ruling superstructure is the only real hope for saving what remains of the Western ecosystems. "The legacy of electing candidates who are only marginally better than their opponents is readily apparent from the West's continuing loss of salmon, forests and natural deserts," says Larry Tuttle.

The green uprising spreading across the West represents a permanent renunciation of the pro-business policies enacted by the neo-liberals who have dominated the Democratic Party for the last two decades. It also signals the birth of a vigorous and principled new political movement that finds its most vibrant expression in the independent and third party campaigns.

This split was a long time coming. But the separation from the Democrats allows environmentalists to return to their roots in community-based, issue-oriented activism, freed from the enervating effects of politics by consensus, compromise and trade-offs. In the West, we may at last witness, to paraphrase . William Kittredge, a politics that is worthy of the landscape.

Chapter 13

THE AMBUSH AT RUBY RIDGE

By Alan Bock

PERHAPS IT WAS INEVITABLE that the longest federal trial in Idaho history would be followed by the longest jury deliberation in such a trial—a 20-day marathon that had news people joking about whether the jury planned to put in for retirement benefits. The eight-week trial of Randy Weaver and Kevin Harris grew out of such a bizarre set of circumstances that it's not surprising it took a while for the jurors to sort things out. It probably also took them a while to come to grips with the idea that government agencies could so blatantly engage in entrapment, lying, cover-ups, and the killing of innocent people. As one alternate juror, excused before deliberations were completed, put it: "I felt like a little kid that finds out there is no Santa Claus."

On July 8, 1993, in what *The New York Times* called "a strong rebuke of the Government's use of force during an armed siege," a jury in Boise found Randy Weaver, 45 and almost always described in the media as a "white separatist," and family friend Kevin Harris, 25, not guilty on six of eight counts, including murder of a U.S. marshal, conspiracy to provoke a confrontation with the government, aiding and abetting murder, and harboring a fugitive.

Weaver was found guilty on two minor counts: failure to appear on an earlier firearms charge and violating conditions of bail on the same count.

The story behind the Weaver/Harris verdict began with government entrapment and continued through 16 months of armed surveillance of Weaver's cabin in the steep, heavily wooded Selkirk Mountains near Naples, about 40 miles south of the Canadian border in the rural "panhandle" region of northern Idaho. It climaxed in a bloody shootout that left three people dead, including Weaver's wife, Vicki, killed by an FBI sniper as she stood in the door of the cabin holding her 10-month-old baby. In the wake of the shootout, federal agents offered shifting and contradictory accounts of the events.

There are several eerie similarities between the Randy Weaver episode and the federal government's deadly confrontation with Branch Davidians near Waco, Texas. Both involved the use of massive force against people with fringe religious beliefs. Both standoffs were initiated by the Bureau of Alcohol, Tobacco, and Firearms based on technical weapons charges. In both cases the FBI eventually became involved. There are two main differences: Fewer lives were lost in Idaho, and the government may actually be held accountable for what it did there.

We might as well begin with the government's indictment, which portrayed a conspiracy by Randy Weaver, his family, and others "to forcibly resist, oppose, impede, interfere with, intimidate, assault, and/or otherwise cause a violent confrontation with law enforcement authorities." In January 1983, Randy and Vicki Weaver left Iowa, where they had been living, and moved to northern Idaho—perhaps, as the indictment reads, "in their belief and prediction that a violent confrontation would occur with law enforcement officers involving a 'kill zone' surrounding their property," or perhaps, as friends and supporters say, to get away from the rat race and find a place where they could raise their children apart from the hustle, bustle, and immorality of American society.

It has been pretty well established that Randy and Vicki were loosely affiliated with or sympathetic to the Christian Identity movement, which holds, among other off-center beliefs, that the true descendants of the tribes of Israel are the modern nationalities of Europe, that today's Jews are impostors, and that Yahweh has fierce punishment planned for sinful America and its Babylonian Occupational Government. Christian Identity believers claim to live by Old Testament laws, to be the true heirs of Israel. Many or most are white separatists. (Unlike white supremacists, separatists say they simply want to live apart from other races, rather than persecuting or subjugating them.)

Naples may not be the remotest place in Idaho, as some early media reports had it, but it's pretty rural. About 15 miles south is Sandpoint (population: 5,200), a lovely resort community on the shore of the Pend Oreille Lake. About five miles north is Bonner's Ferry (population: 2,000), founded in 1863 as a trapper's outpost, with an economy now based on lumber, farming, mining, and recreation. Fewer than 2,000 people live in the Naples zip code. It's about 10 miles square, but because mountains rise on either side of the valley through which State Highway 95 runs, only an area about two miles by eight miles is inhabited.

A general store and a small sawmill are the only signs of commercial activity. Naples first "boomed" in the 1930s; in the '70s it tolerated an influx of hippies getting back to nature. Many of the residents are retirees. Others are attracted by the beautiful mountains, the low cost of living, the friendly, small-town quality of life, and, as Earl in the general store puts it, "the freedom." It's a place where every other resident, it seems, is a hunter, and most households own guns.

In January 1984, the Weavers bought 20 acres pretty far back in the woods and up in the mountains, on what was called Ruby Ridge. To get to the property, you have to drive about three miles on a decent dirt road off the main drag, then another couple of miles on a much steeper and heavily rutted dirt road. Yet it's only a few minutes from the town store, which in traditional general-store fashion stocks a little bit of almost everything, including classical-music tapes and compact discs. At Ruby Ridge, Randy and Vicki built a cabin on a small, rocky bluff, planted extensive gardens, built a couple of storage sheds, and lived, schooling their children at home. Randy would take occasional odd jobs to pay for things that required cash, but you can make it on relatively little money in the area if you garden and hunt.

The Weavers taught their children their unusual religious beliefs, but they weren't particularly active in either Christian Identity or white separatist events. They went to a few Aryan Nation meetings—there's an active organization around Hayden Lake, about 50 miles south of Naples—and to some Christian Identity summer camps. A sign at the entrance to their driveway reads "Every Knee Shall Bow to Jahshuah Messiah" (a.k.a. Jesus). They weren't regular churchgoers.

Around October 1989, Randy Weaver was introduced to "Gus Magisono," an alias for Kenneth Fadley, a paid undercover BATF informant in the Aryan Nation. "Magisono" asked Randy to sell him two shotguns with the barrels sawed off, even showing him where to cut. Randy was reluctant, but "Gus" was persistent and Randy was strapped for cash. Weaver finally sold him two shotguns for $300. Eight months later, a couple of BATF agents approached Weaver and asked him to serve as an informant within the Aryan Nation.

They told him they didn't have a warrant, but they did have incriminating conversations on tape. They threatened him with arrest and confiscation of his truck or house if he didn't cooperate. He refused.

In December 1990, Randy Weaver was indicted for manufacturing, possessing, and selling illegal firearms. The difference between legal and illegal in this case was about a quarter inch of barrel per gun and a $200 tax stamp. On January 17, 1991, two BATF agents, posing as a couple having engine trouble with a pickup truck hauling a camper, parked on the one-lane bridge leading to the Weaver property. Randy and Vicki stopped to help. When Randy looked under the hood, the male agent stuck a .45-caliber pistol in the back of his neck and announced he was under arrest. Other law-enforcement agents piled out of the camper. Vicki Weaver was thrown face down into the snow and mud. Randy was taken into custody and later released on a $10,000 bond. Vicki was not arrested.

The trial was originally set for February 19, 1991, then changed to February 20 for the convenience of the BATF. But Probation Officer Karl Richins sent Weaver a letter, dated February 7, instructing him to appear on March 20. Although Assistant U.S. Attorney Ron Howen, who later acted as prosecutor, knew Weaver had been sent an erroneous notification, he appeared before the grand jury on March 14 (six days before the date Richins gave Weaver) and won an indictment for failure to appear on February 20. That set the stage.

There's some question about whether Randy Weaver ever received a notification, even the one giving the wrong trial date. In any case, Weaver apparently decided not to appear, fearing he would be railroaded into prison on the basis of false testimony without an opportunity to defend himself properly. He spent the next 18 months on his mountain, hardly even venturing outside the cabin. Friends brought food and other supplies for the family, which by August 1992 included Sara, 16, Sammy, 14, Rachel, 10, and a 10-month-old baby, Elisheba.

Meanwhile, the feds began an elaborate 16-month surveillance of the cabin and surrounding area. Federal agents testified in court that they never seriously considered simply knocking on the door and serving the arrest warrant, because they feared an armed confrontation. Instead, they paid a neighbor (a relative term in this terrain but the house was on the only road to the Weaver property) to record the comings and goings of visitors and write down license numbers. They paid for a phone line to be installed at the neighbor's house.

They placed agents of the BATF and the U.S. Marshals Service on and around the property, usually in full camouflage gear. Agents went to the cabin in the guise of people interested in an adjacent piece of property that had no source of water and hadn't had a serious prospective buyer in years.

Two concealed video cameras, one solar powered, were set up to monitor the family's activities and visitors. Sniper positions were scouted The feds discussed various plans, including the use of stun guns and tear gas, cutting the water supply and kidnapping Sara, who slept in the "birthing house" (a shed several yards from the main cabin) during her menstrual period. About 160 hours of videotape were recorded. Agents rented a whole condominium building in Spokane as a base of operations. Neighbors and friends were questioned. Planes and helicopters were rented for aerial reconnaissance and photography. The habits of the family dogs were studied. Phone taps were ordered for several residences and for the phones at the general store.

Your tax dollars at work. All to capture a man accused of a minor gun offense, a charge that might well have been rejected had it come to trial. Even if Weaver had been found guilty on the weapons charge, he would probably have gotten a shorter sentence than the one he imposed on himself by holing up in his cabin.

The Weavers were aware of being watched, although they may not have known how extensive the operation was. They saw low-flying aircraft, and Vicki even invited a couple of obviously nervous "real estate prospects" into the cabin for coffee one day. Some friends report the family believed they would all be killed eventually, while others say the Weavers expected the feds to tire of the game. Likely their attitude shifted back and forth.

Finally, on August 21, 1992, the ultimate tragedy began. A six-man team from the Special Operations Group of the U.S. Marshals Service came onto the Weavers' property at 4:30 a.m., dressed in full camouflage and ski masks, carrying night vision goggles and silenced 9-mm pistols and M-16 machine guns with laser scopes. Three deputy marshals, Lawrence Cooper, William Degan, and Art Roderick, poked around close to the cabin, while the other three, in radio contact, were placed at observation points. The agents testified that they were doing surveillance for a possible future operation. A medical team was on alert at the bottom of the hill.

It's not easy to picture the Weaver property if you haven't been there. I spent several hours there in July of 1993 with Jackie Brown, who was one of

Vicki Weaver's closest friends and the cabin's caretaker during the trial. The Weaver cabin is on a stony outcropping, above most of the surrounding terrain, though the slope of mountain some 200 yards to the north towers over it. The road leading to the driveway is fairly steep; the driveway curves around a huge rock and up to the cabin. Except for a few acres cleared for gardens, the whole area is thickly wooded. In addition to the dirt road, an old logging road encircles much of the property. A trail runs more or less straight down from the cabin about a quarter mile to meet the logging road at a place described in testimony as the "Y" (it looked more like a "T" to me). The trail from the "Y" up toward the cabin is overhung with a canopy of leafy branches. The woods are so thick that you can't see the cabin from the "Y" or vice versa.

After poking around the property for a while, the three deputy marshals stood behind the rock near the driveway, well below the cabin, and started throwing little stones up toward the cabin, to "see if they could get the dogs' attention." Soon Striker, the family's yellow labrador, began following the agents, who circled the property along the logging road to the "Y," where there's a dense stand of trees.

Sammy Weaver and Kevin Harris, apparently believing the dog had sniffed out a deer or some other game (the family was out of meat), followed the dog along the logging road. Randy Weaver went down the straighter, easier trail. It's a fairly standard hunting practice to get a deer surrounded and trapped.

Cooper testified that before the deputy marshals could take cover (he said they feared being shot in the back), they saw Randy coming down the trail and ordered him to stop. Randy yelled at Kevin and Sammy to head back for the cabin, that it was an ambush. He fired a couple of shots in the air and ran toward the cabin.

Cooper and Degan took cover in the stand of trees. The dog and the two boys came to the "Y" and turned up the trail toward the cabin. What happened next remains in dispute.

Cooper told the jury that as the boys passed their concealed spot, Degan crouched on one knee and yelled, "Stop, U.S. Marshal!"—whereupon Kevin fired his .30-06 rifle from the hip and shot Degan in the chest. But Idaho State Police Capt. David Neale testified that shortly after the battle, Roderick told him that he, Roderick, had fired first, wounding and then killing Sammy's dog, Striker. And although the government initially claimed that Degan was killed by the first shot of the battle, seven shells from his gun were found near the deputy marshals' hiding place.

What is certain is that the dog was shot in the rear end (suggesting that he was running away) and then killed by a second shot. Sammy Weaver, who was running toward the cabin, wheeled around, yelled something like "You shot my dog, you son of a bitch," fired a couple of rounds, and started running again. Sammy was shot twice—first wounded in the elbow and then killed by a bullet in the back. Kevin fired his .30-06 at the marshals and believed he had hit Degan, though he insists the marshals started shooting first and he was firing in self-defense after Sammy was hit.

Roderick went for help. His report seems to have given those who weren't there the impression that a massive, continuing gun battle was going on. The authorities seemed to believe that the agents were "pinned down" by gunfire from the cabin, a very unlikely scenario given the terrain. Kevin made it to the cabin; he went back later to confirm that Sammy was dead. Toward evening, Randy and Kevin retrieved Sammy's body, wrapped it as best they could, and put it in the birthing shed near the main cabin. A siege that was to last 11 days was under way.

What happened the next day may have been determined by an airplane taking Richard Rogers, commander of the FBI's Hostage Rescue Team, from Washington, D.C., to Idaho. The law ordinarily permits the use of deadly force by law-enforcement officers only when the officers or others are in imminent danger of death or serious bodily injury. But in writing the "rules of engagement" for the siege to follow, Rogers, who had not yet spoken to anyone who had actually been at the cabin, didn't know about the 14 shots fired by the deputy marshals. He seemed to be under the impression that a fierce two-way gun battle was going on even as he wrote. So he decided that any armed adult outside the Weaver cabin should be subject to "shoot-to-kill" sniping, whether or not that person was menacing anyone.

Perhaps unbeknownst to Rogers, videotape surveillance showed that all members of the family, including the children, routinely carried a weapon when outside. The family owned 14 weapons—all legal until a couple of shotguns were sawed off at a government snitch's behest. That may seem like a lot of guns to some, especially city dwellers, but it isn't unusual in rural areas.

The arrival of the hostage team marked the beginning of the buildup. At least 400 people equipped with sophisticated military hardware, including "humvees," armored personnel carriers, and various aircraft, were eventually deployed in the woods around Randy Weaver's plywood cabin.

The rules of engagement required a warning before any shots were fired, but that didn't happen. On August 22, the day after the shootout, Randy Weaver left the cabin for the little outbuilding that held his son's body. As he raised his arm to unlatch the door to the shed, he was shot by a sniper posted on the mountainside. The bullet entered his right shoulder area and exited near his armpit. He and Kevin Harris, who was also outside, ran for the cabin. Vicki Weaver stood in the doorway, yelling for the two men to hurry, cradling baby Elisheba in her arms. She was unarmed.

As Kevin Harris tumbled into the house, another shot from the sniper went through the glass window and entered Vicki Weaver's temple, killing her instantly. The bullet and fragments of Vicki's skull went on to injure Kevin Harris's arm and torso, breaking a rib and puncturing one of his lungs.

The sniper, Lon Horiuchi, was a West Point graduate armed with state-of-the-art sniping equipment and trained to be accurate to within a quarter inch at 200 yards. He claims he missed Kevin and hit Vicki by accident. But Bo Gritz, the former Green Beret commander who eventually negotiated Randy Weaver's surrender, said that after he became a negotiator the FBI showed him a psychological profile of the family prepared for the Marshals Service before the siege that described Vicki as the "dominant member" of the family. "Vicki was the maternal head of the family," Gritz told the Spokane *Spokes-man-Review*. "I believe Vicki was shot purposely by the sniper as a priority target....The profile said, if you get a chance, take Vicki Weaver out."

In any case, Vicki Weaver was dead. Her body remained in the kitchen, covered with a sheet, for a week. Gritz, who thought he remembered Randy Weaver from Weaver's days as a Green Beret, arrived on the scene and offered to try talking Randy out peacefully. At first the FBI ignored him, but eventually they let Gritz approach the cabin. Gritz secured a promise from Wyoming trial lawyer Gerry Spence, whose previous clients had included Imelda Marcos and the family of Karen Silkwood, to represent Weaver if he surrendered peacefully.

On Sunday, August 30, Vicki Weaver's body was removed, and Kevin Harris, whose wound was infected, was taken to a hospital under heavy guard. Around noon the following day, after lengthy discussions with Gritz, Randy

Weaver and the three girls came out. Randy was arrested, and his daughters were met by their maternal grandparents, who later took them back to Iowa.

Ron Howen, the assistant U.S. attorney who had been on hand during the siege, secured a 10-count grand jury indictment of Randy Weaver and Kevin Harris in September. As the trial began in April, U.S. District Judge Edward Lodge told the seven-woman, five-man jury: "This will be one of the most interesting cases you could be asked to sit on as jurors." As Dean Miller, staff writer for the *Spokesman-Review*, wrote later: "If anything, Lodge's remark was an understatement."

The first of 54 government witnesses was Deputy U.S. Marshal Lawrence Cooper, who appeared in court wearing the same paramilitary full-camouflage regalia he had worn the day Sammy Weaver and William Degan were killed. A couple of witnesses detailed the confusion about when Randy Weaver's original court date had been scheduled. Then came a long string of witnesses testifying about the Weavers' beliefs. Although no evidence was presented to tie the Weaver family to neo-Nazi activities, the full panoply of right-wing anti-Zionist, anti-Semitic beliefs was trotted before the jury. Spence objected, saying the prosecution was attempting to "demonize" his client, but the prosecution was allowed to spend several days describing conspiracy theories, interlocking groups, and violent activities.

Spence and the other defense attorneys used cross-examination to smash holes in the sometimes shifting stories of government witnesses and to put the government on trial indirectly. They uncovered the embarrassing fact that some bullets had been removed from the scene, then brought back later to be dropped on the ground and photographed. They made sure jurors got a close up look at photographs of the dead dog, Striker, with tracks showing that tank-like vehicles had run over his lifeless body several times. They got the original snitch to admit that it was difficult to persuade Randy Weaver to sell sawed-off shotguns and that Weaver had little inclination to break the law.

Judge Lodge issued a formal reprimand and imposed a fine on the prosecution after background information on the sniper and his initial reports—ordered to be made available to the defense—was sent by fourth-class mail from Washington, D.C., arriving the day *after* the sniper had testified. The defense team got a government ballistics expert to admit, after poring over maps and diagrams of the "Y," that the physical evidence supported the defense's version of events as easily as it did the prosecution's.

At one point, with the jury out of the courtroom as attorneys argued whether a witness should be called, Judge Lodge wondered aloud why Spence was objecting. By Lodge's estimate, about 75 percent of the testimony from government witnesses so far had helped the defense. When the prosecution rested, the defense declined to call a single witness, saying the government had so manifestly failed to prove its case that no defense was necessary.

On the final Friday of the case, *Spokesman-Review* writer Dean Miller reported, lead prosecutor Ron Howen "was 15 minutes into his response to the defense motion for dismissal when he appeared to lose his train of thought. Up to that time, his left hand was shaking violently and his delivery lacked its characteristic vigor. After a long pause, he sighed loudly, shuffled through his notes and looked over at co-prosecutor Kim Lindquist, who smiled encouragingly back, raising his eyebrows. Howen turned back to his notes and then stopped. 'I'm sorry, judge, I can't continue,' he said, his voice unsteady." He left the courtroom and did not return after a recess. Lindquist had to present the closing argument the following Tuesday.

Spence was pleased by the verdict but not satisfied. "A jury today has said that you can't kill somebody just because you wear badges, and then cover up those homicides by prosecuting the innocent," he said. "What are we now going to do about the deaths of Vicki Weaver, a mother who was killed with a baby in her arms, and Sammy Weaver, a boy who was shot in the back? Somebody has to answer for those deaths."

If the holocaust in Waco hadn't happened even as the Weaver trial was under way, all this might be an essentially regional story of government bungling with tragic results. But Waco did happen. The lead agency there was the BATF, determined to make an arrest of dubious public-safety importance with an overwhelming show of force. The FBI got involved when the confrontation became a siege (Dick Rogers was on the scene at Waco too), and massive amounts of military and paramilitary equipment were deployed against American citizens. The option of a simple arrest was rejected in favor of a military-style attack. Innocent people were killed.

If you talked to some of the self-styled patriots who hung around the Boise courthouse, you would hear all kinds of scary theories. The Weaver operation was just a dress rehearsal for Waco, which was part of a government campaign to shut down, intimidate, or terrorize minority religious groups and political dissenters. Now and then, you'd hear that the real problem was Zionist control of the government.

But the reasons for what happened in Naples and Waco are less sinister and more mundane: In their approach to the Weavers and the Branch Davidians, federal law-enforcement officials displayed a mixture of vanity, arrogance, fear, anger, and frustration. An ironworker hanging around the Naples General Store in early July 1993 saw it this way: "All these federal agencies–IRS, DEA, BATF, FBI, FDA–have too many agents trained in paramilitary tatics. They get itchy to see if the training really works, so every so often they have to target some poor sap."

Certainly the BATF, which Reagan and Bush era budget cutters recommended abolishing, seems to be an agency in search of a mission. It began life as the Bureau of Prohibition, but it survived after Prohibition was repealed in 1933. It was reorganized as the Bureau of Alcohol, Tobacco, and Firearms under the Nixon administration. The Bureau currently carries out a mix of licensing, regulatory, tax-collection, and law-enforcement functions that could easily be handled by other agencies, if they are necessary at all. It's doubtful that the republic would be any poorer if the BATF ceased to exist.

But the problem goes beyond the BATF, to a mindset that says people with strange ideas cannot be trusted. The notion that religious nuts with guns are always a threat to public safety becomes a self-fulfilling prophecy. The attempt to subdue these supposedly dangerous people provokes the very violence it is intended to prevent.

It need not be so. Sociologist Jim Aho, author of *The Politics of Righteousness: Idaho Christian Patriotism*, told a Coeur d'Alene newspaper that "the big myth about these people is they are essentially evil." Through years of research and interviews, Aho found that members of "patriot" groups weren't unusually inclined toward violence, nor were they particularly socially isolated. Contrary to stereotypes, they were about as well educated as their neighbors. Aho said his findings surprised him, but "on the whole, I found these people pretty indistinguishable," apart from their "bizarre and unique" beliefs.

This is not to say that you'd want to have members of the Christian Identity movement over for dinner. But people can have odd ideas, even abhorrent and disturbing ideas, and still live peacefully with their neighbors. It's best that we let them.

Chapter 14

IGNOMINY AND RESISTANCE IN IDAHO: LAST STAND IN THE BIG WOODS

By Jeffrey St. Clair

"Every time I've compromised, I've lost. When I held firm I won. The problem with too many environmentalists today is that they are trying to write the compromise instead of letting those we pay to compromise do it. They think they get power by taking people to lunch or being taken to lunch, when in reality they are only being taken."

—David R. Brower, 1994

THERE WAS NO REASON it had to come down like this: Two militant greens standing in the middle of an isolated, snow-crusted road in a place where a road should never be; bracing their bodies against a train of logging trucks, snowmobiles, and Forest Service jeeps groaning at the gate, demanding entry; willingly subjecting themselves to arrest by Idaho troopers armed with guns, clubs, and a draconian and sub-constitutional new law. All in a last-gasp attempt to halt a vastly destructive timber sale in the heart of the nation's largest roadless area, a timber sale two federal judges had already found to be a brazen assault on our national environmental laws.

Charged with felony conspiracy to commit a misdemeanor, Mike Roselle, a founder of Earth First!, and Tom Fullum, of the Native Forest Network, now face possible five-year prison terms and $50,000 fines under Idaho's so-called Earth First! Statute—a law geared to smother popular dissent against the transgressions of multinational timber companies by slamming the jail-house door on anyone bold enough to bodily protest logging on federal lands in the Potato State. The bill was signed into law in 1993 by then-Governor Cecil Andrus, a noted liberal who called the Cove/ Mallard protesters "just a bunch of kooks."

The proximate cause of Roselle's and Fullum's travails, and a new round of logging in the Cove/Mallard Roadless Area, is an act of organizational cowardice committed by one of the country's oldest and wealthiest environmental corporations: The Wilderness Society.

In January 1994, The Wilderness Society and Pacific Rivers Council won a slam-drunk injunction against the Forest Service in federal court. Citing the agency's contemptuous behavior for failing to submit its logging plans for review by the National Marine Fisheries Service after several stocks of salmon were placed on the endangered species list, federal district Judge David Ezra halted all logging, mining, and grazing in salmon watersheds on the Nez Perce, Salmon, Challis, Sawtooth, Clearwater, and Payette National Forest in central Idaho. The Cove/ Mallard timber sale, along with 300 other logging, road building and mining projects, were stopped cold.

The evidence of an imminent ecological collapse of Idaho's river systems is overwhelming. In America's wildest state, more than 70 percent of the streams are out of compliance with the standards of the Clean Water Act, dozens of stocks of salmon gasp along with the bull trout at the brink of extinction. This means that every additional clearcut or mine gouged into these watersheds creates a necrotic wound in the ecosystem. This was the emergency situation to which Judge Ezra responded with his injunction.

Of course, the predictable backlash swiftly erupted in rural Idaho when news of the injunction was leaked to timber contractors, ranchers, and mining companies by the Forest Service. Local papers played up the inevitable chest-beating by a mongrel assortment of loggers, ranch-hands and placer miners from towns with names like Challis, Dixie and Kamiah. Then came the apocalyptic assessments of the ruling by mega-corporations such as Boise/ Cascade, Potlatch, and Hecla Mining: Mills and mines will be closed, they warned, thousands will be thrown out of work, already impoverished communities will be driven deeper into destitution.

The injunction also became a pretext for yet another round of vituperative cant from Idaho's reactionary congressional delegation. On the floor of the Senate, Dirk Kempthorne (who would later become Idaho's governor and then Interior Secretary under Bush the Younger) bellowed that he would seek congressional action to shred the injunction and "the ill-conceived laws it was based on." Meanwhile, Helen 'Call-Me-Congressman' Chenoweth denounced the injunction as the work of "animal worshipping nature cults." And the stentorious Larry Craig, the senator with the wide stance, amplified the volume of his "forest health" crusade—a cruel hoax on the public in which the last roadless forests in the West will be stripped of the meager protection provided them by current environmental laws and opened to indiscriminate chainsaw surgery in the name of medicating the ecosystem.

The Wilderness Society flinched and folded. They beat a rapid retreat, dragging the Pacific Rivers Council and their lawyers at the Sierra Club Legal Defense Fund along with them. What follows is a saga of graveness that undercuts the credibility of nearly every environmentalist working to protect the planet in the dark times.

A week after the injunction came down, Craig Gehrke, the Wilderness Society's Idaho rep, sent an alarum to the Sierra Club Legal Defense Fund office in Seattle, begging them to reappear before Judge Ezra and beg him to retract his ruling. SCLDF was loathe to engage in such a shameful turnabout. They explained to Gehrke that the Judge might interpret such a back flip as a severe breach of legal ethics. After all, only a week earlier SCLDF had persuasively argued that there was an emergency situation unfolding on the ground that needed a drastic legal remedy.

But Gehrke was undeterred. He insisted that the injunction be lifted. Higher levels of the Wilderness Society also phoned Seattle, explaining to SCLDF attorneys the delicate political situation they faced back at their gilded offices on 17th Street, in Northwest Washington, DC. Word is that former Wilderness Society boss George Frampton, then Bruce Babbitt's right-hand man at the Interior Department, also called to suggest that the injunction was counter-productive to his good efforts at the Interior Department to salvage the Endangered Species Act.

For SCLDF attorneys this entire scenario must have seemed like a bad flashback to the notorious Deal of Shame, where 18 months previously lawyers at the same office insisted that the plaintiffs in the spotted owl case release timber sales in old-growth forest that had been enjoined by Judge William

Dwyer. This time, however, the roles were reversed: SCLDF's clients were now twisting their lawyers' arms to jettison an injunction.

By all reports, the conference call with an infuriated Judge Ezra was a bruising encounter for the eco-lawyers. When SCLDF explained the unexpectedly intense reaction the injunction had sparked in Idaho, the judge reportedly pulled out a sheaf of faxes and retorted that he'd been taking heat from Salmon and Challis, too, but he thought the case was about enforcing the law and protecting the salmon. According to a source close to SCLDF, Judge Exra threatened to impose legal sanctions on the attorneys. Ultimately, however, with none of the parties to the case standing up for the injunction or the salmon, Ezra was left with no choice: the judge delayed imposition of the injunction for 45 days. But for all practical purposes the injunction that could have saved the forests of the Salmon/ Selway river watersheds is gone forever.

When queried on the subject, SCLDF attorney Adam Berger reasoned: "We believe our actions served the best interest of justice."

Justice for whom? "Well, everyone understands the meaning of justice and that's all we're going to say," Berger concluded.

With Roselle and Fullum safely locked up in the Grangeville jail and Judge Ezra's injunction aborted at the demand of the Wilderness Society, the road was now clear for the Forest Service and the Shearer Lumber Company to bust into the largest units of the Noble timber sale, deep in the heart of the Cove/Mallard. In a move that reminded many forest activists of the midnight strike on Millennium Grove (a forest stand in the Willamette National Forest that harbored the oldest trees in the Oregon Cascades), Shearer Lumber swiftly attacked the two most lucrative and biologically productive stands of ponderosa pine in the 18-unit Noble timber sale.

Most of the Noble sale was already clearcut prior to March 15, the date SCLDF and the Wilderness Society chose to have the injunction postponed until. In fact, the Cove/Mallard EIS required the Forest Service to terminate operations prior to March 15, since that is the beginning of elk calving season. Ron Mitchell, director of the Idaho Sporting Congress, believes the March 15 date may not have been coincidental. "It sure looks like these groups simply wanted to avoid the politically explosive issue of Cove/ Mallard," Mitchell said. "The betrayal of the Wilderness Society on this point is devastating."

The 90,000 acre Cove/Mallard Roadless Area is a biological cradle in the mountains, a rolling landscape of ponderosa pine forests, meandering streams, and wet meadows that serves as a critical biological and migration corridor between the Salmon River and the high country of the Gospel Hump and Selway Mountains. Its brisk streams are home to steelhead, chinook salmon, bull trout, rainbow trout, and cutthroat, while the broad meadows harbor some of the best elk country in the Northern Rockies. The tall mountains are inhabited by bighorn sheep and mountain goat and the entire area is a key part of the Central Idaho grizzly bear and gray wolf recovery areas. In fact, over the past 10 years the Fish and Wildlife Service has documented numerous confirmed wolf sightings in the Cove/Mallard Roadless Area.

The Noble timber sale was one of nine big timber sales slated for the Cove/ Mallard. These sales called for 200 different clearcuts, the logging of 81 million board feet of timber, and the construction of 145 miles of new logging roads. When completed the Cove/ Mallard timber sale will leave behind only an empty infrastructure: its web of roads a lethal impediment to the migration of wolves and elk; its eroding swaths of bare land quietly smothering salmon and trout. In sum, Cove/ Mallard will be transformed into a crumbling necropolis to modern forest management.

Yet, the Wilderness Society (the organization founded by Aldo Leopold and Robert Marshall, and nurtured by Howard Zahniser) has never objected to the Cove/Mallard logging operations. Indeed, Cove/Mallard was simply a sacrifice area, traded-off years ago by the political brokers at the Sierra Club, Idaho Conversation League and The Wilderness Society in exchange for partial protection of the spectacular, but less controversial, Gospel Hump Wilderness.

The wretched terms of this deal are even now defended with intensity by Sierra Clubber Dennis Baird, of Moscow, Idaho, who in 1992 proclaimed to *The Oregonian:* "If the country need lumber and timber jobs, the Cove/ Mallard isn't such a bad place to get it." Given a chance to retract this comment, Baird instead tried to drive a couple more nails into Cove/ Mallard's ecological coffin. "The Northern Rockies Chapter [of the Sierra Club], which covers all of Idaho and some of eastern Washington, never opposed timber sales in the Cove/ Mallard because the area is mostly flat."

In fact, the relatively flat, rolling terrain of portions of the Cove/Mallard only underscored the area's ecological importance. Yet, we all know only too well that the burghers of the Sierra Club prefer to wage their wilderness fights on steeper terrain, in alpine areas which offer fewer stands of productive forest and less opportunities for political conflict.

Baird was a key author of the Sierra Club's woefully deficient national forest policy, a policy that has been under vigorous assault for years by grassroots Sierra Club activists. Baird also served, along with his friend Craig Gehrke, as a member of Cecil Andrus's secretive 1993 Idaho Timber Supply Task Force, which was chaired by Boise National Forest supervisor Stephen Mealey. The objective of the timber task force was to find ways to provide certainly for timber supplies from national forest lands in Idaho.

"Basically, the intent of the task force was to expedite timber sales in Idaho roadless areas by circumventing NEPA," said Ron Mitchell, whose group was refused access to the background documents generated by the task force. "Gehrke and Baird were there to put a green stamp on illegal timber sales."

The persistent criticism by Mitchell and Dan Funsch, an organizer with the Alliance for the Wild Rockies, effectively checked any official pronouncement from the task force. However, its secret agenda proceeds apace on the ground. At 10 million acres, Idaho retains more unprotected wildland than any other state; yet the Forest Service plans to lacerate the region with 150 commercial timber sales in these roadless areas in the coming decades, despoiling its wilderness character and placine hundreds of species (from salmon to grizzlies) in peril of extinction.

Meanwhile, Steve Mealey perfected the art of expedited timber sales on the ravaged Boise National Forest, where dozens of so-called salvage sales in roadless areas escaped full compliance with NEPA. Mealey's free-wheeling excursions in the forested foothills around Boise served as a disturbing prelude to the looming gotterdamerung for Western roadless areas promised by Larry Craig's forest health campaign.

As the chainsaws were cleaving through the Cove/ Mallard once again, Craig Gehrke defended his surrender (on the very day Roselle and Fullum were appearing at their preliminary hearing) by telling a reporter for the Missoula *Independent*: "We trust the Forest Service to abide by the law."

Various rationalizations and excuses for the release of the Idaho salmon injunction pinballed between the parties. SCLDF, for example, told an incredulous Judge Ezra that the injunction was now unnecessary because the Forest Service had agreed to begin consulting with NMFS. Immediately after the stay, Gehrke announced to the Idaho press that the Wilderness Society "did this voluntarily ... We didn't want to come between working people and their jobs."

The Pacific Rivers Council's Ron Cooper (a former Wilderness Society staffer) told distraught Idaho and Montana forest activists that while he personally disagreed with the decision to lift the injunction "sometimes you've got to come promise in the face of political reality." In Oregon, PRC's David Bayles cast a similar line, chirping that they agreed to lift the injunction only in order to save "the Endangered Species Act."

Meanwhile, Rich Hoppe, a spin doctor at the Wilderness Society's D.C. headquarters, tweeted that they released the injunction to protect Gehrke, who had purportedly received death threats. Back in Idaho, however, Gehrke insisted that he was more concerned about the "safety" of rural activists.

There is nothing especially exculpating in any of these statements. Quite the contrary. SCLDF's comment about consultation is a transparent canard, since it merely relies on the discretionary actions of a discredited agency. In other words, precisely the reason they went to court in the first place. But the legal effects of this surrender extend far beyond merely this case. SCLDF's retreat alienated a sympathetic and friendly federal judge and darkened the prospects for any new environmental suits throughout the Ninth Circuit. Greens may have the legal standing to sue, but now lack the credibility needed to secure difficult legal decisions.

"Maybe the lawsuit was ill-timed considering the new political atmosphere," said Mike Medberry, former public lands director for the Idaho Conservation League. "But it was a good suit, a necessary action. Giving up the injunction so quickly sent the worst possible political and legal message."

The real politick banter of the Pacific Rivers Council also falls flat. It represents the don't-use-it-to-don't-lose-it approach to environmentalism. But of what value is the Endangered Species Act, if the cost of saving the law requires some species to be consigned to extinction? Moreover, there is no evidence that the lifting of the injunction has lessened the rabid attacks against the ESA and other environmental laws launched by Idaho's congressional delegation, and their corporate backers.

Obviously, the political pressure from the wacko right in Idaho was intense, particularly from Craig, Chenoweth and Kempthorne. But there were several angles of effective counterattack against these politicians available to the plaintiffs. Take Rep. Helen Chenoweth, the primped heroine of Idaho's burgeoning population of potbellied punks and middle-aged skinheads, the prissy pinup girl of the Posse Comitatus, a woman who morphed the religio-cosmetic acumen of Tammy Faye Bakker onto the paranoid political sensibilities of Lyndon LaRouche.

Chenoweth is a former legislative aid to former Idaho Sen. Steve Symms (an intellectual neighbor of Dan Quayle's in the lower depths of the Bell Curve), who trounced the ineffectual Democrat Larry LaRocco by running an openly racist campaign, which had as its recurring theme: "White anglo-saxon males are the only endangered species." Chenoweth occasionally grabbed the mic at Don Young's Natural Resources Committee to launch rambling and incoherent *ad hominem* attacks on the evils of environmentalism, along the lines of her now famous aphorism: "Salmon aren't endangered, there are cans of them on the shelf at Albertsons."

Back in September 1994, Chenoweth's strange election campaign (which featured endangered salmon feast, among other mindless amusements) was running low on cash. For salvation, she turned to a traditional source of financial succor for Idaho politicians: mining companies. Chenoweth sold an "interest" in a parcel of land she owned in the Clearwater country to Allen Ball. Ball paid Chenoweth $60,000 for part owner-ship in a property with an assessed value of less than $10,000.

Ball owns the A-B Mining Company. It is possible that A-B Mining purchased the subsurface rights to Chenoweth's property and intends to excavate this mineral-laden land. But A-B Mining also has plans to construct a massive cyanide heap-leach gold mine along Smiley Creek, a salmon stream that flows off the pyramids-shaped Abe's Chair Mountain in the Sawtooth National Recreation Area.

The transfer of cash was not reported to the Federal Election Commission and a new deed was never officially filed with the county clerk. A week after the deal, however, Chenoweth held a press conference to announce that one of her first acts as a "Congressman" would be to open the Sawtooth National Recreation Area to new mining claims. An apparent case of political *quid pro quo*.

Chenoweth's populist protestations about the injunction could have been exposed as nothing more than a thin veneer concealing her pursuit of self-enrichment. Instead, the Wilderness Society opted for appeasement, a strategy eerily foreshadowed by Gehrke shortly after the election when he publicly declared: "I don't want to pick a fight with these guys." But the neurotic pursuit of the political center in a state where the ideological spectrum spans from the well-off xenophobe to the well-armed white supremacist is vain and self-immolating.

This leads directly to the dire consequences of the Wilderness Society's most feeble and lachrymose excuse: By placating vague threats of violence, the Wilderness Society dramatically increased the odds of real violence being visited upon grassroots activists in the near future. Their surrender strengthens the resolve and amplifies the intensity of the most venomous sects of the Wise-Use and Militia movements, not to mention the henchmen of Boise/ Cascade and Hecla Mining. The atmosphere of intimidation against environmentalists in Idaho, and throughout the West, will only be torqued-up by such supplicant behavior.

"Not only did Gehrke help nullify an effective injunction that had stopped the Cove/ Mallard sale for at least a few more months," said Russ Moritz of the Kanisku Bioregional Council in Sandpoint, Idaho. "But he offended a friendly judge, forced Roselle and Fullum to sacrifice themselves, and show the opposition just how weak the national environmental groups really are."

Craig Gehrke, of course, is a merely deserving scapegoat for the real forces that asphyxiate the Wilderness Society's agenda: money and politics. At the center of this dispiriting nexus is Cecil Andrus; and, most importantly, Walter Minnick, CEO of the Boise-based timber company TJ International.

Minnick's transnational enterprise, Trus-Joist, is partially owned by timber giant MacMillan Bloedel, scourge of Canada's forests. Evidence of the nefarious character of TJ International's operations can be found in the company's 10K filings with the Securities Exchange Commission, where Minnick bemoan the facts that successful litigation on federal forests in the West has constricted timber supplies. In order to combat this "problem," TJ's annual report to its shareholders announced the formation of a "strategic alliance" with MacMillan Bloedel and Weyerhaeuser. Booming profits simply aren't enough to satiate these masters of capital.

TJ International's corporate neighbor Boise/ Cascade, which enjoys a near monopoly on federal timber supplies in central Idaho, may soon be folded into this grim oligarchy of timber interests. The debt-saddled timber company (whose products were being boycotted by environmentalists because of the corporation's logging operations at Sugarloaf in a grove of ancient forest the

Siskiyou Mountains of Oregon) is now run by financier George Harad, an old Harvard chum of Minnick's, whom Walt recently described as being "dazzling in his intellectual ability and financial acuity." Boise/ Cascade, it will be recalled, energized much of the so-called popular opposition to Judge Ezra's injunction.

That Walt Minnick might use his position on the governing board of the Wilderness Society to leverage the surrender of the salmon injunction shouldn't surprise anyone familiar with this man's past activities. Many west coast forest activists painfully recall Minnick's performance at Bill Clinton's Timber Summit, held in Portland in 1993, where the CEO seemed more obsessed with advertising his engineered wood products, declaring his opposition to restrictions on log exports, and securing certainly for the federal timber supply, than in advocating permanent protection for ancient forests, Pacific salmon or spotted owls.

From where I sat that gloomy day (buried in the basement next to the then high-flying and frantic George Stephanopolos and Andrea Mitchell, of NBC News, who kept asking me in the latte line: "Murrelet?...Sounds kinky! What's a murrelet?"), Minnick came off as more of a timber beast than Weyerhaeuser's vicious genius Charlie Bingham. As an offer of proof, check out this gem of neoliberalism, delivered as a quasi-threat to President Clinton, where Minnick warns that if timber supplies are not freed from the Dwyer injunction he might be forced to export his mills to Canada: "Essentially what we need the government to do is get out of the way, let the market system work, get some certainly into the west side timber supply because we don't know whether to build another plant here to go to Canada or even whether we should be hiring folks for a month from now, because we can't be assured that our veneer supplier are going to have the raw material we're going to need."

This was hardly the first time Minnick wielded an iron fist to well-intentioned Wilderness Society policy initiatives. Several years ago Minnick helped crush an attempt by former Wilderness Society staffer Larry Tuttle and former board member Terry Tempest Williams to change the organization's archaic policy on public lands grazing. Among other things, Minnick vociferously rejected a proposal that the Wilderness Society oppose livestock grazing in designated wilderness areas. It should be noted for the record that many of the society's board members and large donors own ranches in the West, including new Wilderness Society president G. Jon Roush, who logged off old growth trees on his own big ranch in Montana and then sold the timber to a notorious log exporter.

"The Wilderness Society's founders, Aldo Leopold and Bob Marshall, believed that progress in environmental protection required radical political and economic changes," said Larry Tuttle. "But the new Wilderness Society through its repeated actions has refused to challenge a system where our public resources are controlled by renegade public agencies and multinational corporations, a system that assumes that our natural resources exist solely for the purpose of making money. The Wilderness Society's corporate motto is: Whatever you do, don't offend anyone."

That brings us to Cecil Andrus, former Secretary of the Interior under Jimmy Carter and four-term governor of Idaho (where he signed into the law the unconstitutional statute that threatened to imprison Roselle and Fullum), who was angered at the effrontery of the salmon injunction given his long and fruitful association with the Wilderness Society.

In the revolving-door-milieu of American environmental politics it was probably inevitable that in 1981 the Wilderness Society would hire the unemployed ex-cabinet secretary as a high-profile influence peddler. Andrus' assignment: develop a bridge between industry and environmentalists on natural resource issues. Well, Andrus didn't so much construct a bridge as a one-way interstate down which Idaho's forests have been happily transported ever since.

For this contribution to the Wilderness Society, Cecil Andrus was handsomely rewarded when he decided to run for governor. Grateful Wilderness Society board members invested heavily in Andrus's campaigns, side-by side with mining companies, agribusiness conglomerates, and timber interests, including Minnick, Boise/Cascade, and Dick Bennett, purchaser of the Cove/Mallard sales.

When George Frampton threatened to close down the Society's Boise office as a cost-cutting move in 1992, Andrus rushed to the rescue. He declared that Craig Gehrke was just the kind of moderate, homegrown environmentalist Idaho needed. An emergency fund-raiser was arranged at an exclusive ranch north of Sun Valley. It was attended by the likes of Charlotte Ford, Bruce Vento, Walt Minnick, Andrus, and Pamela Harriman. Tens of thousands were quickly raised; Gehrke's office saved.

Then Gehrke speedily climbed aboard the timber supply task force, gave qualified endorsement to the awful LaRocco wilderness destruction bill, and refused to oppose the Cove/Mallard timber sales even when his fellow environmentalists were being assaulted, hit with SLAPP suits, and hauled off to jail. After Andrus left the governor's office, he joined the board of directors of two mining companies, both of which were eyeing claims in central Idaho that might have been hampered by the injunction.

Connect-the-dots; it's not a pretty picture.

The whole Cove/Mallard affair reads like synecdoche for how the environmental elite operate these days. Each new entry on the bleak tableau of conscience-eating concessions, compromises and trade-offs strikes like a body blow against grassroots environmental activists standing up on the frontlines for salmon, wolves, and wildlands.

Still a palpable resistance survives. Amid the cratered reputation of the national environmental corporations a grassroots insurrection is being incubated under fire. This new movement is symbolized by Roselle and Fullum standing there at that gate, facing off with the police, the logging trucks, and the Forest Service, in the freezing mountains of central Idaho, and by the dozens of other activists who rushed to Idaho to stand in their place.

The grassroots movement is healed and galvanized by the feverish efforts of Ron Mitchell and the Idaho Sporting Congress to uncover new legal angles to save this imperiled landscape. And by the growing troops of rural activists with groups like the Alliance for the Wild Rockies and Kanisku Bioregional Council who have the courage to stand up in their communities and say: Damn it, we've simply got to save it all for our own good.

In the end, the wild land itself is redemptive. This land particularly so. Or that's how it seemed to me on an autumn when my 10-year-old son Nathaniel and I had come to take our stand at the gate in the lower reaches of the Cove/ Mallard: the sky splayed with stars, the air spiced with the scent of ponderosa pine, the sound of the salmon-graced river still flowing free.

Chapter 15

VISHNU SCHIST AND THE WILD WEST

By Josh Mahan

THE FREEDOM OF THE road has always captured the imagination, most people bound to their respective cities, corner coffee shops, and ways of life. With this in mind, Mike and I load our bags into the back of the El Camino and take the back roads to the Colorado River. What are we searching for? Freedom. The open road. We want to find out if you can still ramble the roadways of the American west without seeing too many fences and badges. Yellowstone to Arches was the route. Sister parks with sister cities. Missoula to Jackson to Moab. It seemed a more logical route to the Grand Canyon than following the choked interstate through Salt Lake's nasty urban spread.

Why not? Hadn't Earth First! sprouted in the wilderness of northwest Wyoming. The Thoroughfare Basin, southeast of Yellowstone is still the furthest one can travel from a road in the Lower 48. And didn't Abbey inspire a generation, dispatching from the pre-pavement, slick-rock back of beyond. We were, after all, on our way to the Grandest Canyon left.

We smoked out of Missoula in the rain. Our Lowbagger buddy Hyside Danny was parking cars for the Griz game. Some guy had parked in the whole lot. We couldn't do much more for Hyside than give him a Pabst tallboy from the cooler. Leaving town was bittersweet, but worth it all the while.

Gunning Bozeman bound, Mike wanted to catch up with Finkle, a high-profile writer friend of his. We both wanted to harass Phil Knight, an old EF!er, and like many old EF!ers, now a mainstay in the non-profit world. But as the Stones say, you can't always get what you want, and we missed both of them.

We settle down for the night with Howie and Marilyn south of Livingston. I also call Marilyn mom. Mike and Howie have been buddies for decades, and are somehow tied for life due to an organization called Earth First! they founded in the early '80s. When Mike and Howie get together they still can't agree on what caused the Earth First! tailspin, or tipping point for that matter. The two are still friends, though a silent schism remains. Some things are better not to be pressed too hard.

Yellowstone is snowy, and the Park Ranger at the Gardiner entrance tells me that snow tires and chains will be required on the passes. "Ma'am, these tires are top of the line," I say, knowing full well Mike probably has a bald pair of street tires on the Camino. He confirms my suspicions inside of the park. We roll past the geysers that mark the world's first National Park. We pass part of the last remaining wild herd of bison. We continue on through the sweeping openness, and through the thick patches of forest recovering from the '88 fire. It's October and tourists are in Oahu. The park is quiet. When the snow lets up enough to let the Tetons peak through, I know I'm almost back to Jackson, my hometown, and the longest place Mike ever called home.

Driving into town on Cache Street we pass the Bridger-Teton National Forest Headquarters, where I met Mike in the mid-eighties. Back then the Freddies wanted to drill for oil in grizzly country around Yellowstone. People were pretty pissed, including Mike. He built a prop oil derrick, as I remember—it was large; but I was fairly small, six at the time. The image that stands out the most is Mike dropping the thing in the middle of the parking lot from the back of a pickup truck, and expressing his general frustration with the project. As we rolled past the building in the Camino Mike said, "I remember that place being bigger." I thought the same thing, but we'd both seen a lot since that day.

Jackson, on the other hand, has grown into a circus-freak cluster of facades, stretching south and littering the "Y." The old Wyoming Woolens on the town square has been replaced by a Gap. The old-time soda fountain, Jackson Drug, has fallen to a dealer of Persian rugs, and is now known as Jackson Rug. Even the oil-soaked floors of my dad's small-engine repair shop have been converted to support the $500 soles of high-end home décor shoppers and art gallery goers. My dad, Ralph Mahan, owned it when it was Ceece's Small Engines. Ceece owned the shop in the '70s and my dad worked for him. Then Ceece had a heart attack fighting the infamous Wort Hotel fire. My dad took over the shop. And if anyone ever called him Ceece when they came into the shop he never seemed to mind.

I think about all this as we park on Jackson's town square. I try to find my favorite tree from when I was a kid. It's been cut down and replaced with a flagpole. We eat a Billy Burger. It's good. Some things you just can't screw up.

It wouldn't have been right to pass through Jackson without stopping at the Simpson House, a Lowbagger haunt of the ages. I'm skeptical that the Simpson House has remained unchanged, since the rest of town has fallen to yuppie convention. But Mike, a graduate of the Simpson House Scene of the Seventies, insists we must visit the Lowbagger refuge. We cold-call with a knock on the door, and are pleased to find the usual Jackson riff-raff waiting on the couch for snowflakes to start falling from the sky in some location besides Mormon Country. Mike inspects the house like an absentee land lord back from Borneo. I stay in the front room, doing my best not to seem too conspicuous. Occasionally I hear an outburst from some secret corner of the house. "Ah, I like the addition of the bunkbeds!" In the end, he discovers a piece of fossilized rock that still stands prominently in the front room. Mike had screwed it into the wall some thirty years ago, the fossil itself now a modern archeological find.

At that moment in time, with October clouds hanging low on the Tetons, it seemed that snow was indeed close. And the Colorado still very far away. Southbound and down. Loaded up and trucking. Good-bye to the Snake. Hello Hoback Country. A quick stop at the Camp Creek Inn, Howie's old haunt. "We're on our way to the Grand Canyon, but used to live here," we tell them, and are met with the instant camaraderie of old-time Teton-folk. A round and we drive on. The Grayback Ridge Roadless Area rises up to the southwest.

Around the same time I met Mike, Howie was doing six months in the Sublette County jail for pulling a proposed Chevron oil road's survey stakes out of National Forest land in the Grayback. A lot of folks thought it was a pretty stiff sentence for opposing an unjust policy of plundering roadless land for marginal economic gain. But the road surveyor who caught him tried to kill him with a hatchet for what amounted to a misdemeanor, so I guess it could have been worse. It was an intense time in the northern Rockies. Another wave of land wars. Back then we pushed for wolves in Yellowstone, and for remaining roadless areas to remain untouched. At the time those positions were considered radical, even crazy. Today they're mainstay. In that sense, I guess it's all been worth it. Driving the Hoback Road south toward Pinedale reminds me of runs my mom and I used to make over the sagebrush highlands to see old Howie in the slammer.

It's up on over the divide, now, into the Green River's headwaters, and the Oil Patch of southwest Wyoming. The landscape is dark by now, and my wingman snores, eminating stale Pabst and cigarettes. The road runs straight. I do my best to dodge the Jackelope, only females out tonight—no sign of antlers. Occasionally black is broken by the glow of an oil derrick. We lay out somewhere near Green River, Wyoming, dusty cowboys in the sagebrush.

The next morning we shoot past the Flaming Gorge, and rocket up an arid plateau. The El Camino purrs like a tiger on acid staring at Vishnu Schist exposed at the bottom of the Grand Canyon. You see, Vishnu Schist is some of the oldest rock exposed on the planet at 1.7 to 2 billion years old. It's the roots of an ancient mountain range once as tall as today's Rockies. I couldn't wait to see it. But for the time Mike and I were on an 8,000-foot, modern-day Rocky Mountain plateau with mile-long groves of aspen trees; white trunks solid, leaves quaking in full golden glory. We were visitors in Indian Country, Uintah and Ouray, and it still didn't feel like we were in Utah, a good thing.

Dropping into Highway 6 we encounter a town named Friend and suddenly it's apparent that we are indeed in Utah. On to Price, another Green River, and finally we cut south with Highway 191 and roll into Moab late in the afternoon. We detour for a quick drive up the muddy Colorado, our first view of the river, and then zip into town. While Moab has grown over the past decade, it has yet to mushroom with the same grotesque lavishness that swallows Jackson.

Kicking around, we run into a couple other guys who will be joining us in the Canyon: Dirty Dayton, former wilderness ranger and bona fide Lowbagger, and the kilt-wearing Colonel Abe, a Missoula legend. Dayton is in town on business. A lady friend from Estes Park has agreed to meet up with him. We go for drinks. The kid who waits on us at the Rio spends most of the night watching, and cheering for, pro wrestling on the television. Always prepared, the Colonel pulls out his personal remote and turns off the television. I wander off to see just how cold the beer is at the famed Woody's Tavern. I sit in a barber's chair and watch the tail-end of a Monday Night football game. A rowdy crew of young locals is drunk and playing pool. Good to see. I spend the rest of the evening moseying around in a dark, creek-side city park.

Early morning finds me with Mike hiking the front-country of Arches. Edward Abbey's back yard. It's hard not to be impressed. So many have seen the beauty of the untrammeled west through Abbey's words. Out here, as in Abbey's writing, it's easy to understand the importance of the palatial expanses of arches and desert scrub-brush. Abbey wrote from the back of beyond, from solitaire. Today the paved roads of Arches are choked with people on a pil-grimage to the place the desert anarchist found so valuable. The fact that they come in shiny SUV's and clog the trails is a paradox too profound for me to pick apart at this juncture. But at least the word is out in Ohio. "There is beautiful, unspoiled land out there that should stay that way," they say back at the office.

I met Abbey once at the '88 EF! Rendezvous on the North Rim of the Grand Canyon. Howie was always good about getting me a little face time with the greats. As I remember we didn't have much to talk about. He wore a big white hat and the signature beard. Years later I would pay my respects at his graveside, alone at sunset, deep in the open desert. Abbey has passed, but his legacy lives on. During a long stretch of road toward Bluff I think of a couple questions I would have asked him back in '88. Maybe something like, why did the Mormons get southern Utah?

Roselle and I blaze on toward Bluff and Navajo Country. Two rocks perched on spires pull me into a nearby café for coffee. Hoodoo voodoo. The Camino drops down across the San Juan River, through Monument Valley and into Arizona. Storm clouds lay out a light veil of rain. I push the accelera-tor and tune the satellite radio to Outlaw Country. On through Page, bang a left, then a right and drop into the pink walls of the Marble Canyon of the Grand. We grab a shuttle rig at the put-in and drive down to the South Rim. We grab drinks at the El Tovar. The service is terrible and it is apparent that the joint is long overdue for a lousy review. Mike spends the night in the front seat of his El Camino, a bold Lowbagger move, proving that, time-and-again, he's the king. A bit softer, I seek shelter on the bench seat of the van I drove down from Marble Canyon.

If you've ever thought of spending much time anywhere near the South Rim, don't. It's a hell-hole maze of worthless gift shops, sloppy over-priced eateries, boring bars and over-used trails. That being said, the vista of the canyon from the South Rim is breath-taking. Lowbaggers appear out of the woodwork the next morning. Big Country comes in from Alabama, and Oko from Texas or India or something. Gia, the Montana mama finds us. Dayton and the Colonel straggle in last, taking an extra day to arrive from Moab. Dayton glows like I've never seen before, so we take the Bright Angel Trail down into the canyon.

And the trail goes down, down, down. Past where the tourists stop. Past Indian Gardens. Past the Devil's Corkscrew. And down to the place that Mike and I have been running to reach for the past five days: the bottom of the Grand Canyon, man. One of the seven natural wonders of the world. Deep and wide. Mike had toted a block of ice, wrapped in his sleeping bag and stuffed in his dry bag down the full 5,000 vertical feet and presented it as a birthday gift to Trip Organizer Wayne Fairchild. Wayne is a modern day Powell, in more ways than just the fact that they both prefer to float the Canyon without ice.

We meet up with the rest of our crew at Phantom Ranch. They've been pacing and drinking beer for a couple of hours, so they are happy to see us, and even help us carry our bags to the boats. The line-up includes a hardy bunch of current and former Salmon River guides, a Santa Montanican kayaker, Roselle (whose been down the Canyon before) as a trainee, and Gene and Chuck Fairchild to keep everyone in line. In all, a pleasant crew.

We row upstream that night and camp above one of the more renowned white-water sections in the country. Tomorrow Big Country will be tossed out of his boat in Horn Rapid and Mike Roselle will ace the rapids in a cataraft. But tonight we have no idea what will happen, and I go to bed early.

I can still feel myself splayed out on my Paco Pad, perched upon the metal deck of my boat frame, the constantly fluctuating river rocking the garish yellow, 18-foot craft. The Colorado can be a loud river from shore, its waves constantly lapping on the small shoals of sand that 16 people call home. The spits are communal sanctuary from the deep, green ribbon that rockets side-slope across the Colorado Plateau.

It's ten days into it now and we've braved thick stretches of whitewater, late morning shadows, and the hardships and joys of Old World life. Today I find Vishnu Schist in all of its seasoned wisdom and glory. Who thought that an ancient black chunk of rock could change somebody's life? Furthermore I was staring at the Great Unconformity. No I'm not talking about Mike Roselle.

The Great Unconformity is where Tapeats Sandstone lays directly on Vishnu Schist with over a billion years of geological record missing in between. Some say an inland sea is to blame for the robbery. But who really knows. The Grand Canyon will steal your mind and show you your soul. It's a bold statement, I know. But the Canyon is a unique stretch of water. Such immensity, day after day. The labyrinth and depth ripple the mind. One searches for true meaning, true importance with each thundering rapid.

Lava Falls makes me re-examine a few things. When our crew ran it, the flow was relatively low, 6,500 c.f.s. to 9,000 c.f.s., but Lava was still kicking. The Colorado River drops thirteen feet in an abrupt mess of frothing waves and holes. We run right. We zag above the nasty, two-thirds river wide keeper hole. Then, square into the lateral just below a more forgiving, but formidable hole. We stick it—and slam into the infamous V-Wave. Coming through that drop and froth, it's on to the final maneuver: a school-bus-sized rock waits below, and next to it, a twenty-foot surging wave. The trouble is that the river wants to throw us on the rock, and we just want to run that wave straight. Team Lowbagger somehow gets it done. Fingers in D-ring, ass on bow, Mike Roselle rode the bull all the way through.

The party below Lava is as crazy and liberating as the rapid itself. We pull over with dangerously high endorphin levels. Joe pulls out a bourbon handle and feeds it to the circling sharks who are whooping, embracing hands knuckle-to-knuckle, and ripping into last night's smoked brisket, one of Garland's famous hunks of meat. Nobody had really been able to eat breakfast.

The night flows like honey with beers, baked ziti, and vodka passion-fruit. The crew shares a bottle of whiskey and a bottle of tequila for dessert around the campfire. At some point clothing becomes ridiculous, and naked moonlight volleyball the only option. We all awake the next morning knowing we have taken another step from society's conventions, and are a little closer to the tribes that once thrived in this canyon.

Reflecting on the journey in the twilight beneath the not-to-be-underestimated Mile 205 Rapid, I wonder where the time has gone. All of the side-canyon hiking in Deer, Mat-Kat, and Havasu Creeks has been as spectacular as the rugged big-drops of Crystal, Hermit, Granite, Horn and Ruby rapids. If time is ever lost on the Grand Canyon, it is only because you can't remember every foot step and oar stroke in such a place. Just be thankful we didn't lose this gem to a dam.

River time ends sooner than later, especially for those of us expected to punch words into a rectangle of plastic plugged into the wall.

Rain is dumping out of the sky and has been all night when we near the take out. For some of the crew it is Day 18 in the wild.

For Wave Two, it's Day 13. The outboard engines of the Hualapai pontoon boats whine as we approach the ramp. We trade the sweet desert air for the aftertaste of engine exhaust. A commercial outfit scrambles to break down its gear and get its clients out of Diamond Creek.

The push to get up Diamond before it flashes, as in floods, is growing death-defyingly dim. Sixteen people scurry in the mud and break down nine rafts with an eighteen-day-tough intensity. Turn it up a notch. The mood is electric as we caravan up the tight wash, not sure if the next blind corner conceals a wall of water, rock, and mud rolling down the hill.

Once again we are visitors in Indian Country. Hualapai Land. People of the tall pine trees. The road out of Diamond Creek leads to Peach Springs, a canyon-top Native town. It's a stark contrast from the canyon. A post-colonial slap. There are no peaches and no springs, just run-down cinderblock homes and hard stares. The rain has stopped drilling the earth, and the temperature has dropped to forty degrees. People are cold. Fellow guides Jimmy, Meredith, and I huddle in a muddy parking lot keeping watch on 15 river bags, shivering and waiting for the rest of our crew to climb back to the New World. Roselle found his El Camino, fired it up, and turned on Outlaw Country.

The ride to Vegas is blustery. Roselle rips apart the newspaper like it's a plate of baby-back ribs, gleaning each section like a man would slide the flesh off a bone. I swear he licked his fingers before he said "This storm decimated southern California yesterday." The Camino shudders in another gust of wind. Up through Kingman, and then we're stopped at a Homeland Security checkpoint. "Any cartridges in that box?" the Homeland Security officer asks me. It's Roselle's ammo can, used as a man purse on the river. "No ma'am." With that the Camino rolls over the Hoover Dam. The river we've ridden for days sits plugged and stagnant in Lake Mead.

The rain won't relent. Over a pass, and down into the sprawl of Henderson. We pull off the expressway at Las Vegas Boulevard, and descend into the infamous city of sin. A wrong turn on Fremont Street puts us straight into North Las Vegas and skid row. Junkies line the streets, wandering absentmindedly in front of the Camino. Though only hours from the canyon, we've come a long way.

Vegas is a Lowbagger heaven: cheap rooms, never-ending rows of cheap food, and free booze for playing a game. Bet slowly, my Lowbaggers. Roselle and I finally find the Golden Nugget. The lobby is busy with rich people checking in. I stand in line, still wearing wet river pants and Chacos. I think I may have stood out.

Surreality sets in by nightfall, as we hit the Black Jack tables, playing with the best of them, full of Canyon stories. Dudley and I share hot seats at the Golden Gate and chips pile up, at least for a couple of poverty-stricken Montanans like us. Then it's off to Caesar's Palace in a stretch limo, a far cry from my 18-foot craft. Walking around amidst the neon lights, it seems like a dream. I half expect to awake with sand in my hair, the rosy light of dawn above an ocotillo skyline, and the descending call of a canyon wren. I mean, this had to be a dream. The bar won't close.

As it turns out I am awake after all, and it is time to return to Montana. This place houses the walking dead. Mike and I split north, stopping at a small eatery just off the main drag in Alamo. I have one hell of a sweet-pork sandwich, and we push north. Leaving Las Vegas the city quickly succumbs to Desert, which gives way to Great Basin. Fifteen hours to home. No sleep 'til Missoula. We hadn't left Vegas until well after one in the afternoon. The delay was worth it. Mike had reunited with his Dad, Lee Roselle, for the first time in 27 years. It was all hugs and war stories. But now it's dark and we are in Ely. We hit Jackpot by midnight. I keep pushing and Mike starts dozing near Twin Falls. Up through Carey, a quick stop at Wild Rose Hot Springs, just to check the temperature (it gets colder every year). The Camino rumbles through Craters of the Moon, past the country's first atomic city, over the Big Lost River (site of the '86 rendezvous) and below Mount Borah, Idaho's highest peak, shining in the moonlight.

Somewhere near what I call Challis Pass, Mike gets cold. He's tired, too. And probably needs a beer. But shit, I've been driving all night. Mike wants the heater on. I can't stand the heater at this point. He pushes the heat up. After ten minutes, I bring it back down. It goes on like this for awhile. Finally Mike freaks out. "Don't touch that fucking thing." I ask him if he could put on a jacket. "I don't need to put a fucking jacket on in my own fucking car," he explodes. Maybe he wouldn't have been so defensive if his jacket hadn't been soaked still from the rainstorm at the takeout. I'll spare you the ensuing conversation, but Mike decides he should drive, and promptly slams into a deer. Near Salmon I convince him to hand over the wheel again, and fly us into Hamilton, Montana for breakfast at the Coffee Cup. Inside the old men are talking about pulling a shotgun on any environmental regulators who want to look at their woodstoves. For some reason the tough redneck words ring comforting. It's good to be home.

Heavy-eyed, I finish the drive, as the sun comes up over the northern Bitterroot Valley. Thick frost coats the fields and windshields of trucks that have lay dormant throughout the night. It's the first frost I've seen this autumn. Fall in the northern Rockies. It feels clean. A fat fog hangs low on the river. Almost back to Missoula.

Chapter 16

THE ELEMENTARY SCHOOL VS. THE STRIP MINE: ED WILEY'S LONG MARCH

By Mike Roselle

TONIGHT SOMETHING VERY STRANGE and wonderful is happening here on this warm fall evening. The sidewalk in the front of the Harry's Bar at the aging and slightly dilapidated Hotel Harrington is alive with the sounds of mountain music. It is so loud the sound is drowning out even the noise of the downtown traffic. The banjo player is wailing and the guitar player is picking, strumming and belting out ancient hillbilly ballads. A small crowd is gathering around the musicians, their curiosity getting the better of them. These are not your normal buskers or your normal Washington street musicians. Rather than facing the audience, the musicians are ignoring them, facing each other, staring at each others fingers in order to detect the next chord change. They are reaching for that high and lonesome harmony that is as much a part of the Appalachians as the rivers and mountains themselves. You can hear them hollerin' over two blocks away.

As we listen, a slew of young activists circulate through the audience and pass out literature and campaign buttons to the passers-by explaining to them the dangers of strip mining in the Appalachians and why we they had come here to *Warshington*, as the denizens of Appalachia pronounce the name of our Nation's Capitol. We are all here for Mountaintop Removal Week with over 60 citizen lobbyist from 13 states who have traveled here to work for passage of H.R. 2719, the Clean Water Protection Act, a bill sponsored by Rep.

Frank Pallone that would prevent the dumping of mine waste into streams and curtail mountaintop removal. Most of these folks came to town on their own dime and by this evening had held over 50 meetings with members of congress.

This morning, Floyd and I, along with Ed Wiley, a West Virginia grandfather and former coal miner, and over one hundred supporters marched the final mile of Ed's epic 455-mile walk from Marsh Fork Elementary School in Sundial, West Virginia to the steps of the Senate Office Building. Ed left Charleston on Aug. 2 to raise awareness about the school's location next door to a coal refuse pond and preparation plant; and to build public support for the construction of a new school in a different location.

Marsh Fork Elementary School is on the front lines of the controversial practice known as mountaintop removal coal mining. It's students are becoming the casualties.

An active 1,849-acre mountaintop removal coalmine surrounds the school area. Marsh Fork Elementary sits just 225 feet from a Massey Energy coal-loading silo that releases high levels of coal dust and saturates the air in the school. Independent tests have shown that coal dust is hazardous to the health of school children. And a leaking earthen dam holding back 2.8 billion gallons of toxic coal-sludge is also located above the school site. What's more, Massey Energy wants to build another silo. Much to the chagrin of people like Ed Wiley.

One of the more exciting developments in the fight for Marsh Fork School came last month, when the West Virginia Department of Environmental Protection denied a permit from Massey Energy to build the second coal silo beside the school. For the residents of the West Virginia coalfields, this was a big victory for the community, the kids, and the larger fight against mountaintop removal. The West Virginia DEP has twice denied the application to build another coal silo next to the elementary school. The existing silo has been found to be even closer to the school than company maps had indicated. Suddenly Massy no longer seems invincible.

To help pay for a new school, Ed Wiley began a local fundraising campaign called Pennies of Promise in an attempt to raise $5 million. He now has a vanload of pennies in jars and plastic jugs. Ed will find the five million even if he has to ask five-hundred million people one at a time. Because of Ed's campaign, and the support he got from folks in West Virginia and along the way, he has become something of a symbol, even a hero of the struggle. No one is more qualified than Ed Wiley to talk about the effects of mountaintop removal or to represent the people of Appalachia.

At the press conference, which was well attended by members of the Washington media. Wiley was joined by U.S. Rep. Pallone (D-NJ); Lois Gibbs, the Love Canal housewife who alerted the nation to the dangers of toxic communities, now known as the mother of Superfund; Teri Blanton of Kentuckians for the Commonwealth; and Mary Anne Hitt of Appalachian Voices. The press conference was featured on news broadcast across the state of West Virginia, where over two-thirds of the residents are opposed to Mountain Top Removal.

Earlier this morning Ed had hoped to meet with West Virginia Sen. Robert C. Byrd. One of the purposes of the walk was to seek help from the powerful Senator. Outside his office Ed announced to the media, "Senator Byrd is an honorable man and a true Appalachian who cares about the people of West Virginia," Wiley said. "I hope he will stand with us to help the children at Marsh Fork Elementary School, because our children have been sacrificed long enough."

Ed had an appointment to meet with Byrd's staff, but not with the Senator himself. But after a few minutes meeting with the staffers, he was summoned into the inner sanctum of Byrd's spacious office. The two spent nearly forty-five minutes talking about the school, mountaintop removal and other issues. Before the meeting was over, both of the West Virginia natives were on their knees in prayer. Senator Byrd promised to do what he could to help move the school. He also issued a press release in which he stated, "I admire the determination and dedication that Ed and Debbie Wiley have shown, the Bible teaches that if we have faith of a mustard seed, we can move mountains. I believe that the Wileys have that faith."

Ed Wiley didn't talk to any consultants. He didn't even hold a meeting. He just got up one morning and told his wife Debbie that he was going to walk to Warshington even if he had to eat grass and drink out of a ditch. Along the way, he rallied thousands of supporters, garnered media attention in each town, and received the support he needed to continue his journey. Now Ed and Debbie are sitting in downtown Warshington and tapping their feet to some raucus mountain music and having a well-deserved beer. I think I'll have one with him.

Lenny Kolm, my good friend and someone who has organized over thirty lobby weeks on issues ranging from the Arctic Refuge to logging Old Growth forests confided to me that of all the events that he has organized or attended, Mountain Top Removal weekend topped them all when it came to the dedication and enthusiasm of this group of people. I had to agree. It seems to me, with just a few thousand dollars, Ed and his friends have accomplished more in a few months than anyone has been able to in the years that Coal Valley residents have demanded action on this issue. Ed is also working to build the kind of movement necessary to address not only mountaintop removal, but the damage that mining and burning coal does to our planet.

Log on to iLoveMountains.org and see how you can get involved.

Chapter 17

THE FIGHT TO SAVE THE ROCKY MOUNTAINS: A VIEW FROM COLORADO

By Joshua Frank

I CAME TO COLORADO to put a few miles between my overburdened mind and the mechanized drone of city life. The allure of the Rocky Mountains has once again compelled an escape. A tempered abandonment from the rat race. This spot, just south of the summit town of Breckenridge, at an elevation of around 11,500 feet, is alpine country. Up here one comes to appreciate that we truly are a product of the soil and not the other way around. It is just too bad that the gluttonous developers below the tree line don't value this geomorphic wonder for the same reason.

Colorado is best known for its winter resorts. Well-heeled vacationers from all over the world fly in to the sleek Denver International Airport so their families can experience the fresh powder of these sloping ranges. Thus the contractors expand the ski runs, build condos, five star hotels, steak houses, shopping centers, and coma inducing day spas. All the luxuries of New York City right here in the heart of the Rockies. But I wouldn't call these gracious comforts; I'd call these privileged communities monstrosities of the worst kind.

If there ever were a reason to resist the *triumphs* of capitalism, these little industrial vistas studded in the pristine Rocky Mountains would be it. The sheer destruction of biodiversity is not something that need be celebrated. Instead it must be challenged.

In 1998 angry Earth Liberation Front (ELF) radicals allegedly torched some buildings and ski lifts in Vail, not all that far from here. In 2006 a few of these activists, after being targeted by the Feds and a FBI collaborator (many argue the fires at Vail were an inside job), began serving prison time for the arson. Others who still face indictments remain at large. But sparking matches in the middle of the night isn't a strategic action, it was reactionary and impetuous—not to mention shortsighted. Vail later rebuilt its resort with even grander and more damaging results for the endangered lynx and other declining species in the area. Insurance pays.

In order to halt the ruination of these untamed places, a concerted campaign among the citizens of Colorado must lead the way for the effort to have any real, lasting impact. Colorado Wild, an environmental outfit that focuses its energies on fighting ski hill expansions, has taken the helm and has had more success than the Vail arsonists in fighting the purveyors of unbridled expansion.

The group, along with Friends of Wolf Creek, is aiming to stop the construction of a 10,000 person village in the middle of the San Juan Mountains, one of the snowiest wilderness regions in the country. The primary investor for the project is Texas billionaire Billy Joe "Red" McCombs who owns the Minnesota Vikings and co-founded Clear Channel Communications. In 2005 *Forbes* rated McCombs as one of the 400 richest Americans.

The Village at Wolf Creek is to be constructed just below the Continental Divide, where the mighty rivers of the West split and race to their respective homes. McCombs' vision, not unlike that of Pete Seibert and Earl Eaton who built the township near Vail, is sustained by greed and a rampant disregard for the wild. Like most industrialists, McCombs seems to be in it for the money and status. Nothing more.

The fight over the blueprints for Village at Wolf Creek still remains in the courts. Colorado Wild and their allies seem to be fending off the moneyed interests of Red McCombs. In October 2005 Colorado 12th District Judge O. John Kuenhold threw out the Mineral County's approval of the resort development on the grounds that it would not have suitable access to the highway. Colorado Wild had one small victory in its pocket and was hoping that more would come.

After a long awaited appeal by McCombs and company to Judge Kuenhold's 2005 decision, and with a cross-suit by Colorado Wild and Wolf Creek

Ski Area, the three members of the Colorado Court of Appeals finally heard the appeals and focused almost solely on the issue of road access. The district judge in the previous hearing had upheld the other portions of the county's approval for development.

The only road that accesses the 287-acre McComb property is Forest Service Road 391. Like most skid roads and other rough Forest Service paths cut through these alpine regions, FS 391 is narrow, unpaved, and closed for most of the year due to impassable snow accumulation. McCombs and company would like to expand 391 and make it available to intrepid tourists year-round.

During the August, 2007 court hearing, McComb's team argued that their client has legal access to his property. On the other hand, Andrew Shoemaker, the ski area's lawyer who has sided with Colorado Wild, said the dirt road is not suited for grandiose development, which even includes a power plant.

"If one occupant of the 10,000 occupants is traveling out and you're traveling in, you don't have access. You're obstructed," Shoemaker told the court. "It would be different if they had proposed a hunting lodge. But this is a Texas-sized development. They wanted the whole shebang."

Besides 391, the Forest Service has authorized two additional roads, to which Colorado Wild challenged in federal court and was victorious. For a while anyway, U.S. District Judge John Kane stopped McCombs from developing the proposed roads.

"There's no immediate threat [that construction will start]," Ryan Demmy Bidwell, executive director of Colorado Wild, told the *Durango Herald*. "There's roughly two months left of snow-free season, and then that window rapidly closes again."

In late December, 2007 the United States Forest Service and Colorado Wild were in negotiations over the development, with the primary focus again on road development. Rocky Smith of Colorado Wild says the Forest Service ought to go back and do another Environmental Impact Statement (EIS) that shows not only the impacts from the roads, but also from the subsequent development they will allow.

The process, admits Colorado Wild, has been tainted due to the development company's backroom dealings with Tetra Tech, the contractor that was hired to prepare the EIS. In a leaked email Tetra Tech executive Mark Blauer asked the development company for tickets to a Washington Redskins football game for his staff that had worked on the Wolf Creek EIS project.

Money and power don't just influence Washington politics; they also trump the public interest across the breadth of the West. In response to this reality, Colorado Wild and Friends of Wolf Creek have turned up the heat and produced an online "white paper" that exposes the Forest Service's collaboration with McCombs and his contractors.

Rocky Smith of Colorado Wild said the impending settlement will be good news for Wolf Creek and will likely halt development. However, Smith also noted that this victory is only round one of a fight that will likely continue at a different level over the course of the next few years.

So the battles rage on by a courageous few to protect the freedom of the wild in these desolate, iconic parts of the Rocky Mountains. If the courts don't side with the legally-inclined environmentalists that want to preserve this wilderness for black bears and not for vacationers, Red McCombs and his investors can be certain that other radical activists will take to the Forest Service roads to confront the development of our untrammeled public lands.

PART THREE: DESERT RATS

Chapter 18

DESERT AUTONOMOUS ZONE

By Jesse Walker

SOMEWHERE IN THE NORTHERN New Mexico desert, a grizzled gardener called Robbie is praising the prickliness of his home. "The cops don't like to come out here," he says proudly, "and this place is built on being left alone by the authorities. People say to the government, 'Fuck you. *Chinga tu madre.* We don't want your government, and you can get out of here.'"

Robbie is a folksinger, a self-described "middle-aged hippie," and one of the rich cast of characters who populate "Off the Grid." Jeremy and Randy Stulberg, a brother and sister team, originally set out to make a documentary about U.S. citizens living abroad. Then they discovered a tribe of expatriates here at home, fleeing the American mainstream in a way that only deepened their American identity. The Stulbergs filmed them instead, with riveting results.

In 15 square miles of abandoned land, about 400 misfits—aging hippies, disillusioned veterans, teenage runaways—have built a community where no one cares if you smoke pot, fire your rifle all day, let your kids drive your car, or walk around naked in the desert heat. It's a landscape of beat-up old trailers, shacks jerry-rigged from recycled materials, solar panels, little farms, greenhouses, and at least one tipi. "Where I live is the last remaining land of America that is left," says Dreadie Jeff, another Mesa resident. "You can do what you fucking want there."

The local culture defies easy stereotypes. "Going into this community with this traditional mainstream liberal ideology," Jeremy says, "we realized all our preconceived notions were bullshit. These people were extremely into their

Second Amendment rights, and they were also into marijuana legalization. They don't fit into these molds." There's a touch of madness to the place as well. Mama Phyllis, a Mesa woman who used to be a psychiatric nurse ("I couldn't do that anymore," she says, and leaves it at that), calls it "the largest outdoor insane asylum." The governing philosophy is a mix of anarchism, patriotism, New Age stoner wisdom, and a militia-style distrust of the state. Early in the film Dreadie Jeff, a veteran of the first Gulf War, exclaims that his military oath was not "to defend this land, it's not to defend the people, it's not to defend the motherfucking asshole president of the United States. My military oath goes, 'I solemnly swear to defend the Constitution of the United States of America from all enemies, foreign and domestic.'" The Constitution's "biggest enemy," he adds, is "this fucking government that is in place right now."

The government in question mostly keeps out of his way. Hardly anyone seems to want the Mesa people's land—the Stulbergs heard several mutually exclusive explanations for who, if anyone, technically owns it—and the citizens of the closest town, 25 miles away, seem willing to stay out of the Mesa's hair if the desert folk will stay out of theirs. But the authorities do fly helicopters over the area, scouting for marijuana growers, and if they think they spot some pot they'll send in the cops. According to Dreadie Jeff, they don't always bring warrants.

A more intimate enemy soon emerged as well. Shortly before the filmmakers arrived, a cultish group of runaways called the Nowhere Kids settled in. "They were extremists," remembers Randy. "They were stockpiling weapons. They had X's tattooed across their face." The new kids' brand of anarchy didn't sit well with the other desert dropouts. "They act like a bunch of revolutionists," snarls one, a pig farmer who frequently takes in teen runaways. "They cuss the system, and yet they've got their hand out...for everything they can get."

Before long, the Nowhere Kids were stealing food from their neighbors. "We don't want to call the cops," Robbie tells the Stulbergs. "But we've got to do something about this. Some people already got their guns." The film cuts to Moonbow, a man who sees no contradiction in talking like a vigilante while wearing a tie-dye. "If you're not a good neighbor," he says, "then we'll band together and chase you out of here."

The rhetoric escalates. The Nowhere Kids declare that they have a right to take anything they please as long as no one is using it at the moment. They also refuse to be filmed, telling the Stulbergs they'll "put bullets" in their heads if they don't keep their cameras off. The other Mesa residents start counting their bullets as well. An informal group of local leaders meets to plan a response to the thefts. At this point, a cynic might accuse the Mesa anarchists of forming a regime of their own.

But a funny thing happens: The standoff ends with no shootout, no bloodshed, and no new government. The desert residents may approve of vigilantism in principle—"we don't dial 911," says one, "we dial .357"—but they preferred to address the conflict by sending a delegation of unarmed women to reason with the runaways. The Nowhere Kids backed down, and so far the peace has held.

The Mesa, says Randy, represents "everything about America we loved and feared." The love, in her brother's words, is for "that pure sense of American democracy. Even though they were disillusioned with the government, they still loved the concept of America." The fear reflected the constant potential for violence, which at one point led the filmmakers themselves to think about getting armed. (In the end, Jeremy says, they decided their "camera was enough of a weapon.") It's telling, though, that the movie's big confrontation is resolved nonviolently. For all their fearsome rhetoric, the Mesa men aren't nearly as violent as, say, the visitors from the drug squad.

Even as it melds different subcultures—"it's the crossroads," Jeremy says, "between utopian idealism and a post-apocalyptic world"—the Mesa also represents a subculture of its own. At the end of the movie there's a hint of a larger network hidden somewhere in the folds of the map: One of the film's characters, we learn, has moved to a similar community in Hawai'i. "There's a circuit," says Randy. "There's a whole off-grid underground." The members of that world range from relatively wealthy environmentalists trying to make a statement about sustainability to poorer people in places like the Mesa, people whose central interest isn't going off the grid so much as it's getting off the radar. (Some of them really aren't off the grid. There's a group of Mesa residents who regularly drive to town, get produce from local food banks, and distribute the goods to neighbors who aren't able to fend for themselves.)

But whether it's liberty or ecology that drives them, all those little villages have something in common, something they share with brotherhoods ranging from monasteries to biker gangs to suburban subdivisions. They are what John Stuart Mill called "experiments of living," what Robert Nozick called "a wide and diverse range of communities which people can enter if they are admitted, leave if they wish to, shape according to their wishes." The Mesa merely stands at the far end of a spectrum, rejecting almost any attempt to impose an order on it.

It isn't the only American place that eschews formal rules. The watermen of Smith Island in the Chesapeake Bay, for example, have lived for three centuries with no cops, jails, or local taxes. But the Mesa is not a close-knit community bound by history, custom, and religious faith. It stands at the extreme end of the American voluntary tradition: a transient society of misfits and madmen, united only by their desire to be left alone. In the desert, Dreadie Jeff tells us, "I feel like I'm really in America. There's a real sense of freedom out there."

Chapter 19

THE BORDER DIARIES

By Eric Ruder and Justine Akers Chacón

Nogales and Tucson
ERIC: BORDER CROSSINGS AND BORDER CROSSES

We've made our way to Nogales, Ariz., the site of our first crossing to the Mexico side of the border. On the U.S. side, buses with Wal-Mart *línea* scrawled on their windows beckon Mexican shoppers to board for the short trip to the retailer.

The border wall that separates the Arizona Nogales from the Mexico Nogales is a symbol of border politics. Under the constant gaze of U.S. Border Patrol agents perched on the hills above, we walk along the wall. Crosses commemorate the lives lost. Some bear names—Frankie Silva and Rodrigo Lopez—while others say simply *desconocido*. Unknown.

Colorful graffiti adorns much of the wall here. "Power to the people" in English, and *Deporten a la migra* in Spanish. But the words that speak to the gnawing feeling I've had ever since arriving in California are: "*Fronteras: Cicatrices en la tierra.*" Borders: Scars on the land.

JUSTIN: LAST STOP ON THE GREEN LINE

"*¡ME CHINGARON aquí!*" pleads a young passerby with a neatly shaven head and spotless "south-side" football jersey—annoyed less with his current "statelessness" than with the person on the other end of his shiny silver cell phone. A U.S. Border Patrol bus has just arrived from the Tucson processing center and unceremoniously unloaded its cargo onto the roadway about 150 yards from the border crossing.

A slow-moving mass takes shape on the winding road. Ten bleary-eyed members of a family from Querétaro, led by a diminutive matriarch with dirt-encrusted shoes and water lines below the knee of her denim jeans, march past me towards the Migrant Help Center. The station is a nondescript white tent situated at the end of the strip that returns them to Mexico and uncertainty.

The silent marchers, wearing expressions that alternate from fatigue to bitter frustration, seem to fall into a fear-induced daze as they pass under the giant "Nogales" sign. It is the sudden realization that the last hours, days, weeks or years al otro lado are now memories—and that they are refugees, economic and otherwise, once more.

Looking down over the ravine that separates Nogales from Nogales, we are able to get an eagle's perspective of *la línea* at this common crossing point. There are the omnipresent *la migra* vehicles, a National Guard encampment and batteries of stadium lighting that cut a hot, white line across the exposed earth.

To the east of the ravine is a lonely stretch of road, running across a causeway linking the two sides. It is this road that serves as the point of deportation for migrant crossers rounded up in internal raids from Escondido to Casas Grandes, Ariz.—processed and tagged with "voluntary deportation" orders and dumped unceremoniously by bus.

This is the last stop on the "green line," the extensive system of immigration restriction that amounts to a legally sanctioned program of discrimination against Mexican and Central American migrants.

The Migrant Help Center is a nickel-and-dime operation, run by an umbrella human rights organization called No More Deaths based in Tucson and staffed by a crew of activists—gringos and Mexicanos—each with their own story to tell. What they lack in technology and a sterile medical environment, they make up for in selflessness, good humor and deep concern for the displaced crossers.

The group provides water, food and basic health treatment to those who want it. They also document cases of abuse, harassment and deprivation, and distribute leaflets that map local migrant shelters and other available services.

Between the times when they provide for deportees, they gather around and tell stories, smoke cigarettes and enjoy each other's company. As I speak to them, I notice the glances down the road, waiting for the next busloads.

I learn from the aid workers that it is not uncommon for people to have nothing more than whatever they had with them at the time of their arrest and detention. Some have crossed still carrying grocery bags, having been plucked from their daily lives during raids on markets and shopping centers.

The coordinator of the Migrant Help Center, Maryada, tells us of an occasion where members of a *quinceañera* (a festive party held on a young adult's 15th birthday to celebrate coming of age) were rounded up and deported—still wearing the tropical-colored party dresses, now tattered by the experience.

Other crossers included a pregnant woman with her children—picked up off the streets and deported while her husband sat at home waiting. Mariachi band members and young children who speak only English have also made the journey along the dark road.

As Maryada explains, "We very regularly come across people who have not just been verbally abused, but physically abused...Some people still freshly wincing in pain and have marks from being beaten."

Often, the abuse is at the hands of border agents. She says it is also not uncommon for hospital patients to be dumped into their laps, groggy and still bearing medical tags and IDs.

Maryada can't help but scoff when we ask about the success of the efforts to "close the border." The most determined, she explains, cross daily, sometimes right under the nose of the gringo military machine. Coyotes regularly dig holes under the fence, and the occasional valiente will navigate the array of obstacles directly, thwarting the multi-million-dollar sensors by crawling on their belly.

For a few, deportation is an inconvenience. A cell-phone call away is another coyote and another chance en el norte. For others, it represents the destruction of their hopes and dreams. For the penniless migrants—often indigenous or from the interior, with nothing left to offer for passage and no primos who "know someone" or owe them a favor—the burden of capture weighs heavily.

For the family of 10 we see on the road, it is a long trip back to Querétaro—and back to saving centavos for the next try in a year or two. The matriarch—separated from her husband in Atlanta and four months pregnant with his child—will have to postpone her reunion. She tells her story to Nohelia while Maryada treats the blisters on her feet.

As I look across the faces of the travelers, I see a thousand different stories—loved ones left behind, painful months of separation, and the more immediate concern about the whereabouts of tonight's meal.

The family disappears under an overpass heading south, the somber scene is etched into my mind. While I dwell on speculations about their future, I'm suddenly shaken out of my daze. "Two more buses!" shouts one of the aid workers. Maryada says her farewells and goes to the road. We drive off to el norte.

ERIC AND JUSTIN: A DESERT TESTIMONIAL

To counter the 21 anti-immigrant "field hearings" held across the U.S. by members of Congress this summer, the Tucson-based Coalición de Derechos Humanos (Coalition for Human Rights) is holding its own hearing on August 17.

The three-hour event includes testimony from more than 20 activists, lawyers, experts and advocates for border crossers, immigrant workers and indigenous peoples. With U.S. Rep. Raúl Grijalva (D-Ariz.) heading up the panel of experts that heard them, the testimonials captivate the room with their raw emotion.

Police have set up a huge security perimeter around the building. We learn that before we arrived, Russ Dove, a member of the local anti-immigrant Border Guardians, entered the meeting hall to disrupt the proceedings. After insulting people in the room, he was asked to leave and finally arrested by Tucson police. Dove became notorious when he burned a Mexican flag during one of the massive pro-immigrant protests in Tucson.

The hearing gets underway, and one of the first presenters is Gloria Mitchel, the aunt of Juan de Jesús Rivera Cota. She sobs as she recounts the circumstances that led to her 16-year-old nephew's murder by a U.S. Border Patrol agent on May 11, 2005. A silence falls over the packed auditorium.

Jesús decided to come to the U.S. in search of work to help support his family. He was driving a truck with five other young men and had just crossed the border when they saw dusty tracks ahead. The travelers panicked and turned around. Suddenly, a Border Patrol vehicle appeared on the road, blocking their way.

According to the Border Patrol, the officer shot and killed Jesús because the truck appeared to be barreling toward him without slowing. But Gloria says this couldn't be true because he was shot from behind, not from the front. The bullet that killed him entered through the back of his head and exited through his eye.

"My nephew Jesús moved to the U.S to help his mother and sister, after his father left his family," Gloria said in an interview after the hearing. "He felt the responsibility to fend for his family. He came here to work. His death has had a big impact on his family because he was the sole provider for his mother who was disabled—she only had one leg and walked with a cane—and also provided for his sister who had three children and another on the way.

"With one paycheck, he wasn't able to make enough to feed five people, plus himself [in Mexico]. That's the reason that people leave—and we are treated like criminals and are killed."

Other experts at the hearing testify about labor rights, indigenous rights and the growing environmental crisis caused by U.S. corporations running toxic maquiladora operations.

Yendi Castillo, a Pima County public defender, speaks about the changes she has witnessed since she began representing immigrants in federal court. "Will we allow the continuation of our government to pay for private corporations to profit from Constitutional violations?" asks Castillo, explaining that the average sentence for an undocumented immigrant in Tucson has grown from 10 days in 1998 to 30 days today.

"Once in court, the 'criminal alien' is not a person, but a commodity ... Generally, defendants are not being housed in government-run prisons. They are increasingly held in private-run prisons with stockholders, where the principal incentive is profit..."

"Two of my clients have died while in prison," says Castillo, her voice tightening and tears filling her eyes. "Both of these men were healthy when they got to prison. How do you quantify the loss of their lives?"

Everyone in the auditorium feels Castillo's raw emotions. We are especially moved by the solidarity she expresses with others who face similar circumstances in different parts of the world.

"Currently, Lockheed, Northrup Grumman and Raytheon are competing for a contract to develop a high-tech border for $2.5 billion," Castillo says. "This is the technology of war—we're talking radar, we're talking sensors, we're talking drones. This is what we are seeing in Palestine."

Yendi isn't alone in this observation. Several speakers make a similar identification with the plight of the Palestinians—a shared sense of the burden of living under the violence of occupation and a stubborn refusal to be worn down by the occupier's hostility to the occupied's language, culture and even existence.

After the hearing, we go out for a late-night dinner with about a dozen of the main organizers and speakers at the event. We sit across from Leilani, a 17-year-old high school senior who's half-Native American and half-African American. She was one of the many volunteers who made the event a success. Her activism began a short time ago—with this spring's pro-immigrant protests—but her assessment of the world and her role in it has developed quickly.

"Our generation has seen a lot—from Katrina to the war in Iraq to the big protests this spring," she explains. "We are waking up."

She quickly produces pages of e-mails exposing the links between the Border Guardians, their race-baiting congressional candidate Joe Sweeny and various white supremacists. "I've got a target on me," she says. "Whenever they see me, they say, 'Hello, Leilani.' But I'm not going to stop what I'm doing."

About 2,000 of the 3,000 kids in her high school participated in the largest of the walkouts for immigrant rights, which happened almost every day during one week in April. Students from six or seven Tucson high schools marched downtown for joint demonstrations of many thousands.

The memories and inspiration of those days seem to fuel everything about Leilani, from her rapid speaking style to the intensity of her drive to keep up the fight, no matter the intimidation.

Tucson and Sasabe

JUSTIN: RECLAIMING A STOLEN PAST

Piercing the Tucson skyline, the white adobe steeples of a towering Catholic Church reclaims *la tierra* for Arizona's Spanish-Indigenous past.

We were told that the meeting is at a white Catholic Church, so we are immediately drawn to the most impressive one. We soon find out this isn't it, so we move on. It becomes apparent that several of these rustic churches— now squeezed between strip malls and other trappings of urban living—form the silhouette of the old pueblo.

We finally locate Santa Cruz Church several blocks further south. It is here that we find a meeting in a courtyard, with the participants taking refuge from the heat under a corrugated tin canopy.

This is a gathering of ex-braceros organizing to tell a story that has been buried for 40 years. The grassroots coalition, called the *Alianza Braceroproa* (Bracero Workers Alliance), is seeking both dignity and withheld wages robbed from them in their youth.

They are a few of the more than 4 million workers who were brought from Mexico as "temporary workers" to labor in the fields (and occasionally on the railroads) from 1942 to 1964. Set up to satisfy a labor shortage during the Second World War, the bracero program quickly evolved into a semi-permanent fixture in the countryside.

The meeting has brought together men and their wives from both sides of the border, from Phoenix to Hermosillo. They had established roots across the region, but are now being pulled back together by the desire for closure and the hope of passing their lessons on to the next generation of Mexican workers looking north.

At stake is the disappearance of an estimated $1 billion to $3 billion (including interest) in bracero wages into the coffers of U.S. and Mexican banks—hard-earned dollars that have never found their way into workers' hands. Under the bracero program, U.S. authorities deducted 10 percent of the migrant workers' wages and placed them in savings accounts, which were supposed to be given to the farmers upon their return to Mexico.

Designed as a way to "entice" them to return home, the money trail passed from Wells Fargo Bank and Union Trust Company of San Francisco to the Bank of Mexico and then to the Banco de Credito Agricola in Mexico—and into oblivion.

Under the program, workers were brought in and dispersed directly to growers and tied to them for the duration of their contract, stripping them of their freedom of movement. Government oversight amounted to using *la migra* to police unruly workers while ignoring the increasingly criminal farm labor conditions.

By creating a group of workers deprived of democratic rights, the growers hoped to drive unions into permanent exile from the fields. Having absolute control over their workers, with little or no government oversight, encouraged agricultural capital to degenerate more into a class of gangsters—with immigration agents as muscle.

This corrupt relationship reached its pinnacle with the theft of bracero wages—used by U.S. banks to rack up short-term interest and likely siphoned by their Mexican counterparts into personal accounts (in Switzerland or back to the U.S.). Like then, braceros are still finding ways to resist. Weathered, wizened and still favoring pains as old as the crimes committed against them, they congregate and plan.

Since the late 1990s, the ex-braceros movement has grown, holding hundreds of meetings, protests and marches to bring attention to their cause. In 2004, more than 1,000 stormed the Guanajuato ranch of Mexican President Vicente Fox to demand the return of their money.

During the mass marches of May 1, 2006, dozens of braceros joined other protesters in shutting down the northbound lanes of the Tijuana-San Diego border crossing—effectively closing the port to the sparse traffic that failed to heed the call to boycott.

Taking seats at the back of the group, we see a young woman addressing the group seated atop a picnic table. Violeta, who hardly appears older than a college student, is a bespectacled organizer who was won the respect of the braceros through her impassioned commitment to their cause.

Despite her thin frame, a powerful voice resonates above the rows of sun-parched cowboy hats. Each sentence is punctuated with a forceful "Uh?" (a Mexican colloquialism equivalent to ¿verdad?).

True to the Mexican tradition of "testimonials" in working-class politics, the men periodically break out in story to illustrate history. The most painful memories are not the sore backs, swollen hands or pesticide-filled lungs, but the indignities suffered at the border and in the fields—from having their heads shaved and being "de-loused" with gas like animals at the border, to being treated like slaves by bosses who saw them only as expendable work-horses.

These images from a stolen past are seared into the collective memory of the bracero, experiences they recall with the most precise and vivid detail. It is this message they are especially interested in communicating to the next generation of workers, especially as a new bracero program is being discussed by rich men in Washington who have likely never had to work a single hard day in their lives.

"*¡Hay que luchar!*" (We have to fight!), concludes one of the men, and the rest of group nods in agreement.

South to Sasabe

ERIC

There's a game that Kat Rodriguez plays when she makes the drive from Tucson, where she staffs the office of the *Coalición de Derechos Humanos*, to Sasabe, Mexico, one of the most active staging grounds for migrants making the final push over the border through the Sonoran desert. Kat keeps a running total of the number of Border Patrol vehicles she sees moving along the two-lane highway that connects the 60 miles between Tucson and Sasabe. The most she's ever seen in one trip is 34.

Kat has accompanied lots of people curious about border crossers to Sasabe—especially reporters and elected officials. "I took a delegation of elected officials from New Jersey down to Nogales," she explains, "and there's a hill where you have a great view of the land with the fence, this scar, running through it.

"Suddenly, this guy runs out, leaps up on the fence and is running along the top of the fence, and he jumps into Mexico. There's a Border Patrol vehicle sitting at the top of the slope. And these elected officials are stuttering, aren't they going to do something about that?"

Kat laughs at the idea that a Border Patrol agent would care about someone crossing to the Mexico side. "What would they do about it?" she asks. "This guy is going back—besides the agent would have to get out of his air-conditioned car into the hot sun."

I ask Kat why someone would cross to the Mexico side in such a fashion. Her reply encapsulates an entire worldview that goes with living on *la línea*. "We're bicultural, we're from both sides," she says. "Maybe he lives on both sides, maybe he needed to go buy something, and he didn't want to go through the line.

"That's the thing that people don't get. We don't recognize that border in the way that they want us to. You don't just draw a line and tell somebody to pick a side. It's like asking somebody to cut their body in half and pick which side they want. You don't live without both of the sides."

Kat interrupts herself. "Is that 10 and 11 or 11 and 12?" she asks as two more Border Patrol vehicles pass us going north.

"We're Tejano, we're from San Antonio," she continues. "My family is from the same land in San Antonio that we've always been from. We never crossed. I don't have relatives in Mexico. My family doesn't have a history of immigration.

"We never 'came' to this country, we were already there, we were where we are. The border literally crossed us, and we were assimilated. And I say 'assimilated' because we were told not to speak Spanish. My parents didn't teach us Spanish because they were told not to.

"So I had to learn it at school, and in my job, I learned a lot of Spanish, of course. People forget that there are millions of us who are Tejanos and Chicanos, and we never 'came' anywhere."

Kat's story starts Nohelia, who grew up on both sides, from Mexicali to San Diego, thinking about her friends and family. For them, the border represents an annoyance, or even a barrier, but one that fails at its purpose of separation.

"In San Diego, there's a lot of people who cross the border daily," says Nohelia. "To go to school, to work, to shop. A lot of my friends have to cross the border on a regular basis. So even after school, they're not staying in the U.S. They have to go back to Tijuana and make that trek the next day and the next and the next."

Kat asks why people cross to go to school. "Are they U.S. citizens?" she wonders.

"Some of them are U.S. citizens," Nohelia replies. "Or people like me—we had relatives or friends who had homes in the U.S., and we borrowed their address and went to school in the U.S."

We pass through an internal Border Patrol checkpoint as we're heading south on Highway 286. Kat says they may tell me to stop taking pictures, but we'll just play dumb. She almost seems eager for them to see me, welcoming the opportunity to defy, even in this small way, the regime of militarization and border enforcement.

In the end, they don't see me snapping photos. It's just as well. I don't have anything to hide, but I'm not eager to find out if the agents are as unfriendly as they look.

I ask Kat if the five vehicles at the checkpoint should add to the running total, but she says that's cheating—they have to be moving. And just as she says that 15 and 16 pass, going the other direction.

ERIC: THE STAGING GROUND

Kat's stories make the time fly right by, and we're arriving in Sasabe, crossing over *la línea*, and rumbling through the dusty streets of Sasabe, Mexico. It takes just a couple minutes, and we're already on the edge of town heading towards a *colonia*—one of the hundreds of neighborhoods that have sprung up along the U.S.-Mexico border, with few to no services like electricity or water.

Residents of this *colonia* eke out a living making bricks or collecting and selling scrap. And coyotes, or guides, use the area as a staging ground for crossers. The coyotes demand huge sums—$1,500 to $3,500 per person—to take people across the border.

The inherent dangers and illegality have turned border crossing into a huge underground economy, which even legitimate businesses cater to. As we melt under Sasabe's sun, a huge Pepsi truck pulls up to stock *la tiendita* (little store) with beverages that will undoubtedly sustain someone across days of walking through the desert.

Kat explains that some will walk 70 miles over three days—almost all the way to Tucson. Others walk about half that, make it to a safe house, then get picked up and taken to Phoenix.

But the coyotes invariably lie about how long it will take. They say it'll take eight or 10 hours, or just a day, because they are competing with one another to land "clients." Truth in advertising is hard to come by, especially on the border. "But it's not the coyote who gets the money," says Kat. "He's just a pawn. The money is going to a few big bosses."

The first group of would-be crossers we approach is from the southern Mexican state of Veracruz. There are about 10 who shift nervously as we approach.

Kat has a stack of "Know your rights" cards that she hands out when she goes to Sasabe. The cards, written in Spanish, of course, explain the rights that people have if they are picked up by Border Patrol—the right to remain silent, the right to an attorney and the right to a deportation hearing. But, the card suggests, if it's your first time crossing, and you don't have any possibility of legal entry, it's better to agree to "Voluntary departure" rather than go to a hearing, which could carry serious consequences.

The group from Veracruz is waiting for their coyote. This evening, they will try to cross for the third time. They've arranged to work off their debt to the coyote once they arrive in the U.S., which gives a sense of just how vast the border-crossing economy is. It's likely that they already have a number to call when they arrive to line up work—an arrangement of indentured servitude in the "land of the free."

The next group we talk to is from Chiapas, which lies on Mexico's southern border with Guatemala. The group of 12, most of whom are friends, each paid 675 pesos (about $65) for a bus ride to Sasabe.

They answer our questions with clipped phrases. They say they're not too nervous, but the anxious smiles give them away. They are all between 18 and 25 years old. They say they are bound for California and are willing to work anywhere—in a field, a factory, whatever.

And they say that if they are apprehended, they will certainly try to cross again.

For several years running now, the Border Patrol has apprehended more than one million people a year. Agents apprehend about 700 each and every day in the Tucson sector—all of whom end up being dropped in Nogales, where we visited the Migrant Help Center two days ago.

It's impossible to say how many individual people are behind these statistics, because some will make it across on their first or second try, while others won't until their sixth, seventh or eighth try. But one thing is certain—none of the border militarization and enforcement measures will succeed in discouraging people from trying, so long as the demand for labor remains higher in the U.S. than in Mexico.

Wayne Cornelius is the director of the Center for Comparative Immigration Studies at the University of California-San Diego, and in early August, he testified at the field hearing in San Diego. "My research findings," he said, "based on highly detailed, face-to-face interviews with 1,327 migrants and their relatives in Mexico during the last 18 months, support earlier research showing that tightened border enforcement since 1993 has not stopped or even discouraged unauthorized migrants from entering the United States."

What's more, Cornelius continued, the enforcement measures have the consequence of forcing migrant workers who would prefer to return to Mexico after coming to the U.S. and earning money for a while to adopt a different approach.

"With clandestine border crossing an increasingly expensive and risky business, U.S. border enforcement policy has unintentionally encouraged undocumented migrants to remain in the U.S. for longer periods, and settle permanently in this country in much larger numbers," he said.

Border enforcement is worse than ineffective, however—because it has had the intended consequence of stirring up anti-immigrant sentiment. By focusing on the crossers instead of the social forces that impel people to cross, politicians of both parties legitimate anger at "the illegals." Border militarization allows this drama to play out at the national and local levels.

At the local level, forcing immigration into more desolate areas puts small towns and communities right in the path of huge migratory flows. Kat points out that this has the effect of overwhelming small hospitals with cases of dehydration, hyperthermia, hypothermia and more.

"The federal government is forcing all this migration through here, but the federal government doesn't give any money to the local hospitals," she says. "So some people start resenting the migrants. But who should we be blaming?

"It's the federal government that should be helping local governments with the cost, especially the border hospitals in Bisbee and Douglas. They can't handle the increased traffic anymore. People scapegoat immigrants for bleeding off our health care system. But they're not recognizing that this is an intentional process that's taking place.

"And no one asks the question why the migration itself is happening—what's displacing people. That would mean we would have to re-evaluate NAFTA and CAFTA and all these free trade agreements that have been the real forces behind migration."

At the national level, politicians from both parties have turned border militarization into a "national security" issue—as if the great mass of would-be gardeners, busboys, field hands and assembly-line workers looking to send money to their loved ones are about to launch a wave of "terrorism."

As Kat puts it, "Terrorism and immigration have nothing to do with each other, but most of America right now has that in their head. The media pushes that forward, and nobody questions that. And I blame our supposed friends in Washington, the liberals, for letting it get to the point where migration and terrorism are even thought of as the same issue. How the hell did we get to this point?"

Living in a border state with Janet Napolitano, a Democratic governor, Kat is no stranger to the political game. In a letter to her "supporters," Napolitano recapped some of her accomplishments. "We were the first to deploy the National Guard to assist at the border and have been relentless in our pressure on the federal government to do its job," she wrote, sounding straight out of the land of the Minutemen. Napolitano also talks of successes in deploying new technology to detect "illegal immigrants and drugs on our highways."

"We got her in," Kat laments. "She would not have been elected without people campaigning for her, and then she forgot about us. She declared a state of emergency and called in the National Guard. It's a political move. People say that she and Bill Richardson, the Democratic governor of New Mexico, have their eye on Washington. She's as conservative a Democrat as you can be. She knows she's got the left already, and so she's pandering to the right. She figures who the hell else are we going to vote for?

The same dynamic is at work in California. Gov. Arnold Schwarzenegger resisted the idea of declaring a 'state of emergency' on the border, says Justin, "even though he also says he 'salutes' the Minutemen. But the speaker of the assembly, Fabian Núñez, says we should call for a state of emergency in California. And he's a Democrat, a traditional 'liberal' Democrat."

These debates are more than just debates for people living on the border, says Kat. "For a lot of folks from Washington, it's a line in a bill," she says. "But to us, it's an actual wall that we're going to have to literally live and die with.

"I've had people from D.C. say to me that we've got to be 'realistic'—that nothing is going to pass without some measures regarding national security and enforcement, that you've got to be able to give something up to get something.

"But what they don't understand is what they're willing to give up is us. We're the sold-out piece. Forgive us for kicking and screaming all the way to the fire, but we're going to do it. And on top of that, we're being sacrificed for nothing because these measures aren't going to change anything unless you address the national migration issue and get to the roots of it."

Chapter 20

CAT-AND-MOUSE WITH LA MIGRA: A DARK RIDE ON THE BORDER

By Andrea Peacock

THE SIRENS WOKE ME up. The dogs broke into a howl, abruptly as though it woke them as well. Gee, that sounded close, I thought. Then the howls turned into barks, and Donna was outside calling them in.

A few moments later, shouts. Doug was out of bed, struggling with the inside-out sleeves of his robe, and I followed, tossing on a t-shirt and pair of shorts. We joined Donna on the back patio, where I peered around the corner of her orchid room and caught sight of a uniformed man standing on alert, next to a gray pickup truck.

"He's trying to keep them all corralled," she said. "I'm just hoping the carport is still there."

I went back inside to make coffee, then started out the front door for the paper. That's when the Border Patrol van pulled up, and I noticed the cruiser sitting in our driveway. "I thought that sounded close," I said to no one in particular.

As we watched, the agent from the backyard marched four short, stocky men wearing layers of dark green and brown clothing, each with their hands on the shoulder of the man in front of him, into the van. Another agent appeared from around the garage, and escorted four more out of the back of the cruiser. Four, Donna said, had gotten away. I saw our neighbors across the street watching from their windows as well.

The second agent, tall and blond, walked over to us and told Donna to call the Border Patrol office if she noticed any damage. He was sorry about all the fuss, he said. It was the second time in as many weeks a truckload of illegal immigrants, chased by BP agents, had turned off into these neighborhood streets, cutting through yards in hopes of reaching the dry Santa Cruz riverbed.

"No problem," she said. "Is my carport still standing?"

Doug and I took our coffee and headed back to bed, luxuriating in a few moments in which we had no other tasks. We had a good half-hour before Donna knocked: "How's your Spanish?" she asked.

I threw a bathrobe on and followed her out the front door. Standing at the side of the house were two girls, dressed in the same bulky camouflaged layers as the men we had seen marched away. Donna handed one a phone. I asked in my pig Spanish: ¿Necessita ayuda? One of the women gestured at the phone. I pointed to the nearly empty water bottle held by the second. ¿Agua? They passed me their bottles, and I took them inside, filled them, grabbed a grocery sack and tossed some bananas and brownies in it. Back outside, the phone was not working. I handed over the food, and Donna coaxed the girls in.

They had a phone number for somewhere in Mexico, but we couldn't seem to get a call through. Our neighbors across the street were outside, talking loudly. "They were just here!" I heard the woman call, a shrill note of excitement to her voice. I expected they would call the Border Patrol, the cute blonde would be back.

But the minutes ticked away, and no one pulled up. The girls gradually began to relax, removing their hoods, then their jackets. They were a little older than I thought-not teenagers. ¿Habla Español? the more assertive one asked me. Poquito, I replied. Very damn little—my restaurant Spanish was not going to be much help.

Donna called a friend of hers, a woman here legally but not a citizen. This put her in an awkward, vulnerable position, but she agreed to speak to our guests. When Donna got back on the phone, Carmen told her she would try calling the phone numbers the young women gave her, in the hope of finding someone who could give us a hint of our next move.

Donna urged them to sit at the dining room table. One was a little older than the other, and seemed to understand a few words of English. They'd been walking (she motioned with her fingers) en el desierto para cinco días, she told me. Sin comida, sin agua.

Let me make you a little comida, I replied.

We'd just had a big birthday party for Doug and the fridge was full of left-overs. I got some eggs, cheese and onions cooking.

Where did you cross? I asked. Misunderstanding, she told me she was from Michoican, Acapulco. Her friend from Guerrero. *Pero,* from *donde* did they walk? Cabeza Prieta? No, she said, understanding now. Sasabe. *¿Donde es aqui?*

After they finished eating, I pulled out a map. I pointed out Sasabe down on the border, Tucson, and just to the south, the mission at San Xavier. *"La Misión,"* I told her. *"Aqui."* They were on their way to Phoenix when La Migra caught them, she said. From there, she was to join her husband in Atlanta. Her friend was destined for Chicago.

More calls followed to Carmen. Doug left a message for a friend with some experience in these matters, choosing his words carefully. We waited. It was Donna's house, and ultimately her choice. "I guess you have to have the courage of your convictions," she said, then suggested showers, the washing machine and fresh clothes. Using mostly nouns and gestures, I got the idea across, dug out a couple pairs of jeans, t-shirts, sweaters and socks and handed the pile over. Fortunately, they seemed to be my size—in fact, the jeans might well fit them better. While they bathed, we considered our options.

We could put them on a shuttle to Phoenix, I suggested. But they don't know where in Phoenix they are going, Donna replied. In the back of our minds, though, we all knew they couldn't stay long. The Border Patrol, the neighbors, all knew they'd been here. One neighbor's children worked for the BP: chances were good someone would call.

The younger woman finished showering first, and we spoke while her friend took a turn in the bathroom. She knew no English at all. *¿Tienes familia en Chicago, o amigos?* I couldn't figure out whether to use the familiar or formal tense, and kept switching back and forth between the two. She didn't seem offended; I figured it didn't matter.

Sí, una hermana.

¿Como se llama? I asked.

Anna.

Andrea, I replied, then pointed and said, *Donna.*

Did I have any brothers or sisters?

Sí, one of each.

And Donna?

A brother, *y nada mas familia. Solo hermano.*

Then the dogs: *¿perro o perra?*

Perro, I said pointing to Kendall, then to Zelda: *y perra.* I laughed to myself: it was the one word that always gave me trouble in high school Spanish class. I never got the hang of rolling my r's with any ease.

Another hour passed with our guests sneaking brownies to the dogs, who now adored them. Another call from Carmen yielded a phone number: the older woman, (whose name we learned was something unpronounceable, but we could call her Jessie) had an aunt in Los Angeles. She called, but got no answer. Her *tia,* she said, was working. She wouldn't be home til after six.

It was the start of an option. Maybe we could put them on a Greyhound and deliver them directly into Auntie's care.

Donna had just been told by a neighbor (the one with the BP children) that a person could lose his or her car for transporting illegal immigrants. It's not like she had one to spare. Maybe we could give them a map, let them hitch.

The early hours of the afternoon rolled by, the possibilities a sequence of waves we rode. Calling *la migra,* I reasoned to myself, was an option that would serve only our convenience. I could imagine parts of their journey: probably a long bus ride all the way from southern Mexico, then the hot desert walk. They'd had to use tweezers to get the cactus spines out of their hands. I had hiked that desert—prepared with a full pack, on cooler days. You couldn't help but brush up against cholla, and gopher burrows turn the ground into a maze of instability. You break through the crust constantly. What a monumental waste of energy to end up back where they had started.

If nothing else panned out, we could give them a good map, bag of food and turn them out at dusk. But I'd heard too many horror stories of those who take advantage of women immigrants. This was no good choice.

I called Greyhound. Yes, there was a bus to Los Angeles tonight. No, my friends would not need to show ID. It would arrive in LA at 8:45 the next morning. I passed this all along to Donna. Should I tell them? I asked her. Sure, she said.

They were sitting in the dining room, looking at the maps spread all over the table. They had no idea of US geography: where they were, how far it was to LA, Atlanta, South Dakota, San Antonio. These all were far, we told them. LA the closest.

I presented my idea: Greyhound, *Tia*, what did they think?

Jessie was guardedly excited, explaining my plan to her friend. *Pero*, she said, they only had Mexican money. We would buy the tickets, I replied, waving off her protests. I had no *otro ideas*—this was the *mas facile* way. Okay, she relented. But they must get a hold of her aunt and let *Tia* know they were coming. That gave us all afternoon to kill. Take a siesta, I suggested. Make yourself at home. Blank looks. *Si necessita agua*, I pointed to the sink, *agua*. *Comida*, I pointed to the fridge, *comida*. *Bano, bano. Todo*. This time they understood. With *gracias* and *de nada*, I retreated to the patio with a book.

An hour later, when I walked into the kitchen to get some water, Jessie said something to me. I caught some conjugation of *comer*. Sure, *sí*. ¿Menudo? I asked. Pizza? It did not matter, so I heated up both, and they ate it all. We talked more: was Donna my sister?

No, ella es mi amiga. Vivo en Montana. We were just here visiting.

¿*Vacaciones?* Jessie asked.

Sí. It seemed the easiest explanation.

Jessie explained that she planned to spend the summer in South Dakota. Doing what, I could not figure out. I told her *la paisaje, la tierra es muy bonita*, and resisted the urge to suggest she drop by if in the neighborhood.

More hours passed and they slept, curled together on the couch. Come evening, Doug took the car on several test runs, certain that the BP could be lurking in the neighborhood still. If they wanted us, I told him, they'd knock at the door and tell us so. But it made him feel better about The Plan. At 6:30, *Tia* was home. First Jessie spoke to her, then handed the phone to me. The woman, Beatrice, thanked me profusely, said her daughter was sick and her husband not home. Could we wait til he returned at nine so she could talk to him about it?

I explained nine would be too late; that we had no other options. Could we please put her niece on a bus bound for LA? With more thanks, she offered to wire money, but we refused. They can do someone else a good turn, I said, feeling and sounding trite. Will they be stopped on the way? Will there be checkpoints? I thought not and told her so, but that was just going to be out of our control.

The 30-minute drive to Tucson felt unreal, like a dream or a movie. The whole day has passed this way, as though the hours were lifted out of ordinary time. Immigrants walk through the Santa Cruz every night: we see their tracks in the pecan groves, find their belongings discarded (backpacks, children's shoes) and reason that they must have had to run; we avoid dense brush while walking the dogs, preferring not to disturb anyone hiding out the daylight hours. But other than these signs, their lives never cross with ours. The entire day, I realize, has been a gift.

It was a dark ride, and the city lights seemed to be floating, moving. Donna at first drove like normal, then checked her speed. We did not need to get pulled over tonight. At the bus station, I went in first and bought the tickets. The agent wanted names: I was too tired to think on my feet and gave her my own, Donna's too. I scanned the waiting room: no police, no border patrol. It was, oddly enough, clean and comfortable. We could all wait in here.

Back out in the parking lot we gathered their gear. Wearing my clothes, Donna's makeup and carrying some old travel bags and purses we pressed upon them, they looked like *Americanas*.

I gave Jessie last minute instructions: I had gotten them on an earlier bus-they would arrive sooner than we planned. The bus would make some stops, *altos, para mas gente, mas personas*. They should stay on. I had to look up this last word: *quedarse*. She understood. Donna bought a bunch of candy and stuffed it-along with a change purse full of cash-in their bags. We hugged, and Jessie held me in a long, strong grip. Their bus was called; they headed for the door: *puerto tres*. We stood back, held our breaths as they passed the ticket taker, then waved one last time as they passed the window on their way to board.

Note: Some of the names and places have been changed in this piece.

Chapter 21

HOW TO BEAT A MINING COMPANY: A GOLD GOLIATH THROWS IN THE TOWEL

By Jeffrey St. Clair

OF ALL THE STATES across the West, Oregon—particularly its eastern half—has been the only one to escape the ravages of the big mining companies. It lacked the opulent gold deposits that prompted torments of the land from the California Sierras to Montana's Northern Rockies.

The high deserts of eastern Oregon are among the most remote, thinly populated and driest in the West. In 1987, two hikers, Gary and Carolyn Brown, were backpacking west of the Owyhee River canyon near the border between Oregon and Idaho when they came across hundreds of survey stakes. To the mining industry's considerable misfortune, the Brown's took an immediate interest in the purpose of these stakes. Carolyn was a botanist and both were active in the environmental movement.

The Browns began a probe. They soon discovered through the Bureau of Land Management (BLM) that the surveyors had been working on behalf of international mining companies laying claim to hundreds of thousands of wilderness acres. By the end of 1988, no less than 21,000 separate mining claims had been filed around the geological formation known as the Snake River Graben. (A graben is a mineral-laden depression between two faults in the crust of the earth.)

Of these thousands of claims the richest prospects were held by the Atlas Corporation—an international mining giant—on public lands overseen by the

BLM in an area called Grassy Mountain. On the basis of their exploratory drillings, geologists for Atlas forecast that the deposits held as much as a million ounces of gold, valued at nearly a billion dollars.

Under the giveaway provisions of the 1872 Mining Law, Atlas could patent these claims for a mere five dollars per acre, pay no royalties on the value of the gold removed and have no obligations to clean up their mess.

The exact nature of the impending mess became of central importance. One of the reasons eastern Oregon had escaped the trauma of mining was that the gold deposits were so splintered in the rock that their extraction was uneconomical with the technologies then available. These were not veins of gold at Grassy Mountain so much as capillaries, yielding only .023 ounces of gold per ton of rock—about a teaspoon of gold for every dumptruck load of rubble.

It was only with the advent of open pit cyanide heap leach mining in the late 1970s and early 1980s that extracting gold in these tiny amounts became a practical proposition for the big companies. The economic math comes out at about $150 in labor and machinery costs for every ounce of gold removed. Gold is now selling for about $400 an ounce.

In 1992, Atlas sold its Grassy Mountain claims to the Denver-based Newmont Mining Company, the largest gold mining enterprise in North America. Atlas made a quick $30 million and a sense of relief that it wouldn't have to undertake the sort of expensive fight against environmentalists that Newmont had the treasury and political clout to wage.

Newmont enjoys $2 billion in assets and was backed by money from Jacob Rothschild (in the English branch of the banking dynasty), Wall Street investor George Soros and Sir James Goldsmith, an Anglo-French tycoon noted for his extreme rightwing views, his brace of mistresses, his food empire Cavenham, his palace on the west coast of Mexico and former ownership of the Crown-Zellerbach timber empire, which he later renamed Cavenham Forest Industries. James's brother Teddy is the publisher of *The Ecologist*, which survives in part due to subventions from his nature-raping brother who now sits in the European parliament and who backed a fascist presidential candidate in a recent French election. Goldsmith acquired his interest in Newmont by trading his 99 percent ownership of Cavenham Forest Industries for Hanson PLC's 49 percent stake in Newmont.

While these shifts in mining ownership were taking place, Carolyn and Gary Brown were building up grassroots opposition from their home in Ontario, a small town on the Oregon-Idaho boarder, where Gary managed a local outlet of a Boise-based tire company. The Browns were eager to politicize the mining issue and take it directly to the people. In this strategy they found common cause with Larry Tuttle. Tuttle is an interesting man who has led a switchback career from banker to congressional candidate to Wilderness Society executive to director of the Oregon Natural Resources Council to founder of his own political green group, Citizens for Environmental Equity. In 1996, Tuttle completed an 1,872 mile walk across the West to call attention to the evil consequences of the 1872 Mining Law.

By the mid-1990s, the battle of Grassy Mountain was truly joined. Newmont had unveiled its intention to dig an 800-foot deep pit a half-mile wide into the heart of Grassy Mountain. The Browns and Tuttle struck back with a state-wide initiative on the Oregon ballot to impose stringent environmental safeguards on chemical gold mining in the state, including rigid reclamation stipulations forcing mining companies to spend millions cleaning up their cyanide mess and refilling their vast pits in the earth. The earliest voter polls showed the initiative being favored by as much as 67 percent of the Oregon voters.

Then Newmont struck back. The company saturated the airwaves of the state with $5 million public relations campaign designed to portray the Browns and Tuttle as green extremists intent on snatching money away from the dinner tables and infant platters of rural Oregon families. The pro-mine faction went after the Browns, isolated in the Oregon outback, in a number of nasty ways. They received numerous threats against their lives, their home and their jobs. Eventually, Gary arrived at work one day to find that his employers had reassigned him to an outlet in Boise, landing him with a 120-mile daily commute.

Newmont won that battle, but they soon lost the war. After a blitzkrieg of deceitful television ads, the mining initiative went down by a narrow margin. The company spent $5 million for their victory, the enviros spent less than $100,000. But amid the rubble of defeat, Tuttle and the Browns announced that they were refilling the initiative with even stronger provisions for the next election.

Faced with the prospect of another prolonged campaign, Newmont instead decided to throw in the towel. In its corporate filings, Newmont announced that it was taking a $35 million tax write off ($30 million for the purchase price and $5 million for the ballot fight) and was putting their Grassy Mountain claims up for sale. Tuttle pressed forward the mining initiative for good measure.

For the time being, eastern Oregon remains free of gaping pits, cyanide ponds and 600-foot tall mounds of crushed rock. The Browns and Tuttle showed that determined opposition and a belief in attacking corporations head on can win the day, as they banished North America's largest gold mining company from the state of Oregon.

At the height of their struggle, the Mineral Policy Center—the national, Washington-based group timidly seeking to reform the archaic mining law—bizarrely sang the praises of Newmont, calling their plans for Grassy Mountain the kind of eco-friendly mining they would "like to see more of in the future." No national environmental organization raised a finger to help Tuttle and the Browns, which is probably why they won.

Chapter 22

SLAB CITY LIVING: AN ELEGY TO THE SALTON SEA

By Saul Landau

IN 19TH CENTURY ENGLAND, William Wordsworth strolled through his garden. "I am at one with Nature," he declared. Hemingway's 20th Century hero Nick Adams paddled with his father in a canoe in the unspoiled Michigan lakes. He put his hand into the ice cold water "It was good." I sometimes try to kid myself like the great writers who felt they had some organic relationship with Nature despite the pervasive encroachment of industrial technology on all areas of life.

Could I aspire to become a 21st Century Nick, as I looked at the unruffled picture post card water? The pristine blue landscape reflected the desert sun. The tamarisk trees cast flimsy shadows on the lake's surface. Southern California's largest body of water, the Salton Sea, exudes calm and natural beauty as long as you have a clothes pin on your nose.

Pull it off and the stench threatens to ramrod its way through your sinuses. This invasive redolence combines residues from agricultural runoff (pesticide and chemical fertilizer), sewage from surrounding desert cities (Palm Springs, Coachella and Indio) and even some toxic waste from maquiladoras in nearby Mexicali across the border.

The lake measures 35 miles in length, up to 15 miles in width and has about 115 miles of shoreline. On the western shore, tens of thousands of carcasses of dead and festering birds and fish belie its tranquil image and add to the pernicious odor.

In 1996, government agencies affirmed that 1,200 endangered brown pelicans died of avian botulism. In addition, 19,000 waterfowl and shore birds from 63 species perished. In 1997, 10,000 plus birds from 51 species died. From January through April, 1998, 17,000 birds from 70 species caught Newcastle's disease and avian cholera. The immune systems of thousands of eared grebes became weak, probably from ingesting selenium, and they succumbed to avian infirmities. Their carcasses decompose on the shore alongside the skeletons of fish. Some biologists predict that all the fish will begin to die as salt levels increase.

But a flood in the 1960s preceded the overwhelming stink. Surrounding agribusiness owners had irrigated their overly-chemical drenched soil with a huge increase of water. They did not consider the impact of their action on the Salton Sea. Residents had to abandon modest retirement homes and vacation cottages. These vacant edifices loom like graveside monuments to the lake side community that had mushroomed on the edge of Salton City after World War II.

The origins of the predicament date back to 1905 when a dam in the Colorado River broke and water raced through mineral heavy canals for two years to collect in a pre-historic dried-up lake bed. The new body of water contained a high salinity level. This new culture proved ideal for certain saltwater fish, as well as a place where birds and ducks and geese could migrate and breed. Indeed, scientists have observed almost 400 species of birds at the sea. During the 1950s, experts estimated that in winter some four million birds used this artificial water body. Indeed, for flying non-insects, it became the most utilized sea in the nation. New flora grew on the shore: Desert scrub, creosote bush, saltbush, and tamarisk.

Developers and speculators built tourist facilities that serviced some 200,000 visitors a year, including campsites, trails, playgrounds and boat ramps. The lake became a virtual speedway for boat racers who took advantage of the high salt content that gave their craft more buoyancy. Water and jet skiers roared past annoyed fisherman. By 1958, the North Shore of the lake sported a Yacht Club, with one of the largest marinas in Southern California. In the 1950s, Jerry Lewis docked his boat there. Desi Arnaz and Johnny Weissmuller played on the 18 hole course and hung around Salton Bay Yacht Club. Bulldozers paved the streets.

These forsaken structures have shed their paint. Motels and yacht clubs, places from which water skiers once took off, have also lost their essence: the neon has dripped out of their signs.

Like other ghost towns that once vibrated with life and crackled with festivity, some of the Salton Sea communities now symbolize ecological disaster: conditions that arise when hustlers attempt to manipulate Nature for profit without acknowledging that the future may involve very high costs. Like Melville's white whale, the Salton Sea today threatens to become a metaphor for Biblical punishment. "You have gone too far," the great voice in the sky might have roared. "You are threatening Nature!"

"Hey, that's the nature of capitalism," the developers might well have replied.

To regain their profitable relationship with people and Nature on the Salton Sea, the "men of progress" call upon "science," the ubiquitous magician, to solve environmental messes.

"Fix it," they metaphorically order the men in white lab coats. "And get the government [taxpayers, not corporations] to pick up the tab." So, EPA, The Department of the Interior, the Bureau of Land Management and various California agencies contacted scientists who dutifully began to study this putrid body of water more than three decades ago. They differ about how to apply their magic to sections of the lake, in some areas fifty feet deep, covered with thick layers of viscous silt. Some marine biologists wonder if anyone can clean up this peanut butter like deposit of chemical slurp that looms as a major ecological calamity.

Nature seemed to rebel in the form of an ecological chain reaction. Altering the flow of Colorado River water to create the Salton Sea also led to the diversion of River water to irrigate the Imperial Valley. The ensuing runoff flowed naturally into the unnatural Salton Sea. When farmers poured their "excess" water into the Sea, the Sea rose having no outlet for the excess water—and flooded the shoreline residents, including those on land belonging to the Torres-Martinez reservation.

Geologists call the Salton Sea a "terminal" water body, one that receives water flow, but has not outlet. So, it had no place to send the agricultural run off, post irrigation water that contains chemical fertilizers, pesticides, selenium and other minerals and salts other than onto the shore, with its people and edifices.

The levels of poisonous materials have risen steadily. The Sea diminishes only through evaporation. Allowing it to dry up would mean that poisonous selenium dust would infect all living things in the area. In 2004, scientists estimate that the Salton Sea contains 25% more salinity than the ocean. Even most saltwater fish cannot survive in it. Today, the Sea's ecosystem suffers from significant stress. Several million fish and birds have already died from disease and depressed levels of dissolved oxygen.

Not all the nearby residents have fled, however. In the eastern shore communities of Bombay Beach and the Slab City trailer community, some people live on meager social security checks. "I like it better here than in rural Alabama," says a man with confederate flag sewn on his trucker's cap.

The bar flies at Bombay Beach's Ski Inn drink, smoke and gossip about daily life. They have become accustomed to living in an environmentally challenged area. From the bar, they drive in Mad Max vehicles to their trailers or small homes. The disgusting odor that pervades the western bank occasionally infiltrates their community as well. It seems worse in the summer when the thermometer rises above 110 degrees.

Some fishermen still drop their line in the lake and duck hunters hide in the blinds on the lake shore. "I sure hope they don't eat what they catch or shoot," says a man who has watched the Sea deteriorate over the decades.

The residents wait for the conflicting interests, like urban water authorities, conservationists, agribusiness, and native peoples, to figure out a "cure" for their ecologically diseased Sea.

One interested party, the Torres Martinez tribe, had to change their life in 1905 when the Colorado River water overflowed their reservation. Like the fauna, flora and people in the area, these Native Americans adapted to the new environment and abandoned their traditional hunting and gathering culture for fishing and modest farming, as they debate whether to build a Casino. In the 1960s more flooding and increasing salinity and pollution of the Sea further threatened their future.

The Salton Sea, like the Aral Sea in Central Asia, which is 400 times its size and shrinking fast, symbolizes ecological catastrophe. Soviet industrial "planners" had treated Nature just as the California capitalist developers did: they employed "productive" technology without calculating or even thinking about consequences. Nearby residents animals and plants suffered horrendous consequences.

But humans learn slowly. They know that reproduction of the species requires a healthy environment—clean air and water and uncontaminated soil. But some of the smartest engineers can lose sight of that truism when offered the chance to manipulate Nature for short-term profits.

Indeed, these "forward looking" individuals view Nature as something to dominate, not nurture. Will it take the rule of romantic poets to teach that tornadoes, hurricanes, El Ninos scream metaphoric messages? "Hey, there's something more powerful than all of you!"

Environmental nightmares like the Salton Sea have not humbled those who exude "progress" but lack the sensitivity to understand that serious lessons follow the modification of the earth's ecology.

Wordsworth's Nature was:
"the language of the sense,
The anchor of my purest thoughts, the
nurse,
The guide, the guardian of my heart,
and soul
Of all my moral being."

—"Lines Composed a Few Miles Above Tintern Abbey"

Chapter 23

TORQUEMADAS IN BIRKENSTOCKS

By Jeffrey St. Clair

MY DEAR OLD FRIEND David Brower must be fuming in his grave. The Sierra Club, the organization he almost single-handedly built into a global green powerhouse, has become so cowardly since his death two years ago that now it refuses even to take a stand against war, which Brower believed to be the ultimate environmental nightmare.

Even worse, its bosses—like petty enforcers from the McCarthy Era—are now threatening to exile from the Club any leaders who step forward to voice their opposition to the bombing, invasion and occupation of Iraq.

It is a telltale sign of the enervated condition of the big greens that there's precious little dissent in the Sierra Club on the prospect of another war in the Persian Gulf. Indeed, it took four activists from Utah, of all places, to light the fire. Let them be known as the Glen Canyon Group Four: John Weisheit, Tori Woodard, Patrick Diehl and Dan Kent.

They bravely announced that they opposed the war and identified themselves as leaders of the Sierra Club's Glen Canyon Group, based in Moab, Utah, former stomping grounds of Edward Abbey.

"The present administration has declared its intention to achieve total military dominance of the world," says Patrick Diehl, vice-chair of the Glen Canyon Group. "We believe that such ambitions will produce a state of perpetual war, undoing whatever protection of the environment that conservation groups may have so far achieved."

This noble stand was soon followed by a similarly principled anti-war resolution enacted by the Club's San Francisco Bay Chapter.

Then: slam! The long arm of Sierra Club HQ came down on them, clumsily as usual.

There's scant room for free speech inside the Sierra Club these days, even when the topic is of paramount concern to the health of the planet. Especially then.

The Club's peevish executive director, Carl Pope, and his gang of glowering enforcers, blustered that the Glen Canyon Four had impertinently violated Club rules. The Club executives threatened to level sanctions against the activists, ranging from expelling them from their positions to dissolving the rebellious group entirely. Angry phone calls and nasty emails flew back and forth. The Glen Canyon Four were threatened with a BOLT action—BOLT being the stark acronym for a Breach of Leadership Trust.

"For the board to compel our silence plays right into Bush's mad world, where a nation of police, prisons, bombs, bunkers is better than lowering oneself to diplomacy to save lives," says Dan Kent.

The Sierra Club's Breach of Leadership Trust rule functions as a kind of proto-type for Ashcroft's Patriot Act, designed to stigmatize, intimidate and muzzle internal dissenters. As result, the Club is rife with snoops, snitches, and would-be Torquemadas in Birkenstocks.

In this case, the intimidation isn't likely to work. John Weisheit is perhaps the most accomplished river guide on the Colorado. He's stared down Cataract Canyon and Lava Falls in their most violent incarnations without flinching. Tori Woodard and Patrick Diehl live in the outback of Escalante, Utah, where they routinely receive death threats for their environmental activism. Pompous chest-thumping and bluster by the likes of Carl Pope won't scare off these people.

Peculiarly, the Sierra Club has chosen to invoke its internal policing power mainly against members who have pushed for the Club to adopt more robust environmental policies: ending livestock grazing, mining and logging on public lands; backing Ralph Nader and the Green Party; or opposing the sell-out of Yosemite National Park to a corrupt firm linked to Bruce Babbitt. The most disgusting internal crackdown came last year in a spiteful attack on Moisha Blechman, a Sierra Club activist in New York City, who was smeared with accusations of the most scurrilous kind, mainly because she was too green for the cautious twerps who run the Club.

Meanwhile, the Sierra Club turns a blind eye to renegade chapters in New Mexico and other places that attack and ridicule its current policies, such as the No Commercial Logging plank, as being too radical. Even worse, the Club leadership stands mute as a gang of Malthusian brigands infiltrate its ranks seeking to hi-jack the organization as a vehicle to carry forward a racist anti-immigration agenda that would make Pat Buchanan cringe.

All of this would seem mighty strange, if you remain naïve enough to believe that the Sierra Club is an organization principally (or even parenthetically) devoted to the preservation of the planet.

It's not, of course. Like any other corporation, the Sierra Club's managers are obsessively preoccupied with beefing up the Club's bottom line and solidifying its access to power, the bloodstream of most nonprofits. (Read: a snuggling relationship to the Democratic National Committee, supine though it may be).

So here's a warning: When you join the Sierra Club and affix your signature to that membership card you are also signing a loyalty oath.

Loyalty to what? Certainly not the environment. These days it's loyalty to the image of the Club that matters. And increasingly the desired image of the Club is manufactured by its bosses, not its members.

How important is "image" to the Sierra Club? Well, it spends more than $2 million a year and employs 25 people to work full time in its Communication and Information Services unit, the outfit's largest single amalgamation of funds.

When the *Los Angeles Times* published a story about the Iraq affair, the bosses of the Club froze, like stuffed weasels in the spotlight. This was not the kind of media attention they'd spent all that money to garner. On the one hand, they didn't want to be seen as tolerating internal opposition to a popular war. On the other hand, many, if not most, Sierra Club members probably harbor serious doubts about the war and the way the Bushites intended to prosecute it. So a kind of organizational paralysis ensued. It's just as well.

In a letter to the *Los Angeles Times*, Club President Jennifer Ferenstein exuded some shopworn homilies about US dependence on foreign oil and pronounced that the Club's resolution warned against "Iraqi aggression." This language sounds cagey, but it's actually moronic and craven. Even Bush didn't charge Iraq with plans to invade its neighbors this time around. Moreover, while the Club supports the Bush Administration's purported goal of disarming Iraq, it remains silent on disarming the Pentagon.

Ferenstein attempted to clarify the Club's confused policy a few days later in a primly worded letter to the *Christian Science Monitor*, but she came off sounding even sillier. "In order to reduce oil's influence in geopolitical relations, the U.S. and other nations have to move away from an oil-dependent economy toward a future based on clean energy, greater efficiency and more renewable power," writes Ferenstein. "The Sierra Club has called for a peaceful resolution of the conflict in Iraq, proceeding according to the UN resolutions, and we emphatically believe that long-term stability depends on the U.S. reducing our oil dependence."

Apparently, Ferenstein didn't understand that the UN Resolution gave the US and Britain the green light to whack Iraq with the slightest provocation, real or fabricated. And apparently war is okay with the Club as long as it's the result of a consensus process (even if the UN consensus was brokered by bullying and bribery)—although how the environment suffers any less under this feel-good scenario remains a mystery.

It's not as if the environmental ruin caused by the first Gulf War is unknown. In January of 2000 Green Cross International, a Christian environmental group, released its detailed investigation of the environmental consequences of the Gulf War. Their findings were grim: more than 60 million gallons of crude spilled into the desert, forming 246 oil lakes; 1,500 miles of the Gulf Coast was saturated with oil; Kuwait's only freshwater aquifer, source of more than 40 percent of the country's drinking water, was heavily contaminated with benzenes and other toxins; 33,000 land mines remain scattered across the desert; incidences of birth defects, childhood illnesses and cancers climbed dramatically after the war.

Cruise missiles targeted Iraqi oil refineries, pipelines, chemical plants, and water treatment systems. Ten years later, many of these facilities remained destroyed, unremediated and hazardous.

Months of bombing of Iraq by US and British planes and cruise missiles also left behind an even more deadly and insidious legacy: tons of shell casings, bullets and bomb fragments laced with depleted uranium. In all, the US hit Iraqi targets with more than 970 radioactive bombs and missiles.

More than 10 years later, the health consequences from this radioactive bombing campaign are beginning to come into focus. And they are dire, indeed. Iraqi physicians call it "the white death"—leukemia. Since 1990, the incident rate of leukemia in Iraq has grown by more than 600 percent. The situation is compounded by Iraq's forced isolation and the sadistic sanctions regime, described by UN secretary general Kofi Annan as "a humanitarian crisis," that makes detection and treatment of the cancers all the more difficult. The return engagement promised to be just as grim, if not worse.

Compared to a courageous titan like Brower, timid little people run the Sierra Club these days. In her two years as president, Ferenstein has gone from being the bubbly Katie Couric of the environmental movement to its Margaret Thatcher. In the process, she may have set back the cause of eco-feminism by 20 years.

But Ferenstein is largely just a figurehead, the hand puppet of executive director Carl Pope. Pope has never had much of a reputation as an environmental activist. He's a wheeler-dealer, who keeps the Club's policies in lockstep with its big funders and political patrons. Where Dave Brower scaled mountains, nearly all of Pope's climbing has been up organizational ladders.

This limp state of affairs has been coming for some time. After 9/11, the Sierra Club leadership was so cowed by the events that they publicly announced that they were putting their environmental campaigns on hold and pledged not to criticize Bush, who at that very moment was seeking to exploit the tragedy in order to expand oil drilling in some the most fragile and imperiled lands on the continent.

The same with the war on Iraq. The mandarins who run the Club made a decision early on to let their position float in grim harmony with the DNC's shameless warmongering.

Only two board members have stood up against the war: Marcia Hanscom from Los Angeles and Michael Dorsey, the Club's only black board member and a man with a true passion for social and environmental justice. That's two out of 15. There was more vigorous dissent inside Bush's National Security Council.

All this would have disgusted Brower, who was a veteran of the famous 10th Mountain Division in World War II but a peacenik at heart. I first met Brower in 1980. He'd already been booted out of the Sierra Club for being too militant and had gone on to found Friends of the Earth, where he was about to meet same fate. He asked me to do some writing for him on what he thought was the great environmental issue of our time: war. At the time,

Brower was helping jumpstart the nuclear freeze movement and I was honored to join him.

"If we greens don't broaden our thinking to tackle war," he told me, "we may save some wilderness, but lose the world." He was a master at aphorisms like that. Especially after a couple of martinis, heavily charged with Tanqueray.

Brower was right, of course. A century of wars have ravaged the environment as brutally as the timber giants and the chemical companies. And the nuclear industry, headquartered in DC and Moscow, threatened the whole shebang with what Jonathan Schell in the *Fate of the Earth*, a book Brower ceaselessly plugged, called "the second death": the extinction of all life on earth.

Brower also knew what most contemporary enviros don't: that the day-to-day operations of the military-industrial complex itself—weapons production and testing—amount to the most toxic industry on the planet, as a trip to the poisoned wastelands of Hanford, Fallon, Nevada or Rocky Flats will readily reveal.

For some reason, battling the Pentagon has never had the allure of fighting the Forest Service (an agency that I detest), which by comparison behaves like the Cub Scouts of the federal government.

Back in 1990, Brower and his beautiful and courageous wife Anne came to Portland, just as the bombing of Iraq had gotten into high gear. There were demonstrations on the streets nearly every night over the course of that war. Together we joined a crowd of several hundred activists gathered in the December rain. We stood shoulder-to-shoulder on the old Hawthorne Bridge for an hour, shutting down rush hour traffic out of downtown. We sang "We Shall Overcome" as the police stared us down, the Browers' unmistakable voices sailing above it all.

Those days are gone. Both Dave and Anne are dead. But a new peace movement is rising and Brower helped give it life and meaning.

The spirit of this new movement won't be found within the confines of any club. It's out on the streets and in the woods, where it's always been. Hurry. It's not too late to join. No membership card required.

Chapter 24

MONA IN THE FIELDS

By Greg Moses

"EVERY VOICE THAT COMES behind Cindy Sheehan sparks a new voice, and someone else stands up. Someone else is not afraid anymore." Mona is speaking from the back seat of a Camp Casey shuttle as the Texas prairie speeds past. Today Mona is not afraid what the President will think. But she is worried to death about her son, who is headed for Iraq next month. Mona's anti-war movement is on a tight schedule indeed. Even the big national protests in DC may have come too late.

"I was on Air America earlier this week," says Mona, answering to the usual round of "where you from?" She called the radio station from Ohio to defend Cindy Sheehan's protest action, and someone asked her if she was planning to go. "Well, if I can arrange it, I'll go," Mona recalls. After she hung up, the station got calls. Someone offered a plane ticket from Ohio to Texas. Another offered the rental car. "So I'm here for at least a week, but I can always just turn in the car and stay longer."

As we debark the shuttle on a recent afternoon, Deputy Kolinek from the McLennan County Sheriff's Department is looking jovial. "You've got a question written all over your face," says the khaki starched Kolinek to a t-shirt clad protester. "What is it?" As Kolinek listens to the question, a woman hands the deputy a chilled bottle of water which he opens right away.

A mist of cool water hits me in the face. It's Fran, one of my traveling hosts. She has grabbed this delightful contraption from a CodePink bag of tricks. It's a spray-gun mini-fan combo in bright plastic colors. All I can say is "do it again!" Days out here are like this. Juxtapositions of worry and joy, anger and delight, water and tears.

Over on Prairie Chapel Road, beneath a few freshly erected white crosses, some flowers have been placed. For 24-year-old Kelly Prewitt of Alabama, someone has placed a collection of colorful cut flowers on the ground. Florist delivery trucks are not uncommon out here. According to a CBS News report, Prewitt wrote his dad to say he was homesick. Back in the fateful month of April 2003 when Kelly was killed, his dad Steve was quoted saying he hoped his son's death would mean something, that the war would do some good. Out here in the blazing light of August, Kelly's mother Jean tells a French wire service that her whole attitude toward the war changed in December 2003 when the reason for starting the war was exposed as "a big lie."

For 22-year-old Irving Medina of Middletown, New York, someone has cut wildflowers from the prairie—a sunflower and a purplish bulb from a nettle or thistle. Irving's twin brother Ivan had just survived an 11-month tour in Iraq when a West Point officer and chaplain, dressed in their best uniforms, knocked at the family home. They were soon followed by TV cameras. Irving had been killed by a "homemade grenade" while on patrol in the streets of Baghdad in late 2003 reported the *Times Herald-Record* of Hudson Valley. He was going to propose to a woman when he returned. All the family knew was her name: Leslie. Was it Leslie who cut the wild flowers today? As I search to find a Crawford connection, all I come up with is Medina, holy city of the prophet.

A rose and a daisy have been placed at the cross of 20-year-old Christian Schulz of Colleyville, Texas, who was stationed at nearby Ft. Hood. His death is attributed to "non-combat" causes, but he died in a war nevertheless, July 11, 2003. Finally, although no flowers yet appear at the cross of Pablito Pena Briones, Jr., who died from a "non-hostile gunshot" in Falluja, something about the name Pablito reminds me how young a 20-year-old can be.

By the time I reach the end of the line, Mona is bent over, trying to rattle loose one of the crosses from a pull-cart. From a string, hanging around her neck, dangles a laminated photo of a young man in uniform.

"Mona, is that your son?" I ask. She looks up, slightly startled, then, "Yes, that's him." Standing up, she twirls the picture to show me the flip side, a photo of her three grandchildren. Two of them are from her son's family, one is from her daughter's, but she has made a group photo for her son to take with him, to give him hope, to encourage him to come back alive. Back to her work with the crosses, she says in a wavering voice, "I sure hope I don't have to put out one of these for him." And we both stand there crying. "Where are all the mothers," she asks, "that these crosses belong to?" A Korean reporter looks at us, and he is also frozen stiff by this grief. His pen hovers over his notebook, but what exactly is there to say?

"Ma'am, do you want me to help you put names on those crosses?" asks the gentle voice of a brand new volunteer who has just walked the line. Which helps to get us all moving again. Under the high sun, with cicadas and crickets buzzing from their invisible homes in the grass, Mona, with her hat brim pulled down, returns to her work among the field of crosses at Prairie Chapel Road.

PART FOUR
INDIAN COUNTRY

Chapter 25

THE LIFE AND DEATH OF LEROY JACKSON

By Jeffrey St. Clair

NAVAJO ENVIRONMENTALIST LEROY JACKSON had been missing for eight days when an anonymous tip led New Mexico state police to a white van, its windows concealed by towels and blankets, parked at a rest stop atop the Brazos Cliffs south of Chama, New Mexico. The doors were locked, a putrid odor emanated from inside.

Patrolman Ted Ulibari broke the driver's door window and looked inside. In the back seat, under a thick wool blanket, he found the sprawled body of Leroy Jackson. He had been dead for days.

Jackson was the charismatic leader of Dine CARE, an environmental group of traditionalists on the big Navajo reservation. He was also my friend. Jackson was on his way from Taos to Washington, DC, where he planned to confront the Clinton administration over logging in the old-growth ponderosa pine forests in the Chuska Mountains, a mysterious and beautiful blue range that rises out of the high desert in northern Arizona and New Mexico. The Chuskas are a sacred place for the Navajo and Hopi, an earthly anchor of their complex cosmology.

Only days before Jackson disappeared, he had spoken out against the logging plans at a public hearing in Window Rock, Arizona. The Bureau of Indian Affairs had just requested an exemption from the Endangered Species Act, which would allow the Navajo Forest Products Industries to clearcut old-growth forest habitat for the Mexican spotted owl, a threatened species, in the Chuska Mountains, near Jackson's home.

In the exemption request to the U.S. Fish and Wildlife Service, the BIA had arrogantly claimed that because owls are "symbols of death" to some Navajo, the extirpation of the bird from reservation lands could be legally justified on religious and cultural grounds. During the hearing, Jackson eviscerated the Bureau for promoting a racist ruse to sanction the destruction of sacred forest lands.

More critically, Jackson hinted publicly at possible corrupt practices by the tribal logging company and officials at the BIA. He urged the Navajo Nation to return to its traditional respect for the land and to support practices that preserved local jobs and forests.

Jackson's remarks were greeted with angry gestures and threats of violence from loggers and millworkers. He received threats from NFPI executives and from employees at the Bureau of Indian Affairs. Leroy and his wife Adella, a nurse, were rudely awakened by late-night phone calls threatening to burn down their home. Jackson dismissed them at the time, but these and other threats led many of Jackson's closest friends to conclude that he was assassinated because of his environmental activism.

Although initial reports indicated that blood, possibly in large quantities, was found at the scene, state police later said that there were no obvious signs of foul play. A cursory autopsy ruled out most natural causes of death, including stroke, heart attack and carbon monoxide poisoning. The results of a toxicology report showed trace quantities of marijuana and methadone in Jackson's blood and tissue. Even though Jackson was not a known drug user, the police swiftly dismissed his mysterious death as a drug overdose.

Jackson's friends claimed that the investigation into his death was cursory at best and point to irregularities and possible cover-ups. For example, the police refused to look into several credible reports that Jackson's van had not been parked at the Brazos overlook during the proceeding week. The police also failed to photograph the crime scene or dust the van for fingerprints. For nearly a week, police left the van outside in a parking lot at Chama before towing it to the crime lab in Santa Fe.

Although the New Mexico state police told Jackson's wife, Adella Begay, that only a small amount of blood was found on a pillow near Jackson's body, a source who was at the scene shortly after the van was discovered said the interior "looked staged. There was blood on the carpets and the seats and the body seem posed."

Responding to a request from Jackson's friends, Bill Richardson, then the congressman representing northern New Mexico, sent a letter to the director of the FBI asking the agency to investigate the circumstances surrounding Jackson's death. In his letter, Jackson cited the recent threats Jackson had received for his environmental activism and suggested that "a major crime may have been committed." Ultimately, the FBI declined to launch an inquiry, citing the conclusion of the state police that Jackson had overdosed on methadone.

At Jackson's burial, his friends vowed to continue the search for his killer and to intensify the fight to protect the old forests on the Navajo reservation. "Those who killed Leroy thought they could silence him," said Earl Tulley, a traditionalist Navajo who co-founded Dine CARE with Jackson. "But they only made his cause stronger than when he was alive."

I met Leroy Jackson three times and talked to him often on the phone. We were friends. Kindred spirits. His voice radiated a rare combination of power, eloquence and humility.

Leroy Jackson cared about his culture and the Navajo people as much as those forests on the slopes of the Chuskas. Indeed, for Jackson the future of the Navajo forests was inseparably tied to the future of the Navajo people and their religion. That's what motivated his struggle.

The last time I spoke to Jackson was about two months before his death. He described in sharp detail plans by the Bureau of Indian Affairs and Navajo Forest Products Industries to clearcut much of the last remaining old-growth ponderosa pine forest on the Big Reservation.

Jackson was angry, but not discouraged. He explained that his new alliance of traditionalist Navajo leaders and energetic young activists was growing in strength and power on the reservation. He believed that Dine CARE was on the verge of dramatically reshaping logging practices on Navajo lands.

"They are going after the heart of the old forest in the sacred mountains," Jackson told me. "But they will not get it. There is a new respect for the old ways."

Ultimately, Jackson was aiming to change something much broader and more fundamental than simply the layout of a timber sale. Like other traditionalists, Jackson understood that outside forces, including the BIA, uranium and coal companies, oil and gas corporations and the timber firms, had assiduously corrupted the Navajo tribal council. Under the banner of jobs, sovereignty and future prosperity, these forces had begun stripping the reservation of its natural resources and cultural and spiritual heritage. This path had put millions in the pockets of the corporations, a few tribal leaders and some officials at the BIA, but had left the reservation itself impoverished: economically, ecologically and culturally.

In response, Jackson and his companions were seeking a return to traditional Navajo values about the land and its use. This was dangerous ground and Jackson knew it. He told me about weekly death threats and about how loggers had hung him in effigy from their trucks the previous summer.

I remember telling him to be cautious. Yes, most hard core environmentalists get threatened and we treat the threats almost as badges of honor, something to laugh and brag about, but not lose much sleep over. But I warned him that in the Southwest it's different. There the threats have a history of being backed up by violence.

I wasn't telling Jackson anything that he didn't already know intimately. One of the last times we spoke he told me that he believed he would probably die in the fight to save the Chuskas.

***

Leroy Jackson was buried under ancient ponderosa pines high in the Chuska Mountains. The way to the burial site was marked by pink ribbons. Some were tied to trees and shrubs, others to root-wads and slash left by the extensive clearcutting, a grim testimonial to the Chuska's ignoble claim as the most intensely logged range in the Southwest.

Under a soft wind, looking out over the blue mountains, etched in the autumnal hue of aspens turning gold, Navajo traditionalist John Redhouse spoke about Leroy's life: "Leroy was no different from the other Dine warriors and patriots who gave their lives. He took a vow to protect the male deity represented by the Chuskas and to preserve balance and harmony for the Navajo people. He saw that the Navajo tribe has not shared this vision, that they have pursued the white man's values. We will continue his struggle. It is a struggle for our destiny and our future."

Chapter 26

STOLEN TRUST: ELOUISE COBELL SOLVES THE CASE OF THE MISSING $10 BILLION

By Jeffrey St. Clair

ELOUISE COBELL COMES RIGHT to the point. "Gale Norton should be thrown in jail." Cobell is a leader of the Blackfeet tribe, and lives along the Rocky Mountain Front in northwestern Montana. Norton, of course, is Bush's Secretary of the Interior and, as such, oversees the US government's relationship with Indian tribes.

Norton also controls the purse strings on federal trust funds holding more than $40 billion dollars owed to Indians across the nation. For her role in the mismanagement of the trust fund, Norton faced a contempt court citation from federal judge Royce Lamberth. She's in bi-partisan company. In 2000, Lamberth hit Bruce Babbitt and Treasury Secretary Robert Rubin with contempt citations for failing to halt the destruction of Indian trust account documents.

The sprawling case begin in 1996 when Cobell, who has been called the Rosa Parks of Indian Country, filed a federal class action suit against the Interior Department, seeking both money that's been owed to Indian people and a radical change in how the trust fund is managed. The case now stands as the largest class action suit in history, with more than 500,000 claimants. And, as it wound its way through the courts, it has tarnished two administrations and exposed the continuing war on Indian people by the federal government.

"We're not after money from the government," Cobell says. "The government has taken money that belongs to us."

Of course, stealing from Indians goes back to the origins of the republic. Mismanagement of Indian trust accounts was first noted by Congress in 1823. But the Cobell suit is targeted at the notorious Dawes Act of 1887, which was a cynical attempt to shatter Indian solidarity and culture by privatizing the reservations into 140 acre allotments put in the names of individual Indians.

Naturally, it was a set up. Soon Indians were swindled out of more than two-thirds of their land, about 135,000 square miles in all. The remaining 57 million acres was put into a trust held by the Department of Interior. This too was a scam. With little or no input from the tribes, the land was leased out to white ranchers, oil companies, mining firms and timber companies. The trust land was stripped of its resources, often left in a ravaged condition.

The revenues from these leases (often sold at bargain-basement rates) goes into a trust fund administered by the Department of Interior. These days the fund receives about $500 million a year. Since 1887, more than $100 billion has gone into the accounts. Although the ranchers and oil companies have made a killing, little of that money has ever reached the tribes, where the per capita income hovers at less than $10,000 a year and unemployment rates hover near 70 percent. A recent study shows that more than 90 percent of elderly Indians across the country are without access to long-term health care.

Lots of people have made money in futile and half-hearted attempts to untangle the mess. In the early 1990s, Enron's favorite bookkeepers, Arthur Anderson was hired to make sense of the trust fund accounts. After two years, they retreated in failure, but collected $20 million for their time.

"This scandal makes Enron look like a pimple," Cobell says. "It's worse than Enron, because it's the government that is lying, covering up and breaching its trust. They stole people's entire life savings. They robbed an entire race of people. If banks had ripped off white people, they'd be shut down in a New York second and everybody responsible would go to jail."

Before filing suit, Cobell tried to meet with Bruce Babbitt, then Clinton's Interior Secretary. Despite his high-minded rhetoric about environmental justice, Babbitt slammed the door in Cobell's face. She then sought out Janet Reno. Reno too brushed her aside. Cobell was disgusted at the hypocrisy and cowardice of the Clintonoids. "They ought to have been ashamed," Cobell told one of Reno's deputies. "People are dying in all Indian communities. They don't have access to their own money."

In 1999, Lamberth ruled that the Interior Department had grossly mismanaged the accounts. "This case reveals a shocking pattern of deception," Lamberth wrote in his ruling. "I've never seen more egregious misconduct by the federal government." It was a huge victory for Cobell, who heard the news as she was driving across the wind-swept Blackfeet reservation. "I pulled over to the side of the road and I cried and cried," Cobell recalled.

But victory didn't prove that simple. After five years, not a single Indian account had been straightened out and the government has done its best to defy the court and subvert its ruling. Incriminating emails were deleted. Subpoenaed documents were trashed, burned and shredded. The recalcitrance and malfeasance was so pervasive that Lamberth cited both Babbitt and Rubin with contempt of court.

Cobell thinks that the Clinton team was simply running out the clock, waiting to hand the mess off to the next administration. "It was crystal clear to me what the Clinton administration was up to," Cobell says. "Stalling, stalling and stalling."

When Gale Norton took over, things got worse. Norton is a protégé of James Watt, who infamously described Indian reservations as "the last bastions of socialism in the western world." Watt desperately wanted to revive the malicious spirit of the Dawes Act and sell off the rest of Indian country to the highest bidder. He was driven from office before he could realize his malign dream, but Norton holds many of the same ideas and prejudices.

A few weeks after taking office, Norton told Judge Lamberth that she was intent on developing a plan that would restructure the Indian trust account system. In the year it took to develop, Norton and her team didn't consult once with the tribes. When the plan was unveiled nearly every tribe in the country denounced it. There was good reason for their outrage. Leaving the Interior Department in charge of a trust fund that they had already looted was like letting the fox in the henhouse.

Judge Lamberth didn't like it much either. He excoriated Norton's handling of the affair and failure to provide even a basic information on the historical mismanagement of the trust. Norton responded flippantly, "I'm no accountant."

Meanwhile, a string of special masters appointed to oversee the Interior Department's implementation of the rulings of the court have denounced Norton and her colleagues for tardiness, incompetence and "government malfeasance."

Norton claimed that the Department's new computer system would provide a quick fix to the problem. But in 2002 a computer hacker successfully penetrated the site to demonstrate how easily the trust fund's records could be manipulated. Lamberth ordered the department to shut down all of its computer systems until the security problem could be fixed.

Norton's flacks used Lambert's landmark ruling as a pretext to withhold sending out the year-end trust fund checks to 40,000 Indians. It was a move designed to punish the tribes and to try to undermine Cobell and her cohorts. Denied their money during Christmas-time, several Indians called Cobell, blaming her for the bleak circumstances. "It was an act of retaliation," says Cobell. "They knew that Indians were starving, because they had no checks. Yet they did nothing."

Only a couple of members of congress objected to these strong-arm tactics. "These people were subject to losing their car or their house," said Rep. Tom Udall, the Democrat from Colorado. "If this happened to security, all of Congress would be in an uproar."

But Lamberth was less tolerant. He threatened to hold Norton and Bureau of Indian Affairs head Neal McCaleb in contempt and hinted that they could face jail and fines. Lamberth warned that the fines will be paid from their personal accounts and not government funds.

But Norton remained undeterred. She engineered the forced resignation of Thomas Slonaker from his position as the special trustee for the Indian trust fund system. Slonaker, a Republican banking executive from Phoenix, had reported that the Interior Department had done little to make corrections to the trust account system. Slonaker had been called to appear before a senate hearing on the mismanagement of the trust fund and Norton instructed him not to submit his prepared testimony. When Slonaker refused, he was handed a letter of resignation by Steven Griles, Deputy Interior Secretary, who was forced to resign in disgrace and was later convicted on federal corruption charges.

"It was like telling the emperor that she has no clothes," said Slonaker. "Sometimes, criticism is not welcome."

With Slonaker dispatched, the Bush administration went after Judge Lamberth. They convinced a panel of federal judges that the conservative jurist was "irrationally prejudiced" against the Interior Department in favor of the Indians. Lamberth was removed from the case he had presided over for a decade.

Cobell, though, won't be so easy to get rid of. In the past, government officials have always counted on the poverty of Indian people as they trample over their rights with near impunity. But Cobell is a creative businesswoman and a master fundraiser. She has raised over $9 million for the trust lawsuit from private sources and foundations, notably the Lannan Fund of New Mexico, which contributed $4.1 million to the cause.

She'll probably need every penny, because there's no indication that the Feds (regardless of who controls the White House or Congress) will ever back down. "The government is going to fight this no matter what, even if it's morally, legally or ethically in the wrong," Cobell says. "That's a real crime in itself."

That's just the way things go in Indian country.

But Cobell also sees the litigation has having served to unite the tribes in a common front. "I actually see it as a miracle," Cobell says. "I've never seen tribes come together and work so hard."

Chapter 27

ACCUSATIONS AND SMEARS: AN INTERVIEW WITH WARD CHURCHILL

By Joshua Frank

Ward Churchill is a former professor of Ethnic Studies at the University of Colorado, Boulder who came under fire for an article he wrote following September 11, 2001 titled, "Some People Push Back." He is also the author of numerous books, including *On the Justice of Roosting Chickens* and *A Little Matter of Genocide*. The following interview was conducted in September of 2005.

...

Joshua Frank: I'm sure that the majority of the readers are familiar with your now infamous essay "Some Push Back," so I won't ask you to explain yourself, but I recently read in an Associated Press article that you wished you had phrased your Adolf Eichmann comment a bit differently. It seemed obvious to me after reading your essay that you were referring to Hannah Arendt's portrayal of Eichmann in her book Eichmann in Jerusalem. *Is that true?*

Ward Churchill: What I meant was that I wished I'd explained the Eichmann analogy a bit, right off the bat. Silly me. I thought it was rather self-explanatory, like maybe a lot of the people professing such strong negative opinions on the matter might have some clue as to who Eichmann actually was and how Hannah Arendt had rather famously analyzed the implications of his career. This is especially true with regard to my self-styled "liberal" critics. I mean, really. Dave Dellinger advanced exactly the same analogy clear back in

1975 without generating anything resembling the same kind of sanctimonious response from the "left." But, then, he was an unabashed white guy, and a pacifist to boot, so...

JF: Your liberal critics have also attacked your scholarship. I remember reading something that Marc Cooper, the corpulent pundit for The Nation, *wrote about it on his blog, hoping that it would get you canned. He, like a lot of liberals, doesn't like your politics and demeanor. But it's not just the liberal establishment that's jumped on the "get-Churchill-fired" bandwagon. The right-wingers seem to think that going after your scholarship could actually do the trick and get you fired— which they've clearly wanted since your 9/11 essay blew up. The most severe of these charges is an alleged plagiarism case, where you've been accused of stealing someone else's work. What's been the fallout of all of this, and are the charges legit? Or has the media simply taken the whole episode out of context?*

WC: Let me reframe that one a little bit. The commonalities linking liberals like Marc Cooper to reactionary jackanapes like Bill O'Reilly couldn't be clearer. At a certain level, and it's not a terribly obscure one, Cooper and O'Reilly share an identical agenda. That's a point I've been trying to hammer home for years, with only limited success, and now Cooper has come right out in full public view and proven me correct. That's been one of the most gratifying aspects of this whole charade, as far as I'm concerned. I'm absolutely delighted that he and liberals more generally have elected to attack me the way they have.

This takes us to the plagiarism "issue." But maybe the best way to address it is to start by clarifying exactly how Cooper has gone about dancing his little minuet with O'Reilly. I mean, he himself was never so out front as to actually appear on *The O'Reilly Factor* to condemn me. What he did instead was quote, approvingly and at length from columns authored for the *Rocky Mountain News* by another self-styled liberal, University of Colorado law professor Paul Campos. Campos repeatedly entered O'Reilly's "no-spin zone" during the 41-day period in February and March when hefty segments of *The Factor* were devoted to my "case" every single night, alternating as talking head with the likes of Newt Gingrich, David Horowitz, and such Clear Channel hacks as Mark Silverman.

Self-evidently, the views Campos expressed fit right in with those expressed by O'Reilly's other "analysts." Otherwise, "Mr. No-Spin" wouldn't have brought him back on. There's no way Cooper could have been unaware of this. So it's fair to say that he knowingly built the O'Reilly/Gingrich/Horowitz/Clear Channel spew into his own material, but without ever owning up to the fact that that's what he was doing. Paul Campos served as his cover (whether wittingly or not, I have no idea). Clever, eh?

In any event, the plagiarism allegation against me originated in one of Campos' *News* screeds in early February. There, and in subsequent columns, he waxed sanctimonious, not only about my supposed plagiarism, but about other "fraudulent research practices" in which he claimed I'd engaged. Among other things, he went on and on about how I supposedly "distorted my sources."

And, of course, since the mainstream media tends to spend most of its time quoting itself, Campos' assertions were endlessly repeated, albeit usually without attribution, thus mutating into "fact," no less for readers of Marc Cooper's blog than for those whose preference is tuning in to O'Reilly or Rush Limbaugh.

Here's where it gets to be amusing in a twisted sort of way. Campos cited a 1999 article by a law professor named John LaVelle at the University of New Mexico as having already accused me of plagiarism, and that he, Campos, was merely repeating the charge. When you look at the LaVelle piece, however, he says nothing of the sort. In fact, he argues the exact opposite, adducing that I've written, or helped write, several pieces that have appeared under other people's names. And, although he's wrong about almost everything else in his essay, John LaVelle scored a direct hit with that one.

So, not only is Paul Campos flagrantly guilty of one of the major charges he's hurled at me—that is, of grossly distorting a source—he now has to suffer the indignity of watching as the truth of what LaVelle actually said is borne out. It's been generally conceded at this point, even in Campos' own paper (although it's been predictably careful not to remind readers that he was saying exactly the opposite a few months back), that I in fact wrote the material I supposedly plagiarized. This being so, the worst "ethical violation" I can be said to have committed is the "deception" of sometimes serving as a ghostwriter and sometimes writing under pseudonyms. That puts me in league with such "unseemly" characters as C.L.R. James, a fate I guess I can learn to live with.

That's not all of it, to be sure. There's a bunch of other pretext charges on the table: when they realized I wasn't going to cave under pressure and, at about the same time, that they weren't going to be able to sustain a firing on speech grounds, they shifted to shotgunning me with "academic integrity" allegations in hopes that something might stick. But it's all going to work out pretty much the same way. Actually, there's a lot more I'd like to get to in this vein, especially with regard to how the liberal "left" has actively collaborated in the right's use of "scholarly standards" as a ploy to accomplish its objectives.

JF: Let's hear it.

WC: It's been going on for quite a while now. In my view, you can probably date the origin of the technique from the David Abraham case of the mid-80s, when a newly-minted assistant professor at Princeton came out with a really excellent book titled *The Collapse of the Weimar Republic*, in which he not only laid out the role played by German big business in bringing the Nazis to power, but the whole complex range of liberal democratic sociopolitical dynamics that contributed to the same result. The study, which was unabashedly neo-Marxian in approach, was really well received, heralded in some quarters as a major methodological breakthrough.

The problem was that Henry A. Turner, a senior historian at Yale, and an arch-conservative to boot, was just then finishing what he viewed as his summative work, a weighty tome called *German Big Business and the Rise of Hitler*, in which he sought to completely exonerate German industrialists from complicity with Nazism. On its face, the situation would seem to form an ideal basis for colloquy, that is, subjecting the two competing interpretations to the process of discussion and debate that supposedly constitutes the backbone of scholarly life. But Turner elected not to play it that way. Instead, he set out to cast the impression that his opponent was guilty of "research fraud," thereby not only eliminating *Collapse of Weimar* as a competitor to his own book, but destroying the reputation of a junior scholar he considered ideologically objectionable in the bargain.

Turner's approach is instructive in that it established the template for what the right has been doing ever since. Joined by Berkeley's Gerald Feldman, another senior and very conservative historian specializing in the German interwar period, he drafted graduate students to go through Abraham's annotation, line-by-line, citation-by-citation. And, of course, they found plenty of trivia: quotation marks missing in various places, inserted where they shouldn't have been in others, wrong dates here and there, and so on. These are the sorts of "endless, minor errors" you'll find in any book, including those of such "greats" as Sir Lewis Namier. But Turner and Feldman kept generating "reports" in which they cast Abraham's missing quote marks as examples of "plagiarism," his inserted quote marks, wrong dates and the like as "fabrications," and his resulting conclusions as "fraudulent."

In the end, Turner and Feldman's allegations against Abraham were shown to be sheer nonsense. All of the documents Abraham cited actually existed, although he'd misdated several. His inserted quotes attended accurate paraphrases. Attribution was given to sources quoted where missing quote marks were concerned, etc. Most of all, it was determined that none of his technical errors had any appreciable effect on either the quality of his argument or the validity of the conclusions he'd reached. But all that took years. Meanwhile, he was denied tenure and *Collapse of Weimar* was withdrawn by Princeton University Press. Feldman actively intervened in several search processes to prevent Abraham being hired by other universities, and even attempted to have his Ph.D. revoked by the University of Chicago. The bottom line is that David Abraham was destroyed as an historian.

JF: What was the response of left historians while all this was going on?

WC: By and large—there were few exceptions—they sought to distance themselves from their colleague or, worse, adopted postures of utmost sanctimony, prattling on about the "sloppiness" of Abraham's scholarship and the need to maintain "the highest standards of scholarly integrity." Although Turner and Feldman had openly committed a broad range of professional ethics violations while pursuing their ideological vendetta, the "left-leaning" American Historical Association (AHA) declined to follow through with an investigation and censure of their conduct.

Even when a group of German historians finally took it upon themselves to document how Turner's *German Big Business* displayed a pattern of evidentiary distortion far more pronounced than any of which Abraham was accused, the AHA maintained a discrete silence. Thus was the issue of "academic integrity" gift wrapped for usage by the right.

And it didn't take long for right-wing ideologues to figure out what to do with the advantage just handed them. While I guess it's fair to say that the "Abraham Affair" was pretty much an in-house tussle among academics, what followed has been anything but. Consider the case of Michael Bellesiles, the young historian at Emory who wrote *Arming America*, a study devoted to debunking many of the more cherished myths of the country's thriving gun culture (for which he won the prestigious Bancroft Prize in 2000). It wasn't other academics who went after Bellesiles, but the National Rifle Association, which commenced a campaign alleging "academic fraud" even before the book was published (there were nearly 250 national articles published on the "Bellesiles Hoax" in less than two years).

Ultimately, the "fraud" claim hinged on a single footnote in which Bellesiles gave the wrong archival location for certain documents he cited to demonstrate that gun ownership in early America was much less common than those of the NRA persuasion—which, by the way, includes me—would have it. The documents actually existed, and they said pretty much what Bellesiles said they said. Nonetheless, in the face of an unrelenting barrage of negative publicity, the NRA was able to orchestrate nearly 250 articles on the "Bellesiles Hoax" in less than two years; a panel of "impartial" scholars commissioned by Emory to "investigate the integrity of Professor Bellesiles' scholarship" concluded that in this instance his handling of data was "less than professional." On that basis, although the university tried to put a happy face on the situation by allowing him to "resign," Bellesiles was effectively fired.

Once again, the performance of the left was something less than exemplary. Although there were a few progressive scholars who publicly defended Bellesiles—Gary Wills comes to mind—I can name none who expressed a sense of outrage that their colleagues on the left weren't joining in. The unfortunate reality is that where a thundering silence didn't prevail among anti-gun liberals, the target quickly found himself as apt to be assailed on "scholarly" ground in *The Nation* as in the *Weekly Standard* or the *New Criterion*.

Then there's the case of Mike Davis, who was accused by real estate interests in Los Angeles of having fabricated much of the data upon which he based his 1998 *Ecology of Fear*. The allegations, which turned out to be false, precipitated a media frenzy surpassing even that to which Michael Bellesiles was subjected, especially on the front and editorial pages of the *Los Angeles Times*. The upshot was that Davis, a major scholar by any defensible estimation, was not granted so much as an interview by either USC or UCLA, both of which had openings for senior historians specializing in California. He had in fact left Southern California altogether in order to secure a faculty position, teaching at SUNY-Stonybrook for several years before finally landing a job at UC Irvine (a decidedly second-tier school in the California system).

Davis received more coherent support from the left academy, as did Edward Said, during the 90s, when Lynne Cheney's ACTA was making him a priority target. But these are exceptions. While Noam Chomsky is by and large always—as he should be—defended at a bedrock level, the rule will be found in the Abraham and Bellesile cases, as well as the current right-wing campaign to drive a number of Arab and Arabist scholars out, not only of the academic context, but of the political discourse more generally. Shahid Alam at Northeastern University and the junior faculty members targeted by Zionist students for elimination at Columbia—Joseph Massad in particular—are good examples of what I'm talking about.

JF: The establishment left seems to ignore all of this history, as well as ignore what's really going on now.

WC: A lot of this is glossed on the left with the rather pious pretense—which a lot of the people saying it may actually believe—that, whatever else may be said, progressives are "ethically obliged," uniquely so, to uphold the very highest standards of scholarly integrity. A standard variation on the theme is that the "credibility" of oppositional politics itself is contingent upon our maintaining an impossible degree of precision in our work. There's a degree of truth to both propositions, of course. We are bound by ethical and factual considerations. We, no more than anyone else, are not entitled to simply invent convenient "facts," suppress inconvenient information, engage in plagiarism, or any of the rest of it.

The way this plays out, however, is that the right, which predictably treats such matters in an utterly cynical fashion, has long since learned that it can use the pretext of "scholarly integrity" to discredit and thus neutralize oppositional scholars on a selective basis, and that it can do so without serious opposition from, and often with the active complicity of, so-called leftists. The right has refined its techniques accordingly, having discovered that all it usually takes is a set of highly-publicized allegations, not just to silence particular voices it considers particularly objectionable, but to deter others from engaging in the kinds of research and articulation that caused the selected individuals to be targeted. Meanwhile, right-wingers are routinely exempted—by the Marc

Coopers of the world no less than by the Billy O'Reillys and Newt Gingrichs—from adhering to the standards imposed upon oppositionists.

JF: Can you give examples?

WC: Take the issue of plagiarism, for example. I'm currently—and falsely—accused of it. The allegations have been advanced in a tone of tremendous indignation from the right and attended for the most part by endless tongue clicking on the left. Everybody's suddenly worried about whether I gave proper attribution to a left environmental group in Canada when using material included in a 12-page pamphlet they produced in 1972. Well, I did. But here's the key. While you've got a feature on this weighty "controversy" in the *Rocky Mountain News*, a follow-up editorial in Boulder's *Daily Camera*, and the area Clear Channel stations having devoted maybe 24 solid hours to it over the past couple of weeks, you've not had a single word said in any medium about Michelle Malkin.

JF: Why Malkin?

WC: Well, she came out with a book titled *In Defense of Internment* in 2004, highly touted in hard right circles, that not only seeks to justify the mass internment of Japanese and Japanese Americans during World War II, but argues that the same procedure could be used against Arabs and Arab Americans today. Setting aside the squalor of her thesis, and the gross distortions of data to which she resorts in "supporting" it, the fact is that the bulk of her argument on the World War II internment derives from a fairly obscure right-winger named Lillian Baker. Yet Baker's material is cited nowhere in Malkin's book. In fact, she isn't so much as mentioned (perhaps because Baker, who passed away some years back, was exposed by Deborah Lipstadt in *Denying the Holocaust* as having employed the same "scholarly methods" as neo-Nazi holocaust deniers).

What's the payout for Malkin? Let's start with a stint as a regular commentator—read, pet "minority" (she's Filipina)—on Fox News and Clear Channel. And let's end with an all but total silence about her "scholarly integrity" from the left. Why? Because she is paid by a right-wing think-tank [ed.'s note: Malkin worked at the Competitive Enterprise Institute until 1995], rather than holding a regular faculty position somewhere? Gimme a break on that one. Her book is used in classes, and she speaks regularly on campuses across the country. If the left is going to indulge in condemning scholarly lapses—real or imaginary—where its own are concerned, it has at the very least an obligation to hold the right accountable to the same standards, and to do so to the best of its ability—through alternative media, if nothing else—using the same tools as the right.

But for the most part it doesn't, and it hasn't even tried for the past quarter century or more. Look at the record. Michael Bellesiles was destroyed on the basis of what amount at most to trivial mistakes while, on the other hand, you've got John Lott, a right-winger who was revealed to have fabricated an entire survey with which to underpin his contention that the use of firearms reduces social violence. His book, *More Guns, Less Crime,* has never been revised to eliminate the fraudulent material, yet it's still listed under the imprimatur of the University of Chicago Press and I don't hear any resulting chorus of outrage from left academics about Goth U's "lack of scholarly integrity." Do you?

Take the case of Allen Weinstein as another example. A few years before David Abraham came out with *Collapse of Weimar,* Weinstein, an unabashed anticommunist, came out with a supposed breakthrough volume of his own. The book, entitled *Perjury,* purported to use "new evidence"—both documents and taped interviews—to "prove once and for all" that 1940s State Department official Alger Hiss was actually a Soviet spy (and, by extension, that wholesale repression of the American left during the "McCarthy Era" was therefore justified). Having thus made his case, with the result that several of his interviewees complained that they'd been badly misquoted, Weinstein simply refused—and continues to refuse—to provide access to his research data, as required by the AHA's ethical canons. Nonetheless, *Perjury* is a text routinely assigned—especially by conservative professors purporting to be devoted to nothing so much as preserving the "highest standards of scholarly integrity"—in classes on the Cold War.

So well did the gambit work for Weinstein in "confirming" his thesis on Hiss that he wrote a sequel titled *The Haunted Wood* in which he covered a broad range of Soviet espionage operations in the U.S. In this instance, he actually arranged for his publisher to pay $100,000 for exclusive access to KGB archives, meaning that other scholars would be barred from confirming the accuracy of his citations and translations (a translator he employed has indicated that some of the documents he ostensibly quotes don't actually say what he claims they do). This embodies another glaring—and obviously calculated—breach of the ethical canon, but, like *Perjury*, *The Haunted Wood* has seen wholesale adoption as a course text by right-wing faculty members across the country.

So esteemed is Weinstein's handling of primary source materials by the right, in fact, that in 2004 George W. Bush nominated him to become the U.S. National Archivist. There are a number of other striking illustrations of "patriotic" historians not being held by either the right or the left to the "strict standards" imposed on dissident scholars. Before his death it was thoroughly demonstrated that the late Steven Ambrose regularly engaged in plagiarism throughout his career, yet neither his reputation nor his book sales appear to have been damaged in the least. The biographer Doris Kearns Goodwin, to offer another example, was proven not only to have plagiarized a lesser-known writer, but to have paid her victim a substantial sum to keep quiet about it. As a "penalty," she was hired as a political commentator by both NBC and MS-NBC (you can see her regularly on "Hardball" and "Meet the Press").

The list of such examples goes on and on. My personal favorite, however, is Edward Pearson, chair of History at Franklin and Marshall College. In 1999, he published *Designs Against Charleston*, a book purportedly analyzing the "transcript" of the 1822 Demark Vesey trial and proving thereby that not only was Vesey the linchpin of a conspiracy to initiate a slave revolt that would slaughter whites in the coastal area of South Carolina, but that the alleged conspirators had ultimately received something resembling due process before being hanged from the nearest tree. This was big news, because no copy of the trial transcript had been previously known to exist.

As it turned out, there wasn't. Pearson had combined two different post hoc summaries as being a single "transcript" of what may have been a non-existent trial (the "conspiracy" itself is also in doubt, but that's another story). Compounding this gross fraud, Pearson was shown to have misquoted or otherwise misrepresented the contents of his documentary sources in "5,000-6,000" separate instances. Acknowledging only that he was guilty of "unrelenting carelessness"—rather than a deliberate deception designed to reinforce a white supremacist historical interpretation—Pearson retained not only his professorship, but also his departmental chairmanship. On this, as always, the silence on the left—most conspicuously among "liberals" of the Marc Cooper/Paul Campos variety—has been absolutely deafening. That, perhaps, is because they've been far too busy building "cases" against oppositional scholars on behalf of the right to say much of anything about the right itself.

JF: Regardless of the double standards involved, you agree that plagiarism, for example, remains a serious issue. Am I right? You addressed some of that earlier when you explained how you'd actually written some of the material you're now accused of plagiarizing. But there's still the allegation concerning Fay Cohen's essay, and now, as you mentioned, the environmental pamphlet. Would you care to respond to those?

WC: Sure. The short version of Fay Cohen is that I didn't write the piece in which her essay was supposedly plagiarized, and I'm not entirely sure who did. I was asked by my ex-wife, Annette Jaimes, to go over a manuscript she had—it was a cut-and-paste job that looked to be collectively authored—and tie it together for style and consistency. In other words, I agreed to serve as a combination copyeditor and what among journalists is called a "rewrite guy."

That's way different from being the author, or even a coauthor. It was in effect Annette's piece, although I'm sure she had collaborators. In any event, the finished product was destined for inclusion in a book Annette was putting together, *The State of Native America*, in which her by-line already appeared several times. She was worried that another piece by her wouldn't look right, so she used the name of a by then defunct research institute I'd founded along with Winona LaDuke (who has nothing to do with anything concerning the offending essay).

The whole thing is peculiar at a number of levels. Annette's book came out in 1992 and has always enjoyed a reasonably broad circulation. Fay Cohen seems never to have said a word to anybody about any plagiarism for five years or so. Then, in 1997, at a point when by her own account she was pursuing a grant—and, I'm told, was up for promotion—she suddenly "discovered" that she'd been plagiarized. Having your work stolen is a kind of backhanded compliment, if you think about it, because it means somebody out there is taking what you're saying is good enough to want their own name on it. Especially if the someone doing the taking has name recognition, such validation can actually enhance a scholar's prospects of research funding, promotion, or both. Soooo...

Cohen took an essay she contributed to a book in 1991 and the piece in Jaimes' book to the legal counsel at her university—she's at Dalhousie, in

Nova Scotia—asking him to do a comparison and render a legal opinion as to whether plagiarism was involved. He then wrote up an internal report concluding that there was. It's important to note, I think, that although it's implied on the first page of the "Dalhousie Report," as the document's been called in the press, it's nowhere stated therein that I myself actually plagiarized anything. If it did say that, Fay Cohen would presently be the named defendant in a defamation suit brought in the Queen's Court of Nova Scotia. But it doesn't.

In any event, that was the end of it for quite a long while. Cohen used the report internally, at Dalhousie, for whatever purpose, and never said another word. Not to me, not to Jaimes, not to the publisher. Nobody. Hell, she didn't even forward a copy to the granting agency to which she was applying when the report was written in 1997. It wasn't until the campaign against me was kicked off in late January 2005—that is, eight years after the report, thirteen after the supposed plagiarism—that she suddenly felt "obliged to come forward." Actually, I can document the fact that she felt no such "need" even then. Not until John LaVelle and Dan Caplis from Denver's Clear Channel KHOW radio went to work on her.

Caplis has reputedly received substantial funding from Christian right organizations in Colorado Springs to convert his daily program—which he hosts along with the earlier-mentioned "liberal" Craig Silverman—into what he calls "All Churchill, All the Time." He's been spending rather lavishly in the effort to get me fired, and I'm not shy about suggesting that that had a little something to do with Cohen's curiously timed surge of "moral obligation" in sending the Dalhousie Report to the University of Colorado.

Maybe it should be mentioned, here, that if you were to ask her about her politics, Fay Cohen would no doubt describe herself as being a "progressive" (just like Cooper, Campos and, for that matter, Craig Silverman).

There of course still had to be some explanation of why, if she actually believed I'd ripped off her material, Cohen had waited well over a decade to mention it. That was given—and on this, the stench of Caplis is unmistakable—with a fable about how I'd called her up in the dead of night and threatened her. With what, was never made clear. But whatever it was, it was apparently so traumatizing that, when asked about my alleged phone call by a relatively independent reporter, she couldn't even come up with the year in which she'd supposedly received it. But, whenever it was supposed to have been, it was years before the Dalhousie Report was prepared and—although it would obviously have served to strongly reinforce the impression that it was me who plagiarized her—she apparently "forgot" to mention it to the university counsel or anyone else.

Pretty compelling stuff, eh? You can see why "progressives" have their undies all in a knot dithering about the implications of my "character." I mean, really, how transparently false does an accusation have to be before it becomes self-discrediting?

Actually, this became something of a media fad for about two weeks or so, back in February. Once Caplis surfaced Cohen's allegation that I'd threatened her via a late night phone call, the Denver press corps went into overdrive, suddenly it turned out that I'd done the same to anybody and everybody with whom I'd ever had a personal or political dispute, most of them self-styled "progressives." Hell, even that famous AIM leader Vernon Bellecourt weighed in, claiming to have been "intimidated" by a message I left on his answering machine about ten years ago. This, from a guy who, according to police intelligence documents released in the Denver "Spy Files" case, appears to have tried to have me and a couple of his other opponents shot during the summer of 1995, and who is generally believed to be responsible for the murder of Anna Mae Aquash back in 1976.

Anyway, the bottom line with the Fay Cohen business is no, I didn't plagiarize her. And, in fairness to Jaimes and anyone else who might have, at least in a technical sense, it should be emphasized that the whole thing has been vastly overblown in the press. About two weeks ago a lawyer specializing in such matters, solicited by the *Rocky Mountain News* to give his opinion on the matter, concluded that there were only three places where what was done might "rise to the level of plagiarism." That must have really dismayed Vincent Carroll and the rest of the editors at the *News*, who've been spinning it as if Cohen's essay had been more or less copied, verbatim. Any way you want to slice it, there's nothing on the order of Ambrose's or Malkin's offenses at issue, and, for all the hoopla, there never was.

JF: Would you like to address the charge that you "invented history" when you accused the U.S. Army of deliberately infecting Indians with smallpox in 1837? There's that, and the allegation that you did the same thing when you claimed that the U.S. imposed a racial definition of their identity upon Indians in the 1887 General Allotment Act.

WC: My response is that I was basically correct on both counts, although I probably should have said "War Department" rather than "Army" with regard to the smallpox. It's important, I think, to point out that, although I've mentioned both matters in several places, I've never done so other than in passing. I've never really stopped to spell out why I was saying what I was saying, or to flesh out the annotation, partly because I mentioned them in the context of developing broader arguments, and partly because I considered what I was saying to be more or less self-evidently true. So, I glad-handed things a bit. *Mea culpa.*

I'm now preparing in-depth essays, both on what happened at Fort Clark in 1837—it turns out to have been much worse than I originally contended, involving not just a couple of low-ranking army officers but the Secretary of War himself—and the identification criteria pertaining under provision of the Allotment Act (I never said the criteria were articulated within the Act itself). Those will be in print within the next year—I've already got a publisher for both pieces—and I think I'd just as soon let them speak for themselves. They'll be far more thorough than anything we'll be able to go into here.

I'd like to say, however, that I don't mind colloquy in the least. Challenges to his or her facticity always prompts a scholar to go back and look at what s/he's said—or it should—and sometimes you find you were wrong about something, in which case you correct the error, and that strengthens your argument. Other times, and this is one of them (or two of them, I guess), it turns out that you were correct in the first place, but you usually learn more about why in the process, and that, too, strengthens your argument. So, in a perverse sort of way, I suppose I owe a debt of gratitude to Thomas Brown for having raised the smallpox issue, and John LaVelle for having advanced his ridiculous claims about the Allotment Act.

That said, however, let's take a peek at my accusers. LaVelle, I've already talked about to some extent, so let's take him first. To begin with, he's a long-time political adversary, having served as a flunky for Carole Standing Elk, Vernon Bellecourt's designated northern California "AIM leader" before finally landing a job at the University of South Dakota law school and then moving on to the University of New Mexico. He's got precious few publications: five essays, I think, and two of them are devoted to attacking me. In a sense, it's fair to say that I *am* his career at this point. It might be flattering if it weren't so pitiful.

More pitiful still is the nature of the argument he employs in trying to prove that my interpretation of the Allotment Act adds up to a "hoax." In effect, he claims that the government was bent upon reinforcing Indian self-determination during the 1880s, at least in terms of setting the criteria for tribal membership. It follows—no kidding, he actually says this—that Indians imposed racial definitions upon themselves, the federal government being essentially powerless to prevent their doing so. You can see why his stuff hasn't achieved much resonance. In academia, you measure the influence of your publications via what's called the "Citation Index," that is, a literal count of the number of times your material is cited by others. Neither of LaVelle's essays on the Allotment Act, the first of which came out in the *American Indian Quarterly* almost a decade ago, has ever been cited by an Indian legal scholar. Not once.

In fact, LaVelle's Allotment Act stuff has been cited exactly three times by any legal scholar, and two of those citations were by the same author, Carole Goldberg, a UCLA law professor who also happens to be the only person the *Rocky Mountain News* could get to vet LaVelle's junk during the current "controversy." Needless to say, the *News* didn't quote people like Robert Porter, a tribal jurist who was on the law faculty with LaVelle in South Dakota, and who has publicly described the whole thrust of his former colleague's legal interpretation—all of it, not just the essays on the Allotment Act—as being designed to "put a happy face on colonialism." Let's just say that his "scholarship" is not particularly well regarded, either by Indians or by anyone else I could name other than the Denver press corps and administrators at the University of Colorado.

Maybe it's appropriate to point out by way of contrast that I was, as of mid-2001, the most cited ethnic studies scholar in the country. I've not checked lately, but that's likely still true. My interpretation of the Allotment Act alone has been cited well over a hundred times, way more, if you add in the stuff I published under Jaimes' name and pseudonyms. And nobody has ever described my work as being in any sense an apologetic for colonialism. Quite the opposite. Which is why the right, including sell-outs like John LaVelle, is so avid to discredit it.

Chapter 28

APACHES RISE TO DEFEND HOMELANDS FROM HOMELAND SECURITY

By Brenda Norrell

Apache land owners on the Rio Grande told Homeland Security to halt the seizure of their lands for the U.S.-Mexico border wall on Jan. 7, 2008. It was the same day that a 30-day notice from Homeland Security expired with the threat of land seizures by eminent domain to build the U.S.-Mexico border wall.

Homeland Security (DHS) declared that it will use the principle of eminent domain to take possession of land currently held by private ownership. DHS has also presented waivers requesting that the landowners grant DHS personnel access to their property for a 12-month period in order to conduct surveys for the intended construction project. The property owners were informed that if they do not voluntarily allow the federal agents on their property, the U.S. government will file a lawsuit to grant Homeland Security authorities unimpeded access to private land, despite the owners' opposition. Homeland Security has stated that it will seize property even without the consent of landowners if necessary to complete the construction of the border fence.

Many landowners, as well as civic leaders and human rights activists, oppose the U.S. government's plans to allow federal law enforcement agents access to private property. The government's demands and aggressive tactics are in conflict with settled rights of private property ownership and are particularly disconcerting to the indigenous peoples' communities impacted by this undertaking.

DEEP ROOTS OF RESISTANCE

The Texas communities along the international boundary zone are largely made up of Native Americans and of land grant heirs who have resided on inherited properties for hundreds of years. Homeland Security plans to complete the Texas portions of the fence before the end of the 2008 calendar year.

"There are two kinds of people in this world, those who build walls and those who build bridges," said Enrique Madrid, Jumano Apache community member, land owner in Redford, and archaeological steward for the Texas Historical Commission.

"The wall in South Texas is militarization," Madrid said of the planned escalation of Border Patrol and military presence. "They will be armed and shoot to kill."

In 1997, a U.S. Marine stationed on the border shot and killed 18-year-old Esequiel Hernandez, who was herding his sheep near his home in Redford. "We had hoped he would be the last United States citizen and the last Native American to be killed by troops," Madrid said during a media conference call on January 7 with Apaches from Texas and Arizona. Instead, the number of people shot and killed or run over by Border Patrol and other U.S. agents has risen sharply as the militarization continues.

Dr. Eloisa Garcia Tamez, Lipan Apache professor living in the Lower Rio Grande, described how U.S. officials attempted to pressure her into allowing them onto her private land to survey for the US-Mexico border wall. When Tamez refused, she was told that she would be taken to court and her lands seized by eminent domain.

"I have told them that it is not for sale and they cannot come onto my land." Tamez is among the land owners where the Department of Homeland Security plans to erect 70 miles of intermittent, double-layered fencing in the Rio Grande Valley.

Tamez said the United States government wants access to all of her land, which is on both sides of a levee. "Then they will decide where to build the wall. It could be over my house." Tamez said that she may only have three acres, but it is all she has.

Tamez' daughter Margo Tamez, poet and scholar, said, "We are not a people of walls. It is against our culture to have walls. The Earth and the River go together. We must be with the river. We must be with this land. We were born for this land."

Margo Tamez added that the recently approved United Nations Declaration on the Rights of Indigenous Peoples guarantees the right of indigenous peoples to their traditional territories.

Rosie Molano Blount, Chiricahua Apache from Del Río noted that many people from the Chiricahua Apache have served in the United States military. "We are proud to be Americans," Blount said, adding that the Chiricahua have always supported the U.S. government. Now, with the increasing harassment of people in the border zone, the local attitude toward the federal government is changing.

"Ya Basta! Enough is enough!" Blount said, repeating the phrase that became the battle cry of the Zapatistas in Mexico struggling for indigenous peoples' rights.

Blount said there needs to be dialogue concerning the issues at the border, but not forced militarization or a border wall. She also directed a comment at Homeland Security Secretary Michael Chertoff. "Don't come here and divide our families, Chertoff. You believe this is the only way to do things."

Michael Paul Hill, San Carlos Apache from Arizona, described how U.S. border agents violated and molested his sacred items, including a sacred stone, Eagle feather, and drum used in ceremonies while crossing the border.

After participating in an Apache ceremony in Mexico, when Hill and other Apaches reentered the United States a SWAT team in full riot gear was waiting for them and interrogated them. "They called me a foreigner, " Hill stated, adding that Border Agents manhandled his ceremonial objects and warned him he might "get away" with crossing the border without intrusive inspections in Nogales, Arizona "but not in Texas."

"It was incredibly frightening," said Margo Tamez, who was also there. She pointed out how the escalating militarization at the border is terrorizing people as they go about their lives, working, taking care of their families, and holding their traditional ceremonies.

Isabel Garcia, co-chair of Derechos Humanos (Human Rights) in Tucson, Arizona, said Arizona has been a laboratory for criminalizing the border. Pointing out that the Arizona border is the ancestral homeland of the Tohono O'odham, she said, "These borders are where people have lived since time immemorial." Garcia described the climate of militarization and abuse by Border

Patrol agents, noting that in 2002 "cowboy" Border Agents ran over and killed 18-year-old Tohono O'odham Bennett Patricio, Jr. His mother, Angie Ramon, is still seeking justice for the death of her son.

Garcia also described the deaths from dehydration and heat in the Sonoran Desert in southern Arizona, where failed border policies have pushed migrants walking to a better life into treacherous desert lands. "Two hundred and thirty-seven bodies were recovered in one year and most were on the tribal lands of the Tohono O'odham."

LEGAL QUESTIONS AND CHALLENGES

Homeland Security recently waived 22 federal laws to build the border wall in the San Pedro wilderness area in Arizona, Garcia noted. Attorney Peter Schey, director of the Center for Human Rights and Constitutional Law in Los Angeles, said America does not need a "Berlin Wall."

Schey, renowned immigrant rights attorney, said Section 564 of the Homeland Security section of the Omnibus Appropriations Bill supersedes earlier legislation. Homeland Security is now required to consult with the communities. Schey said this means real consultation and real consideration of the community's input and data. Schey took his first action by notifying Homeland Security Secretary Michael Chertoff by letter sent by fax on behalf of Texas property-owner Dr. Tamez on Monday, the same day that a 30-day notice to Texas land owners expired with the threat of eminent domain land seizures looming. Schey informed Chertoff to halt the impending seizures of private lands. Schey said Section 564 strikes provisions of the earlier Secure Fence Act and requires Homeland Security to consult with property owners like Dr. Tamez in order "to minimize the impact on the environment, culture, commerce, and quality of life" in areas considered for construction of the border fence.

"Furthermore, we believe that the new statutory provisions invalidate the Draft Environmental Impact Statement for fence construction published on the Department's behalf on Nov. 16, 2007, pending completion of the required local consultations and other requirements as outlined in the Omnibus Bill," Schey told Chertoff in the letter.

Homeland Security has already built walls along much of the California and Arizona international boundary zone with Mexico, despite opposition from the government of Mexico.

Apaches at the Texas border have formed a national working group coalition of supporters, attorneys, and fellow Apaches and other indigenous peoples to resist the seizure of their lands, the desecration of their sacred places and the militarization of their communities. In solidarity, the network opposes the seizure of private lands by Homeland Security by way of eminent domain, the militarization of the border, and construction of the border wall.

Chapter 29

DEFENDING WESTERN SHOSHONE LANDS FOR THE SEVEN GENERATIONS: CARRIE DANN, NEWE SOGOBIA, IN HER OWN WORDS.

By Julie Fishel and Brenda Norrel

IN THE VAST LANDS of the Western Shoshone, where the mountains are now being cored out by gold corporations, Carrie Dann comes through the door like a flame of fire. Gentle and loving, Carrie sits near the wood stove in the home of Julie Fishel, coordinator of the Western Shoshone Defense Project in Crescent Valley, Nevada. When Carrie comes down from the mountain, the power of the struggle comes with her. On this weekend, others gather to support the Western Shoshone, including Louise Benally, Navajo from Big Mountain, Arizona, and longtime resister of forced relocation.

Gathered with the defenders of the land, Carrie Dann remembers the history of her people, when the Shoshone people were nearly wiped out by small pox. "Yellow scarves were passed out to the Western Shoshone people, they were contaminated with the small pox. We were told that our people died like flies. Where the gold mine is today, the people died like flies.

"Today the United States government is offering us bread crumbs for our land—for our life—because that is what land is, it is life."

Carrie remembers the painful history of her people, how they were massacred, raped, humiliated and starved to death. Yet, there has been no apology from the US government, only continued oppression.

Carrie, executive director of the non-profit Western Shoshone Defense Project, lives in the center of Western Shoshone territory, which stretches across two thirds of Nevada, parts of Idaho and Utah, and into Death Valley and California.

The area was recognized as belonging to Western Shoshone by the United States government in the Treaty of Ruby Valley of 1863. However, since that time, the United States has considered the land as public land. It was not through any court proceedings or through the official transfer of title, but through the Indian Land Claims Commission set up by Congress in 1946.

At the end of World War II, at a time when other countries were going through the process of decolonization, the United States established the commission in an attempt to pay off Indian people for disputed land claims. The Western Shoshone was one case taken to the Commission. The payment now sits in the Department of Treasury, as the Western Shoshone remain on their land and continue to fight to retain their original land base.

The area is now the second largest gold producing area in the world, with the world's largest gold companies rushing in to gorge out the mountains and poison the water, including Barrick Gold Corporation, Newmont Mining Corporation, Kennecott and Placer Dome. The Nevada Test Site is also on Western Shoshone lands, where the United States government has carried out most of its nuclear testing and continues to do underground nuclear testing. And in addition, if that's not enough, the United States now wants to place the nation's nuclear waste, as well as some of Europe's nuclear waste, into the mouth of Yucca Mountain.

Carrie, a hard-working rancher and grandmother, worked alongside her sister Mary Dann, mending fences and ranching through the blowing snow and harsh winters. Mary passed to the Spirit World on April 22, 2005, in a ranching accident. The sisters spent their lives battling the United States government, military, nuclear industry and gold corporations. They did it humbly.

In February of 2003, the United States claimed the Danns were trespassing on their own lands and unleashed a helicopter roundup of the Danns' horses and wild horses of Pine Valley. It resulted in a stampede, leading to premature births of foals and horses being crushed. By the end of the day, the US had confiscated 500 horses. Later, the carcasses of 50 of those horses were found. They had starved to death. After that, Carrie says, "Mary went down real fast."

The Western Shoshone took their case to the United Nations in Geneva. The UN Committee on the Elimination of Racial Discrimination, CERD, ruled in March of 2006 in favor of the Western Shoshone. The Early Warning and Urgent Action Decision urged the United States to immediately freeze, desist and stop any further actions against the Western Shoshone people, including efforts to seize or privatize their lands. Although the UN Committee ordered the United States to stop immediately and initiate dialogue with the Western Shoshone, the United States has not complied.

Now, in collusion with the United States government, the gold corporations seek to carve out the most sacred mountain, Mount Tenabo, and continue seizing Western Shoshone lands.

While the United States oppression of Western Shoshone has been relentless, Carrie says, "We've been here since time immemorial. I was born here and this is where I'll die."

Here is Carrie Dann's story, in her own words—Julie Fishel and Brenda Norrell

***

My sister and I have been fighting in a battle we were born into as indigenous people on Turtle Island (United States). The struggle of the Western Shoshone Nation is the struggle of all indigenous peoples. It is not just about abuse of power and economics—it is about the stripping away of our spirit. It is about being forced to live in two worlds—the real world and a world of made up laws and legal constructs which attempt to render us invisible. Laws which claim to transfer power from the sacred things to the almighty dollar. When we have been beaten down, time and time again, when we have to stand by and watch our world and our people collapsing in front of us, the one thing that keeps us going is our spiritual beliefs, our knowledge of the traditional teachings. Mary and I were raised by our grandmother, Mary Hall, who lived a traditional lifestyle until the day she passed to the Spirit World, and our mom and dad.

What our grandmother taught us is that we, the Shoshone people, Newe in our language, were placed here on this land, Newe Sogobia, as caretakers. We were placed as caretakers of the lands, the animals, all the living things; those things that cannot speak for themselves in this human language. We were placed here with a responsibility. In traditional indigenous society, there are four things that are sacred above all. Those things are the land, the air, the water and the sun.

We see the earth as our mother, that which gives us all life. The water is like the blood in our veins, the air, that which nourishes the cycle of life and the sun, that which encourages growth and replenishment. Without any one of these things there would be no life; these things are sacred above all. This is our religion—our spirituality—and defines who we are as a people.

Our people, the Western Shoshone are in the midst of a decades' long struggle to retain our homeland, Newe Sogobia. Our lands were never ceded, "conquered," nor abandoned. We continue to live and pray on these lands.

In 1863, the United States entered into a Treaty of Peace and Friendship with the Western Shoshone, the Treaty of Ruby Valley. At the time, as I have been told, the U.S. did not realize there was anything of economic value in these lands. They simply wanted to cross the land to get to California. Our ancestors agreed to let them cross, we agreed to some ranching, small towns, a railroad, a telegraph line and mining, as we understood it in 1863. In return, the U.S. recognized our land boundaries and agreed to fairly compensate the Shoshone people for U.S. activities and for the minerals taken from the ground."

Newe Sogobia stretches across about 60 million acres throughout Nevada, California, Utah and Idaho—from the Snake River in Idaho down to Death Valley, California. Despite this formal recognition of the Western Shoshone land base, the U.S. now claims that these lands are "public" lands and is attempting to force a one time payment on the Western Shoshone through use of what is called the Indian Claims Commission (ICC).

As a method of intimidation to silence our family and other Western Shoshone, the Department of Interior has been conducting military-type raids on Western Shoshone, seizing hundreds of cows and horses from the mountains and valleys of Shoshone country in the last several years. They have destroyed our economic livelihood and scared many Western Shoshone away from standing up for their rights.

Currently, according to the USGS, Newe Sogobia is the second largest gold producing area in the world. When mining started in Nevada back in the 1800s, when our leaders signed the Treaty of Ruby Valley, it was with a pick and shovel—the damage was very little and the land could heal again. Beginning in the 1960s, with the discovery of a process where companies could extract the microscopic gold in the earth, we had huge mining companies with the open pit, cyanide processes moved into our territory. Newmont, now the world's largest gold company, had its start in Newe Sogobia on what is called the Carlin Trend—in fact the Carlin Mine was built by none other than the now infamous Bechtel Corporation. Currently, we have just about every major gold company in the world here—Newmont, Placer Dome and Barrick. The list goes on and on. So, our sacred land has given billions of dollars to the powerful companies for the sacrifice of the earth, air and water.

So, in this struggle, we see a direct connection between the U.S. failure to uphold its agreements to respect our rights and the mining industry's effort to accumulate wealth. When it comes to mining, the U.S. government claims that according to the 1872 Mining Law they cannot say no to a mine, even if it is a spiritual area, even if there are burial sites and even if they will contaminate our waters. They can only tell the mining company to "be careful." I think that is ridiculous. The Western Shoshone never agreed to the 1872 Mining Law. That law is only applicable to federal or "public" lands—not Western Shoshone lands.

When we look at what the mining is doing to Newe Sogobia, we see not only the disrespect given to our people, but also the destruction of sacred things. The mines take down whole mountains and dig huge open pits over a thousand feet deep and over a mile wide where they pump tens of thousands of gallons of water per minute, detonate heavy explosive to loosen the rock, then crush the rock and pour cyanide over it to extract the gold. We have lost hunting and fishing areas, food and medicinal plants, the wildlife is disturbed by the toxins in the air and the lights and noise made by 24-hour mining drill rigs and digging. Burial sites have been disturbed and many cultural artifacts have disappeared.

The destruction of the water is especially painful to think about. In our traditional way, that our people have told us, the water in the Earth's body is like blood in your veins. It's a life system within the earth. And they're taking it out. They are pumping out the essence of life so the multi-national corporations can get richer. Our water table has dropped with some of our spring drying up. Most of the springs I used to drink from are no longer fit to drink and some are even posted, with the sign, "Do not drink the water."

An example of just how arrogant these mines are is the behavior of Cortez Gold Mine (Barrick/Kennecott) in an area called Mount Tenino and Horse

Canyon. To us, all land is sacred, but there are certain areas that are very important and should not be disturbed. Mount Tenabo and Horse Canyon is one of those areas. Mount Tenabo has a long history of spiritual and cultural significance to our people. Caves on the mountain are part of our Creation story, our people have used the mountain for ceremony. We have gathered clay there for pottery. It is a landmark seen from many miles in every direction, located at the confluence of several Shoshone trails. We continue to use the mountain for hunting and gathering both foods and medicines, it continues to hold a spiritual and cultural relevance to us, in spite of the damage that has been inflicted upon it by previous mining. This mountain and its canyons should be respected and left alone.

What the U.S. did to the Indian people historically was physical genocide—now, as they dump toxins on our lands and destroy our spiritual places, it is spiritual genocide. Our homelands are basically being given to the gold companies at approximately $2.50–$5.00 an acre under the 1872 Mining Law. The land and its minerals are actually worth billions. To us, they are priceless and can never be sold because no one has the right to sell the land and destroy that which is sacred and provides life to all.

So far, our work, through the legal representation of the Indian Law Resource Center and the University of Arizona Indigenous Law and Policy Program, has brought the United States under direct international scrutiny on two separate occasions. One of these occasions was before the Inter-American Commission on Human Rights and the other was this year before the United Nations Committee for the Elimination of Racial Discrimination. In both instances serious questions have been raised and decisions rendered with regard to U.S. Indian policy, its ongoing impairment of Indian rights and its incompatibility with international law and human rights.

I believe that before we can seriously talk with the companies, they must respect our rights as indigenous people to this land. The fact of the matter is that the large scale, open pit cyanide heap leach mining, the pumping of tens of thousands of gallons of water and the purchasing of lands for private property by gold companies has been taking place without our consent and in direct conflict with our concerns—which we have expressed over and over again.

What we do here in the U.S. affects all indigenous peoples. We must always keep this in mind. We must expose the illusions that the U.S. and the corporations have created around us all and we must educate people about the sacredness of things and the importance of protecting those things against any amount of money.

In order to keep our indigenous creator's laws, we have to then break the laws of man. The reason why I say that is because our way of spirituality is tied to our land. We don't look at the land as real estate. It is the mother to life, not only to our life but to the life of all life out there. The wind and those that live in the water and fly through the air. We always refer to them as our brothers and sisters.

Then we also look at the sacred things to us. The sun is sacred. The air is sacred. The water is sacred. And the land is sacred. Because these all pertain to life. You take the water away, there will be no life. You destroy the air, there will be no life. You take the land away, there will be no life. From land comes all the necessities of life. Everything we need in life comes from the earth mother. And during that time when I was growing up, my grandmother used to tell us, 'You girls are like the earth because you do create life and you nurture that life until that life returns to its earthly mother, the earth, for its existence.

So with that, now we have the United States of America offering us 15 cents per acre for our life, because the land is life, water is life. But these are all the earth. The first government in the whole world that is making an offer to buy our birth rights—our rights as indigenous people. I wouldn't be surprised to the years that come, that this type of practice by other nations of the world are even going to somewhere as to say, 'We are going to buy your rights whether you like it or not.' And that is what is facing us today.

I never did want to sell my land because my land is my own. It's always been home. It's been the home of our people. And it will be the home for our future generations. But here now we have the federal government, the federal legislatures, destroying our ways. It is the destruction of our ways, because we don't want to sell our earth. We don't want to sell our mother. And yet through federal legislation, this is what they want to do to us.

Now, let's look at what happened on the land. In the 1950s, they tested nuclear weapons on our land. Soon afterwards, thousands of sheep died and the United States denied that it was nuclear testing. They called it atomic testing at the time. Nuclear testing, atomic testing. Millions of sheep died.

Nuclear radiation causes cancer. Many people do have thyroid cancer. Many people are affected in different ways from radiation from the nuclear testing. Then they went underground with their nuclear tests.

And I saw a lot of difference from the time they did put a test ban treaty into effect because we were in the livestock business. We saw the calves being born, so many born. It was sad to see little babies come out deformed. It was sad. And then, we started to see the mama cows develop sickness within their own bodies. I think if these kinds of deformities are in the livestock, they can also be in the human children. It can happen to any child of the earth. Any one of us. We are all affected.

With this nuclear testing, and nuclear waste dump, I don't feel safe at all. Now we have biological testing done at the test site, chemical warfare, all these kinds of testing are done there. I think it is wrong. I think these are crimes against humanity and crimes against all life being perpetuated by the governments of the world. They have no right to do that. Governments are against the people, especially the poor, whom they think are weaker.

The springs are drier in the mountains. It is devastating. The only life that can be up there is man because he can carry water on his back when he goes up there. The rest of the animals depend on the natural water source which won't be there.

We have to think about the seventh generation which is yet to come. Whatever prior decision we make, we have to think about those that are still of the earth and yet to come. I remember one time my grandmother said to me, "Hey, you're not that important. It's the future generation you have to think about. You have to think about the young babies that are not here yet. You have to think about your own babies that might come. You have to think about your grandchildren and your great grandchildren and so forth down the line."

We have air contamination, mercury contamination. Yet mining goes on. Contamination goes on. This violates the human rights not only of the indigenous people, but all of the people that live here. It's against the health of our people. It's against the health of the people and not only the people but all life thereafter. We have other life out there. We didn't give them their lives so we have no right to take away their life. Those little apples, birds, they have a simple right as we have. In the indigenous ways, our life cannot exist unless they are out there because they are a part of the past. If you ever look at yourself, see how perfectly your body is made. Look at how perfectly everything is made.

We refer to the winds as the air. We refer to sun as the fire for many different places. So when we hear people talk about the winds and the fire, they are usually referring to the sun. So with these thoughts I would like to say as these young people walk through life, that they do think about future generations, which could be their grand babies, great grand babies.

I am really sick and tired of being treated not as an animal, but below the dignity of an animal. Below the dignity of a human being. The Western Shoshone, other indigenous people, and other people need to stand proud with dignity, and with honor of their families, their tribes.

Deep inside, your tears fall. But after awhile you run out of tears. I used to hear the old folks talking about crying from within from your heart. So I assume now that this is all we have left. There are very little tears that we cry from within.

—Carrie Dann

Chapter 30

THE POWER OF THUNDER: AN INTERVIEW WITH CECELIA FIRE THUNDER

By Rose Aguilar

JUNE, 2006

AFTER SOUTH DAKOTA GOVERNOR Mike Rounds signed the state's extreme abortion ban with no exceptions for rape and incest, Cecelia Fire Thunder, the first woman president of the Oglala Sioux tribe, made national headlines after saying she would personally set up a clinic on her tribe's land in South Dakota to preserve a woman's right to choose. There is currently only one clinic in the entire state of South Dakota that provides abortions, and its status, since the ban, is endangered.

President Fire Thunder's decision to take the lead on this issue is nothing short of remarkable considering the number of challenges on the reservation. Almost half of all Native American women in South Dakota are poor, compared with approximately 10 percent of white women, according to the Institute for Women's Policy Research report on the Status of Women in South Dakota. Median annual earnings for women in South Dakota rank last in the nation. Furthermore, the unemployment rate on the reservation is 85 percent and the life expectancy rate is 46 for men and 55 for women.

But President Fire Thunder is a determined woman. Besides announcing plans for the clinic, she has continued to focus on the need to address rape as an issue for South Dakota women, particularly Native American women. One in six American women has been the victim of rape or attempted rape, according to the National Crime Victimization Survey. The average annual rate of rape and sexual assault among American Indians is three and a half times higher than the national average.

I spoke with President Fire Thunder about the clinic, abortion ban and challenges facing women who live in rural areas.

Rose Aguilar: Tell me about the clinic you're planning to build.

Cecelia Fire Thunder: The proposed clinic would be for all women because right now, if a woman needs an abortion, she needs to go all the way to Sioux Falls. This clinic would go beyond abortion and contraception. We're missing out on teaching our boys and men about what they need to do to avoid pregnancies.

RA: I called the governor's office to find out what the penalty would be for women who have abortions if the law goes into effect, but haven't received a call back. If the law is upheld, will women be able to have legal abortions on your reservation?

FT: We don't know. We have five Indian lawyers working on this right now. When we go face to face with the South Dakota lawmakers, we'll be ready.

RA: You've made it a point to talk about rape in your interviews. While the abortion ban has received widespread attention, there's been little talk about how this law would force a girl who'd been raped by a male relative to have his baby.

FT: We need to start talking about those issues. Americans should be outraged about the number of women who are raped in this country. We need to also speak out for women in places like Afghanistan and other war-torn areas where rape is happening. This is not new. Rape has always been a part of life. Unfortunately, the world is not always a safe place for women.

Ultimately, this is a much bigger issue than just abortion. The women of America should be outraged that policies and decisions about their bodies are being made by male politicians and clergy. It's time for women to reclaim their bodies.

Women in America have something that women in other parts of the world don't have. Women in this country don't appreciate their right to free speech. Women in America can be the voice of women around the world. This is a call to arms by women in the United States.

RA: And not only are the anti-choicers going after abortion, they're also going after birth control.

FT: Women should have access to contraception. No questions asked. Contraception is a solution. Why don't they (politicians) get it?

RA: Do the women on the reservation have access to contraception?

FT: We have Indian clinics on the reservation, so birth control is available, but it's not enough. We're going to go ahead with the clinic no matter what. If nothing else, we need to establish a place where women feel comfortable.

RA: How will you fund it?

FT: I'm not concerned about that. We'll get a lot of support. If it's meant to be, it'll happen. We pray a lot. We trust that there will be people who support it.

RA: How do these laws directly impact the poor women on the reservation?

FT: Women of color and poor women have always known that regardless of what happens, women with money will have access to abortion. Women with money will have access to contraception. No matter which way you cut it, it's always on the backs of poor women.

An elder on my reservation said, "So they don't want you to have contraception or abortions after rape? Are they going to step up and take care of that baby?"

RA: Do you think the pro-choice movement does enough to reach out to poor women?

FT: Yes and no. For the most part, we have to empower ourselves. We're becoming much more politically astute, and we're getting a lot more young people involved. We love to get people riled up.

RA: Tell me about your reservation and the realities women living in rural areas face in this political climate.

FT: My reservation is 50 miles by 100 miles long. It's a large rural community of 40,000 people and 60 percent of our people speak our language. Half of our population is under 18.

In a perfect world, if a woman is raped, she will call the police, and the police will take her to the emergency room. The emergency room will have components in place to help this woman, including the morning-after pill to prevent the pregnancy. In rural America, that doesn't happen. Many places in rural America do not know about the morning-after pill.

On the reservation, we have to take a look at the high rates of alcohol and drug use. More often than not, young women who've been raped while under the influence will be blamed for being drunk. If someone is raped, especially out in the rural community, they may not report it. After three days, they've passed the cut-off point for taking the morning-after pill.

How many babies are conceived during the act of violence? We don't know.

RA: Tell me about your background.

FT: I was born and raised on the reservation. Then I went to Los Angeles on a relocation program from 1963 to 1976. The program was the Eisenhower administration's solution to the "Indian problem." What they wanted to do was put us in cities and hope we would disappear. During the 1970s, Los Angeles had the largest Indian population in the U.S.

I eventually became a nurse and was able to provide for my two children. I returned to the reservation in 1987 and eventually worked for the state health department.

RA: And eventually became the first woman president of your tribe.

FT: Yes, it says a lot about my tribe. My job is to look after 2.7 million acres of land. My job is to take care of the water. My responsibilities are not only about the two-legged, but the four-legged. I have to make sure we have an infrastructure in place, that our educational systems are working, that we have healthcare and that our people have enough food to eat.

Right in my own backyard, I have great possibilities. We're very patriotic on my reservation, however, it's time to get out of Iraq. We need to let people make their own decisions about their future. As a woman and a mother, I personally don't want any more women to cry.

RA: Are many men from the reservation in Iraq and Afghanistan?

FT: You bet. We have hundreds of guys over there, and they volunteer to go. We just had a big funeral here last month. It was our first casualty.

RA: How old was he?

FT: He was 22. So many of our resources have been taken away from us to support that war. There's a huge groundswell of Americans that say enough is enough. It's time to get out of there.

RA: What are your plans from here?

FT: I'll continue pushing the envelope and exerting our sovereignty.

A long time ago, we had medicines that were available to terminate a pregnancy. Women like my grandmother were medicine women, and they had it in their possession. So you look at every culture in the world, and there were ways we took care of ourselves. You didn't have people passing laws to control a woman's body.

As a woman, it's my job to support women. It's my job to support my sisters.

Chapter 31

JOHN TRUDELL AND THE LIBERATION OF NATIVE AMERICA

By Michael Donnelly

"When I go around in America and I see the bulk of the white people, they do not feel oppressed; they feel powerless. When I go amongst my people, we do not feel powerless; we feel oppressed. We do not want to make the trade...we must be willing in our lifetime to deal with reality. It's not revolution; it's liberation.

We want to be free of a value system that's being imposed upon us. We do not want to participate in that value system. We don't want change in the value system. We want to remove it from our lives forever...We have to assume our responsibilities as power, as individuals, as spirit, as people...

We are the people. We have the potential for power. We must not fool ourselves. We must not mislead ourselves. It takes more than good intentions. It takes commitment. It takes recognizing that at some point in our lives we are going to have to decide that we have a way of life that we follow, and we are going to have to live that way of life...That is the only solution there is for us."

—John Trudell

JOHN TRUDELL WAS BORN in Omaha in 1946 to a Mexican mother and a Santee Sioux father. His childhood was spent on and around the Santee Reservation near Omaha.

He joined the Navy in 1963. After serving during the Vietnam War, he quickly became involved in the struggle for Native Rights. He was the spokesperson for the Indians of All Tribes reclamation of Alcatraz Island in 1969. Using a clause in the Fort Laramie Treaty of 1848 which ceded abandoned federal lands back to the original owners as legal justification, the group occupied the island and proposed an Ecology and Cultural center for the abandoned prison site. Another more far-reaching demand was made—that the onerous policy of Termination (of tribal identities and title to lands) be rescinded.

After eighteen months, the government forced the Indians of All Tribes off the island. The group failed to get the island converted to the proposed cultural center. But, a more important victory was achieved—the Termination policy was ended and a policy of restoring tribal identities and rights was implemented through some 52 pieces of Federal legislation. In addition, the successful effort led to over 74 other occupations of abandoned federal lands.

John joined the American Indian Movement and served as its (last) National Chairman from 1972–79. In 1972, he was part of the Trail of Broken Treaties caravan that went to DC to present Nixon with an Election Eve plan for Native Rights. They were rebuffed by the Interior Department and settled on a takeover of the Bureau of Indian Affairs (BIA) building in DC. The government responded by providing $66,000 in "gas money" and yet another unkept promise to address their issues. Many angry folks took the gas money and headed to South Dakota. Soon after, the famous 10-week stand-off at Wounded Knee occurred. Trudell did not go to Wounded Knee at first; fearing a trap and thinking it a mistake to leave the high-visibility DC protests for ones where the government could control the media images and where violence was likely inevitable.

Within three years of Wounded Knee, 69 AIM members and supporters were murdered. Another 350 were assaulted. No one has ever been convicted for the spate of bloodshed. On the other hand, Leonard Peltier rots in prison convicted of killing two FBI agents. Two others were acquitted on grounds of self-defense in the same shoot-out with the FBI which left one AIM member and two FBI agents dead.

In 1978, Trudell and AIM organized a 2700-mile march across the continent to bring attention to the failure of the government to honor tribal water and hunting/fishing rights. Some eleven Bills were before Congress that would have lessened those rights or done away with them altogether. After five months, The Longest Walk arrived in DC. Almost 2000 people marched to the Washington Monument and even more joined on in an encampment in Maryland, bussing to DC everyday to lobby against the Rights' roll-back Bills. In the end, a sweeping victory saw not a single one of the bills passed.

Violence is never justified. Violence is always rationalized.

—John Trudell

February 11, 1979, Trudell led another DC march. By this time he was well-known and feared by the FBI. Although warned against it, he gave a speech on the steps of FBI Headquarters while an American flag was burned. Less than 12 hours later, his pregnant wife Tina, three children and mother-in-law died in a suspicious fire which destroyed the home of Trudell's father-in-law Arthur Manning, a Tribal Council Member of the Shoshone-Paiute Reservation of Duck Valley which straddles the Nevada-Idaho border. Tina had been working to preserve tribal water rights and her father was a leader in demanding adherence to treaty rights. Both were opposed by the tribal oligarchy which included the tribal police chief, his brother who was implicated in an assassination plot on Peltier and BIA representatives; all of whom had been on the side of the authorities at Wounded Knee. The fire could have been related to that and not to John's activities. Though the BIA issued a claim that the fire was "accidental," John (and many others) believes his family was murdered.

Much of John's suspicion centers on his support for Peltier. During the Peltier trial in Fargo, John returned to the courtroom one day and was denied entrance. He was arrested and convicted of Contempt of Court and sentenced to 60 days. He was shuttled through five jails during that time and while at Springfield Prison he was approached and warned by another inmate that if he did not give up his efforts on Native Rights, his family would be killed.

By 1979, the FBI had amassed a 17,000 page dossier on Trudell (which he obtained in 1986) with fetishistic notations of his skills as an orator and organizer continually mentioned.

It was during his time of grieving that those skills became ever more present and John began a career as a "spoken word" artist. In 1983, he allied with his friend Quiltman Sahme and formed Tribal Voice with Quiltman singing traditional Native chants as background to John's poetry. Soon, they joined with the great Kiowa guitarist Jesse Ed Davis and produced *AKA Graffiti Man*, a biting social commentary which was remastered by Jackson Browne gaining wide release in 1992 and Bob Dylan's nod as the "best album of the year."

In 1989, Trudell began yet another career as an actor, appearing in the fine film *Pow Wow Highway*. He later had roles in 1992's *Thunderheart* and 1998's *Smoke Signals*. He was instrumental as historian for 1992's *Incident at Oglala*; the Robert Redford-narrated documentary of the events surrounding the FBI shootout at Pine Ridge that saw Peltier convicted. A movie about Trudell, himself, came out in 1995.

John Trudell continues to create politically-charged poetry with his group Bad Dog, including Quiltman. Their most recent effort is the exceptional *Madness & the Moremes*. He and Quiltman continue to travel as Tribal Voice to Reservations speaking and singing to Native Youth groups about the history of AIM and Native Rights efforts. He, his band and Browne have donated their time to many benefits for the environment, as well as peace efforts; and, with fellow activist Willie Nelson are currently holding a series of benefits for the LA-based Women's Cancer Research Center.

Chapter 32

STAR WHORES: ASTRONOMERS VS. APACHES ON MOUNT GRAHAM

By Jeffrey St. Clair

WE WAITED FOR A night when the moon was obscured by clouds. It sounded like a silly plan here in the heart of the Arizona desert, where Oregonians stream each year to worship the unrelenting sun.

But the wait was only two days. Then the sky clouded up, just as the Apaches predicted. These weren't rain clouds, just a smoke-blue skein, thin as morning fog, but dense enough to dull the moonlight and shield our passage across forbidden ground.

We were going to see the scopes. The mountain was under lockdown. Armed guards, rented by the University of Arizona, blocked passage up the new road and patrolled the alpine forest on the crest of Mount Graham. Only certified astronomers and construction workers were permitted entry. And university donors. And Vatican priests.

But not environmentalists. And not Apaches. Not at night, anyway. Not any more.

Yet, here we were, skulking through strange moss-draped stands of fir and spruce, displaced relics from a boreal world, our eyes peeled for white domes and trigger-happy cops.

It says something about the new nature of this mountain, this sky island, that we heard the telescopes before we saw them, a steady buzz like the whine of a table saw down the block.

The tail-lights of SUVs streamed through the trees, packing astronomers and their cohorts towards the giant machine eyes, on a road plastered over the secret middens of the mountain's most famous native: the Mount Graham red squirrel.

The tiny squirrel was once thought be extinct. In 1966, federal biologists said that they had found no evidence of the squirrel in the Pinaleno Range (the strange mountains of which Mount Graham forms the largest peak) since 1958. Then five years later a biologist working in the shaggy forests at the tip of the mountain found evidence of at least four squirrels. A wider survey showed an isolated population on the mountain's peak. In 1987, the squirrel was finally listed as a endangered species.

Still, the squirrel population fluctuates wildly from year to year, in cycles largely tied to the annual pine cone crop. But these days the population spikes rarely top 500 animals on the entire planet-which for them constitutes the upper flanks of Mount Graham, the same swath of forest claimed by the astronomers. But the trendlines for the squirrels all point down: down and out. And the astronomers just keep coming. And so do the clearcuts. The new campsites. The unnatural fires. Extinction looms.

We edged along the road, under the cover of a beauty-strip of fir trees, until we came to a fence, tipped with razored wire, and beyond it a clearing slashed into the forest. And there before us crouched one of the mechanical space-eyes, set within a white cube, sterile as a hospital. The structure is so cold and lifeless that it could have sprung from the pen of Richard Meier, the corporate architect responsible for the dreadful Getty Museum blasted onto the crest of the Santa Monica mountains outside LA.

My guide calls himself Vittorio. "That's Vittorio with a 't'," he says. "Like the Italian director." But he calls himself Vittorio in honor of the great Apache leader Victorio. He was 19 when I met him in the mid-90s, hip deep in snow, at a place called Enola Hill in the Cascade Mountains fifty miles or so from Portland. Enola Hill is a sacred site for many of the tribes of the Pacific Northwest—a bulge of basalt covered with Douglas-fir, where from a narrow thrust of rock you can look up a fog-draped canyon to Spirit Horse Falls and beyond to the white pyramid of Mount Hood.

Enola Hill has been a vision quest site for centuries. But the Forest Service, despite brittle platitudes from Bill Clinton about his sensitivities to native peoples, schemed to blast a road through the heart of the hill and clearcut it to the bone.

Vittorio haunted the forests of Enola Hill for weeks, along with a few dozen other Indian activists and environmentalists, bracing themselves in front of dozers, cops and chainsaws. Some were hauled off to jail; others, like Vittorio, faded into the forest, to fight another day. But eventually, the Forest Service had its way. The logging roads went in and the trees came down. But the experience brought us together. It is a friendship sealed in sorrow and anger. And humor, too. Vittorio, who studied art at UCLA on what he calls "a guilt and pity scholarship," is not a grim person. He has a wicked sense of humor and an unerring eye for beauty.

Vittorio mainly grew up in east LA. His mother died young in a car crash with a drunk driver outside Safford, Arizona when he was five. Vittorio was in the car and he still bares a scar, a purple semi-colon hanging above his left eye. He was taken in by his grandmother, a Mexican-American. For a time she cleaned the house of Jeff Chandler, the cross-dressing actor who once played Cochise.

Vittorio's father is a San Carlos Apache from Tucson. He went off to Vietnam, came back shattered in his head, and addicted to smack. It wasn't long before he ran into trouble. He is now parked in the bowels of Pelican Bay, the bleak panopticon-like prison in northern California, another victim of the state's merciless three-strikes law.

"My old man was born with two strikes," Vittorio said. "Just like the rest of us. But after Vietnam, he couldn't run and hide anymore."

That's been the fate of too many Apaches since whites invaded their lands: chased, hunted, tortured, killed, starved and confined. And then blamed for the misery that had been done to them. The Apaches have been relentlessly demonized, perhaps more viciously than any other tribe. Here's how General John Pope described them in 1880: "a miserable, brutal race, cruel, deceitful and wholly irreclaimable." This description, of course, bears little relation to the Apache, but is a fairly apt portrait of their tormentors.

But that's how they were treated, as irreclaimable subhumans, even after they agreed to submit to life on the reservations. Young Apache men were forced to wear numbered badges, just like the Jews of Nazi Germany. Minor violations of arbitrary rules, such as the ban on drinking Tizwin, an Apache homebrew, meant exile to Leavenworth, often a death sentence. Apaches weren't recognized as citizens until 1924. They were prohibited from worshipping their religion until 1934 and couldn't vote until 1948.

But still they resist and their resistance earns them even more rebukes from authorities and locals yahoos. Until the 1960s, it wasn't uncommon to see signs outside stores, diners and bars throughout southern Arizona saying: "No dogs or Apaches Allowed." Now, ain't that America?

In the hip-deep snow on Enola hill, Vittorio told me this story about his namesake, the great Chihenne chief, Victorio. "Victorio was revered by his band and by most other Apaches," Vittorio said. "When he was gravely wounded by federal troops during a raid on his camp in the Black Range, the soldiers called on the Chihenne women to surrender, probably so they could be raped and then sent to their deaths. The women shouted back their refusal and vowed to eat Victorio's corpse should he die, so that no white man would see his body or abuse it."

At the time, the Mexican government had put out a $50 bounty for each Apache scalp and offered the then grand sum of $2,500 for the head of Victorio. The Apache leader survived the battle of the Black Range, but was eventually tracked down, ambushed and killed in the mountains of Chihuahua.

* * *

In the spring of 2002, Vittorio invited me to Arizona to tour the San Carlos Reservation and make a covert visit to the Mount Graham telescopes. At the time, the University of Arizona was in the midst of constructing the $87 million Large Binocular Telescope, billed as the largest optical telescope on Earth.

That's right $87 million. Put this outlandish figure in perspective. That's double the entire annual income of all Apaches in Arizona. The astronomers and priests have never experienced anything approaching life on the San Carlos Reservation, where grinding poverty is the daily fare. And it's been that way since the beginning in 1872, when this bleak patch of land along the Gila River was established as a reservation/prison by the grim Indian killer Gen. George Crook.

The non-treaty Apaches have always hated the place for its brackish waters, infertile soils and robust population of rattlesnakes. The site was a malarial barrens where many Apaches died of what the Army called "quotidian intermittent fever." Here's how Daklugie, the son of the great Chiricahua leader Juh, recalled the early days of life on the reservation:

"San Carlos! That was the worst place in all the great territory stolen from the Apaches. If anybody ever lived there permanently, no Apache knew of it. Where there is no grass there is no game. Nearly all of the vegetation was cacti; and though in season a little cactus fruit was produced, the rest of the year food was lacking. The heat was terrible. The insects were terrible. The water was terrible. What there was in the sluggish river was brackish and warm. At San Carlos, for the first time within memory of any of my people, the Apaches experienced the shaking sickness."

Of course, that was the point. The Army and the Interior Department weren't on a humanitarian mission. The reservations, especially for the Apaches, were always more like concentration camps carved out of the most desolate terrain in a barren landscape. American death camps. Black holes on Earth.

And so 140 years later, San Carlos remains one of the poorest places in the nation. The per capita income is less than $3,000. More than 50 percent of the people who live there are homeless. More than 60 percent are unemployed. Less than half the Apaches have a high school diploma and only one in a hundred Apache kids percent go on to college. The University of Arizona, so anxious to defile a sacred Apache mountain in the pursuit of science, has done almost nothing to help the dire situation at San Carlos, except to raid the reservation for cultural artifacts and to submit the people there to remorseless interrogations by university anthropologists.

***

Our way up Mount Graham seemed simple enough when tracing the route on the map. We traveled logging roads, traversed deer and bear trails and made a steady bearing up a crumpled ridgeline toward the forests of Emerald Peak. Naturally, I was lost within an hour.

Perhaps, it had to do with the otherworldliness of the ascent, moving out of searing desert through chaparral, scrublands and finally into ever deeper forest. As the astronomers trained their lenses deep into the past toward the light of dead stars, we walked through a living relic; the journey up the slopes of the mountain was a trip back into ecological time.

Mount Graham is a sky island, a 10,700-foot-tall extrusion from the floor of the Sonoran desert, which has traveled its own evolutionary course since the last ice age, more than 10,000 years ago. The mountain is a kind of continental Galapagos, featuring seven different biomes, stacked on top each other like an ecological flow chart.

At the very top of the pyramid (and the mountain) is a cloud forest of fir and spruce, the southernmost manifestation of this biome. This is an ancient forest, as stout and mossy as the fabled forests of Oregon. That's where the squirrels hang out. Of course, the forests has been gnawed at over the years by loggers and the like, but there was still more than 600-acres of it left when the astronomers laid claimed to the area, with the ironclad brutality of a mining company.

From an ecological point of view, the astronomers couldn't have picked a worse site in Arizona-partly because the only rival to Mount Graham, the densely forested San Francisco Peaks north of Flagstaff, holy ground for the Hopi, has already been defiled by ski slopes and powerlines. There are more than 18 plants and animals that are endemic to Mount Graham. There are nine trout streams tumbling off its slopes. Numerous cienegas, those strange desert marshes. Rare northern goshawks and Mexican spotted owls. And more apex predators, cougars and black bears, than in any other place in the desert Southwest. When you've got the big predators, it usually a sign the ecosystem is humming along in a functioning state—an all-too-rare condition in the American West these days.

But there's a problem. And it's a big one. It is the curse of ecological islands to suffer from high extinction rates, even in a relative natural state. But when outside forces, such as clearcuts, powerlines, roads, and telescopes, rudely penetrate the environment these rates soar uncontrollably.

The reason is fairly straightforward: the species that live in these isolated habitats have evolved in a kind of vacuum and aren't equipped to handle the shock of such drastic changes to their living quarters. And there's another complicating factor. When endemic animals and plants are wiped out by chainsaws and bulldozer, there's no nearby population to fill the void: a sea of hostile desert separates Mount Graham from the archipelago of sky islands arcing through northern Mexico and southern Arizona.

In a way then, the plants and animals of Mount Graham share this striking vulnerability with the Apache people, who, although masters of desert life and highly skilled warriors, had no ultimate defense against the waves of disease and alien technology marshaled into their realm by whites.

* * *

Mount Graham attracted astronomers for the some of the same reasons it harbors unique wildlife and is revered by the Apache: it is wild, remote, tall and steep. Indeed, although it's not the tallest mountain in Arizona, Mount Graham is the steepest, rising more than 8,000 feet off the desert floor.

The University of Arizona fixed its attentions on Mount Graham in the early 1980s. It had gotten into the astronomy game in the 1920s and had put observatories on several of the peaks in the Santa Catalina Mountains outside Tucson, including Mount Lemmon, Mount Hopkins and Kitt Peak.

The University's Seward Observatory touts itself as one of the top astronomy centers in the world. It not only mans observatories, but also has its hands in the lucrative business of building and polishing the giant mirrors used by modern telescopes.

But the star-gazing business is akin to the expanding universe: staying on top means constantly building new scopes, claiming new, higher peaks, extending your empire.

The University's Seward Observatory had run into another problem. The observatories closest to Tucson had become increasingly less efficient over the years, the image quality marred by smog and light pollution. So they went looking for a new peak and quickly settled on Mount Graham, a 100 miles northeast of Tucson. Of course, they told the Apaches nothing about their intentions.

It turns out that Mount Graham isn't a very good place to probe the secrets of the heavens. There are updrafts of warm air pushing off the desert that distort the images, making them as jittery as the first snaps that came back from the Hubbell space telescope. Plus, Mount Graham is a sky island and though it rises out of one of the driest stretches of land on the continent it is often cloudy on the peak.

"Any Apache could have told the astronomers that," says Vittorio. "It is a stormbringer mountain, summoning up all the moisture from the desert below, pooling it at the peak in a nimbus of clouds."

In fact, the University of Arizona knew that Mount Graham was a poor choice for the deep space telescopes from the beginning. In 1986, a team from the National Optical Astronomy Observatory conducted a two-year investigation comparing Mount Graham and Mauna Kea, Hawai'i as possible telescope sites. The Arizona peak fell far short. "There was no comparison," concluded Mike Merrill, an astronomer at the NOAO. Indeed, the study advised that there were 37 other sites ranking better than Mount Graham for observing stars-even the smog-shrouded Mount Hopkins topped Mount Graham.

This troublesome bit of news didn't deter the University of Arizona. In 1988, it announced plans to turn Mount Graham into a kind of astronomical strip mall, featuring seven telescopes at a cost of more than $250 million. They rounded up a bevy of partners, including the Vatican, several universities in the US and Europe and the odious Max Planck Institute, which in an earlier incarnation as the Max Planck Society gave assistance to the murderous experiments of Dr. Mengele.

This peculiar consortium ran into immediate legal hurdles, the biggest being the small Mount Graham red squirrel. It was a now federally protected endangered species and its last refuge was the very cloud forest the astronomer's claimed for their avenue of telescopes. Federal biologists announced that the project would jeopardize the squirrel's very existence. It's not hard to figure out why they reached this conclusion. The observatory scheme would destroy nearly 30 percent of the squirrel's best remaining habitat.

But the University wasn't going to let extinction stand in the way of science. It took an aggressive and belligerent approach. Officials badgered and intimidated federal biologists and when they wouldn't back down the University and its lawyers went over their heads. For example, in May of 1988, the University summoned Michael Spear, then regional head of the Fish and Wildlife Service, to a closed door meeting at the Tucson airport, for a session of backroom arm-twisting. Spear emerged a few hours later having agreed to order agency biologists to conclude that the telescopes could go forward regardless of the effect on the squirrels. Which is, in fact, what they did.

"Procedurally, it was incorrect," Lesley Fitzpatrick, a US Fish and Wildlife biologist, later testified. "And it was in violation of the law, and therefore it is incorrect regardless of whether its procedural or substantive."

In other words, the Fish and Wildlife Service had committed a fraud and everyone there knew it while they were doing it. And they got caught and even then it didn't matter. Why? Well, a diminutive squirrel doesn't pull at the heartstrings of most Arizonans, who seemed unruffled at the fact that the state's rarest species was slated to become political roadkill.

More tellingly, the University got its way because it has powerful politicians in its pocket, ranging from Bruce Babbitt to John McCain, and they used them relentlessly, especially the vile McCain.

The university tapped McCain to push through congress the so-called Idaho and Arizona Conservation Act of 1988. This deceptively-titled law was actually a double-barrel blast at the environment: it gave the green light to illegal logging in the wildlands of Idaho and for the construction of the Mount Graham telescopes, shielding them from any kind of litigation by environmentalists or Apaches. To help sneak this malign measure through congress, the University shelled out more than a half-million dollars for the services of the powerhouse DC lobbying firm Patton, Boggs and Blow.

The bill passed in the dead of night and, in the words of one University of Arizona lawyer, it gave the astronomers the right to move forward "even if it killed every squirrel."

It also exempted the project from the National Historic Preservation Act and other laws that might have made it possible for the Apaches to assert their claims to the mountain, giving the University of Arizona the dubious honor of becoming the first academic institution to seek the right to trample on the religious freedoms of Native Americans.

In the spring of 1989 with the squirrel population in freefall, the Forest Service, which oversees Mount Graham as part of the Coronado National Forest, began to raise questions about the project. Worried that the astronomers' road might spell the squirrel's demise, Jim Abbott, the supervisor of the Coronado forest, ordered a halt construction at the site. The delay infuriated McCain.

On May 17, 1989, Abbott got a call from Mike Jimenez, McCain's chief of staff. Jimenez informed Abbot that McCain was angry and wanted to meet with him the next day. He told Abbott to expect "some ass-chewing." At the meeting, McCain raged, threatening Abbott that "if you do not cooperate on this project [bypassing the Endangered Species Act], you'll be the shortest tenured forest supervisor in the history of the Forest Service."

Unfortunately for McCain, there was a witness to this encounter, a ranking Forest Service employee named Richard Flannelly, who recorded the encounter in his notebook. This notebook was later turned over to investigators at the General Accounting Office.

A few days later, McCain called Abbott to apologize. But the call sounded more like an attempt to bribe the Forest Supervisor to go along with the project. According to a 1990 GAO report on the affair, McCain "held out a carrot that with better cooperation, he would see about getting funding for Mr. Abbott's desired recreation projects."

Environmentalists lodged an ethics complaint against McCain, citing a federal law that prohibits anyone (including members of Congress) from browbeating federal personnel. The Senate ethics committee never pursued the matter. When the GAO report, condemning McCain, surfaced publicly, McCain lied about the encounter, calling the allegations "groundless" and "silly."

In 1992, environmentalists Robin Silver and Bob Witzeman went to meet with McCain at his office in Phoenix to discuss Mount Graham. Silver and Witzeman are both physicians. The doctors say that at the mention of the words Mount Graham McCain erupted into a violent fit. "He slammed his fists on his desk, scattering papers across the room," said Silver. "He jumped up and down, screaming obscenities at us for about 10 minutes. He shook his fists as if he was going to slug us. It was as violent as almost any domestic abuse altercation."

Witzeman left the meeting stunned: "I'm a lifelong environmentalist, but what really scares me about McCain is not his environmental policies, which are horrid, but his violent, irrational temper. I wouldn't want to see this guy with his finger on the button."

* * *

Despite lawsuits and fierce protests, including a daring attempt to block the access road to by a young Apache mother named Diane Valenzuela, who suspended herself from a tripod, the Vatican and Max Planck scopes went up.

Then the opponents began another tact: a global campaign against universities seeking to invest in the Mount Graham Observatory. It was brilliantly executed and wildly successful. More than 80 universities announced they would have nothing to do with the observatory and 50 prominent European astronomers signed a letter requesting that the project be halted "so that the unique environment and sacred mountain of Mount Graham can be saved." Even the Max Planck Institute scaled back its investment.

All of this began to wear on the head of the Mount Graham project, Peter Strittmatter, the chief astronomer at the University's Seward Observatory. He lashed out repeatedly at the Apaches and greens, referring to them as "essentially terrorists." That's an old slur for the Apaches, going back to the conquistadors, and an increasingly common one for environmentalists. (By the way, Strittmatter's special focus is the all important subject of "Speckle Interferometry.")

But the University pressed on, deploying tactics that seemed cribbed right out of the Dow Chemical Company's playbook: they brought in former FBI agents, including veterans of the bureau's noxious COINTELPRO operation, to train campus police; they tried to infiltrate and disrupt opposition groups; and they hired a pr firm to write phony letters, supposedly drafted by Arizona students, to local papers attacking the Apaches and the enviros.

Then in 1993 the astronomers finally confronted the technical problem that had loomed for so long. The original site for the Large Binocular Telescope was simply untenable. It was too windy and too cloudy. So the astronomers announced they were going to move it to a new site on the mountain, even deeper into the forest.

The enviros and Apaches argued that this sudden change in plans would reactivate environmental laws that had been neutered by the 1988 legislation. But in the pre-dawn hours of December 3, the University unleashed a pre-emptive strike: they clearcut 250 old-growth trees on the new site before the environmentalist could get before a judge. They didn't even tell their own biologist, charged with monitoring the project's impacts on the red squirrel. He found out about it on the evening news.

When the environmentalists finally got into a federal court, the judge agreed with them and halted the construction of the big scope, ruling that the project needed to undergo a formal environmental review. The university appealed and lost.

Then in 1996 they turned to President Clinton. Despite Clinton's pledges to protect the environment and honor the religious practices and sacred sites of Native Americans, he bowed to the demands of the University and signed another piece of legislation overturning the court injunctions and shielding the new site from environmental review and litigation. So even when you play by the rules and win, you can still lose through political connivance and trickery. It's a lesson the Apaches learned long ago.

So work on the big scope resumed, followed by the construction of a 23-mile long powerline corridor up the flank of the mountain. By 2003, he sacred mountain of the Apache had been fully electrified.

***

As we crept through the lush montane forest to the crest of the mountain, Vittorio pulled a small pouch from his pocket. He said it was a medicine bundle that he wanted to bury at the telescope site.

"What's in there?" I asked. "Sage and sweetgrass?"

"Hell, no," he chuckled. "Squirrel shit."

"Uh," I asked nervously. "Do squirrels carry Hanta virus?"

"One can always hope."

He dug a small trench beneath the fence, slid the pouch under, buried in it fir needles and said something in Apache that I couldn't begin to transcribe, though it sounded more like a curse than a prayer.

"The priest said if they spotted aliens in those scopes, it would be their mission to convert them," Vittorio said, speaking of Father George V. Coyne, the head Vatican astronomer. "But they are the aliens here and they're too fucking self-righteous realize it."

Here's a taste of Father Coyne's cosmic eschatology: "The Church would be obliged to address the question of whether extraterrestrials might be brought into the fold and baptized. One would want to put some questions to him, such as: have you ever experienced something similar to Adam and Eve, in other words, original sin? Do you people also know a Jesus who has redeemed you?" And this spaced-out priest has the nerve to denounce the Apache religion as primitive?

The Apache know Mount Graham as Dzil nchaa sian, Big Seated Mountain. The mountain is an anchor point of the Apache cosmology, as vital to their tradition as Chartres, the Wailing Wall or the temples of Angkor Wat. It orients the world, presages the weather, nurtures healing plants and serves as a sanctuary from bands of killers, so often riding under the auspices of the Church. What more do we require of holy places? That they be handmade? Commissioned?

Ironically, that's the position of the Catholic Church. Coyne himself has sneered that unless there are physical relics on the site it can't really be considered sacred, except as a kind of paganistic nature worship which the church finds anathema.

"Nature and Earth are just there, blah!" the cosmic priest wrote. "And there will be a time when they are not there [The Apaches and militant greens] subscribe to an environmentalism and religiosity to which I cannot subscribe and which must be suppressed with all the force we can muster."

Of course, over the past four hundred years the Church has done it's damnedest to eradicate any remnant of Apache culture: villages, clothing, language, ceremonies and the Apache themselves.

"On this mountain is a great life-giving force," declared Franklin Stanley, a San Carlos medicine man, in a 1992 as the bulldozers prepared to dig the footings for the scopes. "You have no knowledge of the place you are about to destroy."

But the priests manning the $3 million Vatican Advanced Technology Telescope dismissed Franklin and the other Apaches. They prevented Apache leaders from meeting with the Pope and even went so far as to suggest that were being used as part of a Jewish conspiracy. "The opposition to the telescopes and the use of Native American people to oppose the project are part of a Jewish conspiracy that comes out of the Jewish lawyers of the ACLU to undermine and destroy and undermine the Catholic church," the Rev. Charles Polzer told Indian activist Guy Lopez in 1992. Polzer, a Jesuit priest, was the curator of ethnohistory at the Arizona State Museum. "Two Phoenix doctors, Robert Witzeman and Robin Silver, are examples of this conspiracy," Polzer told Lopez.

Polzer was as wrong about Witzeman and Silver as was about the sacred nature of Mount Graham. Witzeman is a Lutheran; Silver is a Mormon. Silver has been a friend of mine for many years. He's also the busiest man I know. He's a gifted tennis player, an emergency room physician, a father and the most prolific environmentalist in the Southwest. "Apaches, Jews and greens we're all the same to the Church and the University of Arizona," says Silver.

The astronomers even made it illegal for the Apaches to conduct prayer ceremonies on the summit without a permit and arrested Wendsler Nosie, a member of Apaches for Cultural Preservation, when he exercised his constitutional right to pray there without one.

"These space priests have the same old prejudices that the inquisitors did back when they went after Galileo," says Vittorio. "What's bizarre is that the tables have turned. Now the Church is being used by the scientists to legitimize their rampages. They even have the gall to name their sacrilege the Columbus Project."

Several universities, including the University of Minnesota and Virginia, offered to buy off opposition from the Apaches. It didn't work. "They're asking us to sell our spirit," said Wendsler Nosie. "The answer is 'no, we don't want anything they're offering to us financially.'"

***

In October of 1992, I attended a Columbus Day rally against Mount Graham at the University of Arizona's Seward Observatory outside Tucson. As an Apache leader was giving a speech, a goon squad of University police charged into the crowd, tackled and tried to drag away one of the Native American student leaders. Robin Silver, who among his other pursuits is a first-rate photographer, began clicking shots of the assault. Then the cops turned their attention on him. He was arrested and his camera seized.

Silver wasn't there to protest, but to document. Still, the University cops recognized him immediately as a chief nemesis. Since 1988, there's been more than a dozen lawsuits filed against the telescope project. Silver has had his hand in crafting most of them. Unlike many environmentalists, Silver also deals honestly and respectfully with Native Americans.

For the university, this is a dangerous mix. And they've repeatedly tried to discredit Silver in the press and with politicians. When that didn't work they sent their cops out to intimidate him. But emergency room physicians don't scare easily and the arrest blew up in the face of the University—Silver also knows how to work the press.

But the university (surely one of the sleaziest institutions in the US) didn't relent. In 1993, it hired the Snell & Winter law firm to dig in to the possibility of filing racketeering charges against environmentalist and Apache opponents of the telescopes. And on and on it goes.

Why would the university go to these extreme lengths? Well, the Mount Graham telescope complex isn't just about the pursuit of "pure science"—as if any science could ever be pure—or, as one astronomer put it, "peering through the dark avenues of time to witness the creative spark of the Big Bang."

Astronomy isn't a benign science. Indeed, it's impossible to separate the discipline from its unseemly ties to military applications. Galileo's first telescopes were designed for the war lords of Venice, who used them to spot enemy ships and troops. The giant mirrors that power the Mount Graham scopes have also been touted for their dual use nature: both as stargazers and as a potential component in the Star Wars scheme, wherein the mirrors would reflect laser-beam weapons on satellites and incoming missiles.

Of course, it's also about money. Lots of money. And we're not just talking about the enormous cost of the project. Telescopes are big business. The investment partners for the Mount Graham Observatory are selling viewing time for $30,000 a night. And this figure will climb when the Large Binocular scope goes online-if it does. Then there's the stream of federal research grants, guided to them by political patrons such as McCain, which the University hopes will tally in the tens of millions a year.

"These guys don't just have stars in their eyes," quips Vittorio. "They've also got dollar signs."

Robin Silver calls them simply "the Star Whores."

All in all, the maligned art of astrology does rather less harm and provides a good deal more human solace.

* * *

"Hey, you, assholes!" We'd been discovered. "Freeze, dammit!"

A green tunnel of light swept towards us, like a dragnet scene in a bad James Cagney movie. A corpulent cop rumbled toward the fence, dragging a bum leg and carrying what looked to be an assault rifle.

"This way," Vittorio whispered and took off running. I jogged after him as he bounded through the forest like a bear harassed by hornets. He descended a rough deer trail, then cut cross country, topping a razor-thin ridge and down into a cove of moss-bearded spruce. I stayed within sight of him for a few minutes, but soon lost him in the darkness, as my lungs began to seize. I'm a lowlander and the 10,000-foot altitude took its toll with a vengeance.

Exhausted and disoriented, I tripped over a downed tree and plunged headfirst into a snow bank. Suddenly, I felt overcome with doom. I laid there in the snow, gasping for air that wasn't there, waiting for the fat cop with the club foot and the rubber bullets to come haul me away to some shithole in Tucson or worse.

"Psst. Down here." Vittorio to the rescue once again.

He was crouching in a narrow gorge, about 20 feet below me. I pulled myself out of the snowbank and worked my way down into the ravine. We walked a few hundred yards in silence, absorbing the intoxicating vanilla-like scent of the forest, until the gorge came to an abrupt end at a cliff, towering a few hundred feet above a broad flank of the mountain below us.

We sat down on the ledge, our feet dangling in a kind of space. A rush of air from below warmed our faces. The sky had cleared of clouds. To the west, the desert rolled on in the darkness beneath us toward the Galiuro and Santa Catalina Mountains and the distant flickering tumor of Tucson.

"Look!" Vittorio whispered, pointing to the midnight sky, suddenly streaming with stars. "How much closer do we really need to be?"

PART FIVE: SOUTHLANDERS

Chapter 33

SET THIS FLAG ON FIRE!

By Jeffrey St. Clair

FOR THE LAST 50 years, the state of South Carolina has flown the Confederate flag above the grounds of the state capitol in Columbia, a noxious emblem of the state government's unremitting animus toward civil rights laws and desegregation.

The flag was hoisted in 1962 as a show of defiance against the Supreme Court and the Civil Rights movement. It soon became a war banner for the segregationist minions marshaled behind Strom Thurmond's Southern Manifesto. The flag has remained a shameful glorification of the ante-bellum, slave-holding South and a daily blight for South Carolina's black population ever since.

Recall that South Carolina was not only the ignition point for the Civil War, but the Wal-Mart of the slave trade. Many of the black Africans brought to South Carolina as slaves for the plantation owners were sent into the swampy rice fields, which proved to be malarial death camps, where people perished in nearly unimaginable numbers. Nearly two-thirds of the black children in the rice plantations perished before reaching the age of sixteen.

Black Africans who weren't forced into the rice and cotton fields of South Carolina (the Carolina planters exhibited a peculiar preference for blacks from Senegambia and present-day Ghana) were sold in Charleston's slave market to plantation owners from across the South. These brokers of human beings ended up making millions and enjoying seats as legislators in the statehouse, where they drafted laws to protect their "property." When people talk about the flag as a proud symbol of the state's heritage that's the inescapable and horrific backdrop.

For the past couple of years, the NAACP and local civic rights organizers have led a campaign to get the flag removed from atop the capitol building and entombed in a display case in a nearby museum, which houses artifacts from what is quaintly referred to in Carolina as "the war between the states."

When first broached, the demand was met with derision by state leaders and threats of violence from local yahoos. Then the civil rights groups launched a nationwide tourism boycott of South Carolina. This was no minor threat. Since the NAFTA-driven collapse of the garment industry, tourism (which consists largely of the ceaseless promotion of the Southern plantation lifestyle) has become the mainstay of the state's frail economy. Soon millions were being lost and businesses (which once not so long ago proudly catered only to whites by law and now do so largely based on pricing) started carping to legislators about what could be done to deal with the noisome boycott.

Ultimately, a so-called compromise plan was brokered by Democrats in the state legislature and the flag migrated from atop the capitol dome to a prominent flagpole on the statehouse grounds, where it flies above statutes of Confederate soldiers and generals and other monuments to slavery and the enforcers of racial segregation. Naturally, this satisfied few in the civil rights community and the NAACP boycott remains in place.

In the spring of 2002, black activist and brick mason Emmett Rufus Eddy decided that he had had enough of this ongoing insult and did something about it. Eddy had tried to pull the flag down on three previous occasions. Even though a restraining order barred him from stepping foot on the grounds of the Statehouse, this time Eddy would succeed.

Assuming the guise of his nom de guerre, the Reverend E. Slave, Eddy donned a black Santa suit, carried a ladder bearing the names black rights organizers to the South Carolina State House, set it up next to the flagpole, climbed to the top of the flagpole, cut down the Confederate flag, shouted "this is for the children," and lit it on fire, as state police heckled him from below and tried to douse him with pepper spray.

Apparently, the study of physics and Newton's law of gravity are not requirements at the police academy in Columbia and the cops were duly surprised when the pepper spray failed to incapacitate the Reverend Slave and instead blew back into the eyes of the police officers. The officers later filed injury claims.

Eddy clung to the pole, telling his pursuers: "Anybody down there can promise me that this flag will not go back up until my trial?" Eddy asked. "Anybody can make that promise? Make that promise and I'll come down."

In South Carolina, old times are not forgotten. The local paper reported the comments of a passing motorist as police tried to pull Eddy down: "String him up right there." [For the record, there were at least 145 lynchings of blacks by white mobs (homegrown terrorism) in South Carolina from 1882 to 1930, according to the excellent *A Festival of Violence: An Analysis of Southern Lynchings* by Stewart E. Tolnay and E.M. Beck.]

Eventually, Eddy was arrested, roughed up a little by the embarrassed cops, shackled and hauled off to jail, to taunts and jeers from a crowd of more than 100 (mostly white) onlookers who had gathered at the site. Within the hour, the Statehouse's grounds crew secured another Confederate flag (value: $30) and hoisted the infamous banner once again.

The flag may only cost $30 to replace, but the State of South Carolina is determined to impose a much more severe sanction on Eddy. For this modest act of civil disobedience (which some might call a beautification project), Eddy faced a $5,000 fine and three years in prison.

The Reverend Slave was bailed out, but a few days later he was arrested again, supposedly for trespassing on the statehouse grounds, although he was across the street at the time. He peacefully resisted by laying down on the sidewalk and going limp, as the cops hauled him back to jail.

Chapter 34

CRIME, CULTURE AND RESISTANCE IN NEW ORLEANS

By Jordan Flaherty

YEARS AFTER THE DEVASTATION of New Orleans spotlighted racism and inequality in the US, the disaster continues. New Orleans' health care and education systems remain in crisis. Thousands of units of public housing sit empty or demolished. Nearly half the city's population remains displaced. A report released by the Institute for Southern Studies during the second anniversary of Katrina reveals that, out of $116 billion in federal Katrina funds allocated, less than 30 percent went towards long-term rebuilding—and half of that 30 percent remained unspent. Walking the streets of this shrinking city, you can feel the loss as a painful scar.

The city's criminal justice system, already ranked among the worst in the nation by human rights organizations pre-Katrina has become a symbol of both incompetence and brutality. After the storm, thousands of prisoners were abandoned in Orleans Parish Prison as the waters rose. In the days after Katrina, mainstream media depicted the people of New Orleans as looters and criminals, and a makeshift jail in a bus station was the first city function to re-open, just days after the storm.

For Robert Goodman, an activist for criminal justice reform who was born and raised in the schools and prisons of Louisiana, the demonizing and criminalization of the survivors was no surprise. His experiences have led him to the conclusion that the primary crisis of New Orleans is a discriminatory and corrupt criminal justice system, "Every time a black child is born in Louisiana, there's already a bed waiting for him at Angola State Prison," he tells me. Robert, a big man with a generous nature and a cell phone headset always on his ear, lives with his extended family on New Orleans' West Bank, on the opposite side of the Mississippi River from the French Quarter and the rest of the city's famous sites. He knows New Orleans, both its good and bad, as well as anyone.

On May 9, 2006, Robert Goodman's brother was killed in an encounter with the New Orleans police. This was one in a long list of civilian deaths at police hands, both pre- and post-Katrina. Advocates say these deaths have not received proper investigation, and indicate larger, systemic problems. Robert's brother was mentally handicapped, and family members say that he was no threat to the officers or anyone else.

In conversations about himself and his family, Robert described for me his upbringing in the city. For poor Black kids growing up in New Orleans, the education system is remarkably dysfunctional; a model for what has been called, by advocates nationally, the "school to prison pipeline."

"When I went to prison, I was illiterate," Goodman tells me. "I didn't even know anything about slavery, about our history." In New Orleans, 95 percent of the detained youth in 1999 were Black. In 2004, Louisiana spent $96,713 to incarcerate each child in detention, and $4,724 to educate a child in the public schools.

New Orleans' public defense system is in such poor shape that Orleans Parish Criminal District Court Judge Arthur Hunter complained in 2007 that, "indigent defense in New Orleans is unbelievable, unconstitutional, totally lacking the basic professional standards of legal representation, and a mockery of what a criminal justice system should be in a Western civilized nation."

Louisiana has the highest incarceration rate of any state in the US. If Louisiana were a country, it would have the highest incarceration rate in the world. Orleans Parish Prison, the city jail, was—pre-Katrina—the eighth largest jail in the US. Advocates complain that there is no forum for oversight over the jail or Marlin Gusman, the infamous Sheriff who oversees it. "We've suffered under a policy where the city builds a huge jail that is then required to be filled with human beings, or else it's a waste of money," states civil rights attorney Mary Howell.

Goodman is fighting to change the system that took away his brother, as part of a grassroots organization called Safe Streets Strong Communities. Safe

Streets is struggling not just to reform the entire system, from policing and public defense to prison, but also to reframe the debate around these issues.

Safe Streets began as a coalition of grassroots activists and organizers from a number of organizations who came together post-Katrina to respond to the immediate crisis. "Our first priority was to help those individuals who had been in Orleans Parish Prison prior to Katrina, many of whom were being held illegally for minor, non-violent offenses," explains co-director Norris Henderson. "In the early days, right after the storm, Safe Streets was basically performing triage for a broken system." Henderson, a dedicated and patient man who spent nearly thirty years in Angola Prison before being exonerated and released, has emerged as a powerful leader in the struggle for post-Katrina criminal justice reform. Before co-founding Safe Streets, he founded an organization called V.O.T.E.—Voice Of The Ex-offender—which aimed to help former prisoners regain their voting rights. As with many New Orleanians, Norris seems to know everyone he passes as he walks down the street of his neighborhood. He has known Robert since they were both in reform school together.

Safe Streets has been a vital leader in the struggle for a just recovery for New Orleans. In the transition from the crisis of Katrina to the long-term catastrophe that still grips the city, Safe Streets focused their energy on building their base, ensuring that people in communities most affected—people like Robert and his family—were shaping the priorities and making the decisions for the organization. Shortly after Safe Streets began pressuring on the issue, the city's indigent defense board was completely reconstituted to include people that actually care about poor people receiving a fair trial. After they turned their focus to cop abuse, the city approved and funded an office of the independent monitor to oversee the police. In addition, the city council has begun looking at downsizing Orleans Parish Prison, as well as reducing the sheriff's budget, and tying it to reform and greater accountability—also a part of Safe Street's strategy.

More importantly, they affected the debate around criminal justice in the city. Within a few months after the storm, instead of talk of more prisons, journalists and politicians were looking at the system, and the roots of the problems. Evidence of widespread police misconduct and people locked up for months without charges began to be reported.

For those that have been victimized by law enforcement violence, organizing and talking about what they have faced has already been transformative. "I can't imagine where my family would be if it weren't for Safe Streets," Goodman tells me. "We would have been pushed to the side. This organizing inspired my mother to live another day."

THE CITY

For those who have not lived in New Orleans, you have missed an incredible, glorious, vital, city. A place with a culture and energy unlike anywhere else in the world. A 70 percent African-American city where resistance to white supremacy supported a generous, subversive and unique culture of vivid beauty.

From jazz, blues and hiphop, to secondlines, Mardi Gras Indians, Jazz Funerals, and the citywide tradition of red beans and rice on Monday nights, New Orleans is a place of art and music and traditions and sexuality and liberation unlike anywhere else in the world.

New Orleans was, as more than one former resident has said, North America's African city. It is a city steeped in a culture that is specifically African-American. Many attribute this at least partly to the legacy of the different form that French colonialism took. The existence in New Orleans of a neighborhood (the Treme) of free Black people as early as 1770, meant that African cultural traditions were maintained in a way that they weren't elsewhere in the US.

New Orleans was the number one African-American tourist destination in the US. The Bayou Classic and Essence Festival, two essential Black community events, brought tens of thousands of tourists to the city every year.

It is a city with its own holidays, like Indian Sunday, in which Black men—and some women—dress in elaborate costumes that they have sewed and constructed all year. The costuming began at least in part as a tribute to the Native American community, for the support that community gave Black people during the times of slavery—such as reservations serving as stops on the underground railroad. These Mardi Gras Indians—as they are called—are just part of the cultural tradition of New Orleans that outsiders rarely see. These are neighborhood traditions—put on by members of a community, for the benefit of others in the community.

Shortly after the city was flooded, Cornel West said:

New Orleans has always been a city that lived on the edge...with Elysian Fields and cemeteries and the quest for paradise. When you live so close to death, behind the levees, you live more intensely, sexually, gastronomically, psychologically. Louis Armstrong came out of that unbelievable cultural breakthrough unprecedented in the history of American civilization. The rural blues, the urban jazz. It is the tragicomic lyricism that gives you the courage to get through the darkest storm. Charlie Parker would have killed somebody if he had not blown his horn. The history of black people in America is one of unbelievable resilience in the face of crushing white supremacist powers.

More than anywhere else in the US, New Orleans is a city where people live in one neighborhood their whole lives, and where generations live in the same community. All of this is to say that New Orleans is not just a tourist stop. New Orleans is a unique culture, one that is resilient, and with a history of community and resistance.

The community traditions of New Orleans have generally existed outside the police and white power structure of the city. Mardi Gras Indians, for example, have never had the support of city government, and have in fact faced police repression.

In spring of 2005, as the Indians were parading on another of their official holidays (St. Joseph's Night) scores of officers descended on the scene and disrupted the event, scaring the children present and arresting several of the performers.

Several weeks later, at a city council hearing on the incident, Tootie Montana, the chief of chiefs of the Mardi Gras Indians, spoke. At 82 years old, Tootie had been a Mardi Gras Indian Chief for five decades. He captivated the assembled crowd with details of a long history of police repression, tied into racial discrimination, beginning with a police crackdown at his very first Mardi Gras many decades ago. Tootie ended his speech with the words, "this has to stop." Those would be his last words. Tootie Montana stepped back from the microphone and collapsed to the floor. He was pronounced dead of a heart attack shortly afterwards.

His funeral was a moving combination of cultural celebration and political demonstration. Thousands of people came out, dressed in all manner of costume, to commemorate the life of this brave fighter for freedom. Longtime community activist Jerome Smith roused the crowd, saying "This is about a life that has passed, but it is also about the struggle against institutionalized racism in our city." Smith—a fiery speaker who was friends with James Baldwin and worked with Ella Baker—is an inspiring model of a grassroots organizer. Eschewing headlines and attention, but possessing a quiet but intense presence, he works with youth in his neighborhood, preserving New Orleans' African-inspired cultural traditions and linking them to a heritage of dignity and resistance. As the crowd cheered Jerome's words, it was clear that the link between New Orleans culture, especially the culture of Black Mardi Gras, and liberation was clear to everyone in attendance.

COMMUNITY

I didn't really understand community until I moved to New Orleans. It is a city of kindness and hospitality, where walking down the block can take two hours because you stop and talk to someone on every porch, and where everyone pulls together when someone is in need. It is a city of extended families and social networks filling the gaps left by city, state and federal governments that have abdicated their responsibility for the public welfare. It is a city where someone you walk past on the street not only asks how you are; they wait for an answer. New Orleans is a place where someone always wants to feed you.

It is a city and people who have resisted white supremacy for centuries. A city of slave revolts and uprisings. This is the city where in 1892 Homer Plessy and the Citizens Committee planned the direct action that brought the first (unsuccessful) legal challenge to the doctrine of "Separate but Equal"—the challenge that became the Supreme Court case of *Plessy v. Ferguson*.

Social Aid and Pleasure Clubs, local Black cultural institutions that began during the reconstruction era for both mutual aid and to maintain the community's culture, still thrive today, and were in fact an important force in bringing back residents of the city.

New Orleans activists were on the front lines of civil rights organizing. "Wherever you went across the South," Congress of Racial Equality (CORE) veteran Mattheo "Flukie" Suarez, told New Orleans journalist Katy Reckdahl in 2004, "there were always New Orleans people working in the civil-rights movement."

New Orleans was also part of the more militant post-civil rights era. In 1970 the New Orleans Black Panthers held off the police from the Desire housing projects, and also formed one of the nations' first Black Panther chapters in prison. Nationwide, the Deacons For Defense, an armed self defense group formed in rural central Louisiana in 1964, inspired Panthers and other radical groups.

Despite these rich traditions, New Orleans has long been a city in crisis. It was a violent city. New Orleans had a pre-Katrina population of fewer than 500,000 and was expecting 300 murders in 2005, most of them centered on just a few, overwhelmingly black, neighborhoods. Murder suspects are rarely convicted. Often, a few days after a shooting, the attacker is shot in revenge. Distrust of police is so high, that even when murders happen in front of large crowds, officers often find no witnesses. The DA's office secured just three convictions for the 162 murders in 2006. Despite having just over half the 2004 population in 2007, New Orleans experienced nearly as many murders.

New Orleans had a 40 percent illiteracy rate by some measures, and over 50 percent of black ninth graders did not graduate high school in four years. Louisiana spends on average $4,724 per child's education each year and ranked 48th in the country for lowest teacher salaries.

New Orleans is a city where industry has left, and most remaining jobs are low paying, transient, insecure positions in the service economy. It has always been a city you fall in love with, and a city you have to fight for. Living here can be like a difficult romance with a brilliant but tragic artist.

SHELTER AND SAFETY

Days after evacuating, I went to the River Road shelter in Baton Rouge as part of a project initiated by a grassroots organization called Families and Friends of Louisiana's Incarcerated Children to help displaced New Orleans residents reconnect with loved ones who are lost in the labyrinth of Louisiana's corrections system.

Everyone I met was desperately trying to find a sister or brother or child or other family member lost in the system. Many people who were picked up for minor infractions in the days before the hurricane ended up being shipped to prisons upstate, including the infamous Angola Prison, a former slave plantation where it has been estimated that over 90 percent of inmates sent there will die within its walls.

Most of the family members I spoke with in the shelter just wanted to get a message to their loved ones, "Tell him that we've been looking for him, that we made it out of New Orleans, and that we love him," said an evacuated New Orleans East resident named Angela.

While Barbara Bush famously declared how fortunate the shelter residents were, in the real world New Orleans evacuees were feeling anything but sheltered. One woman I spoke with in the River Street shelter said that she'd barely slept since she arrived in the system. "I sleep with one eye open," she told me. "It's not safe in there."

Christina Kucera, a Planned Parenthood organizer from New Orleans, explained it this way; "Issues of safety and shelter are intricately tied to gender. This has hit women particularly hard. It's the collapse of community. We've lost neighbors and systems within our communities that helped keep us safe." Kucera, who first introduced me to much of the beauty and sorrow of New Orleans, was unable to move back to the city post-storm, but still carries a passion for it.

For many who experienced the shelter system, abuse and re-victimization was rampant. There were widespread reports of racism and discrimination in Red Cross shelters, especially in Lafayette, Lake Charles and Baton Rouge. According to Jodie Escobedo, a doctor from California who was volunteering in the Baton Rouge shelters, "Local officials, including politicians, select Red Cross personnel and an especially well placed but small segment of the Louisiana medical community, have managed to get themselves into positions of power where their prejudices result in the hoarding of supplies, vilification of the needy and substandard treatment of volunteers and refugees alike." As a medical volunteer with a first-hand view, Escobedo painted a devastating portrait.

New Orleans was a blueprint for a new, militarized, relief. The Chicago police camped out in a bar on Bourbon Street, while an Israeli security company named Instinctive Shooting International was hired to guard uptown mansions and National Guard and Blackwater mercenaries were seemingly everywhere. Meanwhile, white vigilante gangs patrolled the West Bank, with tacit permission of local authorities. As one central city resident complained to me, "Why don't they send some of these troops with tools to rebuild instead of just weapons? I guess they don't want it rebuilt."

CRIMINALIZING THE SURVIVORS

If the effort of living in this devastated city isn't hard enough, for the thousands of New Orleanians caught up in the criminal justice system, things keep getting worse. The continuing debacle of this broken system inspires in me a sense of indignation I thought was lost to cynicism long ago.

Ursula Price, an investigator for indigent defense cases, spent months after the storm speaking with several thousand hurricane survivors who were imprisoned at the time of the hurricane, and her stories chill me. "I grew up in small town Mississippi," she tells me. "We had the Klan marching down our main street, but I've never seen anything like this." Price, another co-founder of Safe Streets Strong Communities, lost all of her possessions during the post-Katrina flooding, but never took more than a weekend off from work for two years after the storm.

In March of 2006, Safe Streets released a devastating report co-authored by Price and based on more than a hundred interviews with prisoners locked up since pre-Katrina and spread across thirteen prisons and hundreds of miles. The report found the average number of days people had been locked up without a trial was 385 days. One person had been locked up for 1,289 days. None of them had been convicted of any crime.

"I've been working in the system for the while, I do capital cases and I've seen the worst that the criminal justice system has to offer," Price explained. "But even I am shocked that there has been so much disregard for the value of these people's lives, especially people who have not been proved to have done anything wrong." According to a pre-Katrina report from the Metropolitan Crime Commission, 65 percent of those arrested in New Orleans are eventually released without ever having been charged with any crime.

Samuel Nicholas (his friends call him Nick) was imprisoned in Orleans Parish Prison on a misdemeanor charge, and was due to be released August 31. Instead, after a harrowing journey of several months, he was released February 1. I met Nick soon after, and spent a number of days talking with him, meeting up in his Central City neighborhood, dancing with him at secondlines. A young grandfather who works in construction, Nick is soft-spoken and shy, and talks with reluctance when the conversation turns to those days after Katrina. He told me he still shudders when he thinks of his experience in Orleans Prison.

"We heard boats leaving, and one of the guys said 'Hey man, all the deputies gone,'" Nick relates. "We took it upon ourselves to try to survive. They left us in the gym for two days with nothing. Some of those guys stayed in a cell for or five days. People were hollering, 'Get me out, I don't want to drown, I don't want to die.' We were locked in with no ventilation, no water, nothing to eat. Its just the grace of god that a lot of us survived." As we discuss the details of his ordeal, it becomes more difficult for Nick to remain composed, but he perseveres.

"This ain't just started, its been going on," Nick tells me. "I want to talk about it, but at the same time it hurts to talk about it. It's not the judge, its not the lawyers, it's the criminal justice system. Everybody who goes to jail isn't guilty. You got guys who were drunk in public, treated like they committed murder."

I talked to Nick in a neighborhood bar near his house, just before he was going to Mardi Gras Indian practice. As with many people from his community, Nick is active in creating and sustaining New Orleans' unique culture. "I'm making this interview so that things get better," he explains. "The prison system, the judicial system, the police. We got to make a change, and we all got to come together as a community to make this change. I want to stop all this harassment and brutality."

Before Katrina, the New Orleans public defender system was already dangerously overloaded, with 42 attorneys and six investigators. For almost a year after the storm, New Orleans was down to six public defenders, and one investigator. And these defenders were not necessarily full-time, nor committed to their clients. One attorney was known to spend his days in court working on crossword puzzles instead of talking to his clients. "We have a system that was broken before Katrina," Price tells me, "that was then torn apart, and is waiting to be rebuilt."

"Despite all of the horror we are seeing daily, my hope is this is an opportunity for change," Price said. "OPP corruption is being laid bare. People being held past their time is nothing new in this system, it's just more extreme now. This is something to organize around and fight against."

For many New Orleanians, it's community that has brought security. And that's why the police and National Guard and security companies on our streets didn't bring the security people wanted. That's why locking up our neighbors in prisons and throwing away the key is no solution.

THE NEXT FIGHT

This has been a sad time for anyone from New Orleans, or anyone who cares about the people of the city. It has been a time of increased drinking and depression. By early 2007, the suicide rate in the city had more than tripled. New Orleanians are still dispersed around the US. No one knows how many will come home, or when, but they are missed. In the weeks after the hurricane a friend told me through tears, "I just want to go back as if this never happened. I want to go back to my friends and my neighbors and my community."

It has also been a beautiful and inspiring time, and this is not the end of our struggle. As the recovery drags on, New Orleanians will keep fighting. Whatever the results, there is much for progressives around the world to learn from and be moved by in the spirit of New Orleanians. And, for the next city or region devastated by disaster, there will certainly be lessons from both our victories and our failures.

Every time I see a family moving back to the city, I am inspired by this small act of resistance and courage, this dedication to community and to the further life of the city. Every day, I see other little acts of resistance, in second-lines and other cultural expressions. I see people going to what seems like the thousandth neighborhood planning meeting and still remaining fresh. I see people demonstrating in the streets. I see people being generous in the face of the cruelty of the city's elite who tried to keep them out. I see people giving their neighbors places to stay, food and always ready with a friendly greeting.

What's really going to bring people back to our city are the people themselves, fighting on the front lines to come home. In hundreds of small struggles, in grassroots organizing and demonstrations around the city, the fight continues. As Beverly Wright, director of Dillard University's Deep South Center for Environmental Justice, declared during a 2006 forum sponsored by the African American Leadership Project, "They've underestimated the determination of people like me to fight to our last breath."

The people of New Orleans are standing up and fighting back, joined by progressive allies from around the world, and reinforced by a tradition and culture of resistance. This culture of resistance, of community and caring, continues to inspire those of us who love New Orleans. It has sustained and inspired me when it seems hopeless. In the end, it may be the best hope this city has.

Chapter 35

JIM CROW IS ALIVE IN JENA

By Nicole Colson

IN SEPTEMBER 1957, THE world watched when nine Black students braved a jeering white mob as they walked into the segregated Central High School in Little Rock, Arkansas, in the pursuit of an equal education.

The images from that day show the ugly reality of American racism. Elizabeth Eckford had arrived alone on the first day of school, and was turned away by the Arkansas National Guard on orders of Democratic Governor Orval Faubus. The crowd of whites that surrounded her as she later walked to a bus stop looked ready to lynch her. Each of the Little Rock Nine would face similar harassment.

Coming after the 1954 *Brown v. Board of Education* Supreme Court decision that outlawed legal segregation, Little Rock showed the reality of racism in the U.S.—that equality before the law mattered little in the Jim Crow South, and that racism would have to be fought every step of the way to overcome it. Today, we're told that America has moved beyond its ugly past—that nooses, "separate but equal" and "Jim Crow justice" are relics of a bygone era. But 50 years after Little Rock, the case of the Jena 6 proves that racism is alive and well in the U.S.

The Jena 6 are six high school students who faced decades in prison for their alleged part in a school fight—which itself followed a series of racist incidents endured by the small minority of African Americans in this Louisiana town of less than 3,000 people.

The case has many of the hallmarks of the Jim Crow past—a vindictive white prosecutor, all-white juries, blatant double standards in punishment.

And, of course, the nooses—hung from a tree in the courtyard of Jena's high school to intimidate Black students who dared to expect equal treatment.

The story of the Jena 6 has spread around the country and the world, causing disbelief and anger. On September 20, 2007, that anger found an outlet—with tens of thousands of people mobilizing around the country to stand up for the Jena 6.

Hundreds rallied on college campuses in Nashville, Houston, Atlanta, Cleveland, Toledo, Muncie, Berkeley, and beyond. In Allentown, Pennsylvania, middle school students marched. In Chicago, students from the all-male Hales Franciscan High School on the South Side organized an out-of-uniform day so they could wear black to show support for the Jena 6. Hundreds more marched in communities in Detroit, Philadelphia and elsewhere.

And then there was Jena itself. Tens of thousands of people descended on the southern hamlet. From early in the morning, protesters came pouring down the sloping road into Jena. They rallied in the town park and marched to the courthouse and, then, to Jena High School to witness the spot where the "whites only" tree once stood. The tree has since been removed, although the school's burned-out auditorium, set on fire by an unknown arsonist, remains.

Ashleigh Randle, a student at the University of Michigan, drove 22 hours with a group of fellow students to stand in the courtyard. "We wanted to come and stand up for what is right, because we're tired of what's been going on, the racial injustice," she said.

"People act like racism is in the past, but it's not. It's subtle or it's blunt, but it's out there. We want people to know that we're tired of settling for less. I say look around. How can you look at Hurricane Katrina and say racism doesn't exist?"

Ashleigh's fellow student, Shanika Steen, pointed to the spot where the tree once stood. "The noose that was hung on the tree. And another one at the University of Maryland a couple of days ago. You can't look at these things and say, 'It's not racism, it's just something that happened.'"

Shavette Wayne Jones journeyed to Jena from St. Louis with a group of about 60 people. "I came because I have two sons of my own," she said. "I have a 2-year-old and a 9-year-old. My mother and I came together. This could very well be one of my children."

Among everyone in the streets of Jena that day, there was a determination to take a stand—if the racism of the Jim Crow days had returned, they would stand up against it, just like the civil rights marchers of 50 years ago. The sign Shavette held summarized the mood: "Jena, La., today. Anytown, USA, tomorrow. Not on our watch!"

The double standards that run through the case of the Jena 6 are unmistakable. The schoolyard assault that the six Black students are charged with was preceded by a series of racist incidents, beginning when three white students hung nooses from a tree in the courtyard of Jena High School. The nooses appeared the day after some Black students asked for and received permission from an assistant principal to sit under the tree, traditionally "reserved" for whites only. Dismissed as a "prank" by LaSalle Parish Schools Superintendent Roy Breithaupt, the white students who hung the nooses received merely in-school suspensions.

But to Jena's Black residents, those swaying nooses indicated a clear threat. "It meant the KKK, it meant 'Niggers, we're going to kill you, we're going to hang you 'til you die,'" said Caseptla Bailey, whose son is also among the six.

When Black students attempted to address the school board about the noose incident, they were turned away—with the board apparently deciding that it had dealt with the issue.

After Black students staged a sit-in under the tree in response to the nooses, LaSalle Parish County District Attorney Reed Walters was called in to address a school assembly. According to Black students, Walters said to stop "fussing" over an "innocent prank"—and then, looking specifically at them, said: "See this pen? I can end your lives with the stroke of a pen."

In late November of 2006, Robert Bailey, a Black student, was beaten up at a party attended by mostly whites. According to the Louisiana Public Defenders' Association, police initially refused to let Bailey make a complaint against his attacker and warned Black students at the party to "get their Black asses out of this part of town."

A few nights later, Bailey and two others were threatened by a white student with a sawed-off shotgun at the town's "Gotta Go" convenience store. The three young Black men wrestled the gun away and fled, but instead of police arresting the white student who pulled the gun, Bailey was initially arrested and charged with second-degree robbery, theft of a firearm and disturbing the peace.

At school the following week, a white student, Justin Barker, allegedly taunted Bailey. After lunch, Barker was knocked down, punched and kicked by a group of Black students, said to include Bailey, Theo Shaw, Carwin Jones, Bryant Purvis, Mychal Bell and another unidentified minor. Barker was taken to the hospital, though he was well enough to attend a party that night.

As Walters promised, there was instant retaliation against the six Black students. They were immediately expelled, and slapped with charges of attempted second-degree murder—punishable by 30 years in prison. Several of the Jena 6 remained in jail for months because their families couldn't afford bail, which ranged from $70,000 for Purvis to $138,000 for Bailey.

The injustices didn't end there. Mychal Bell was the first to come to trial. On the morning his trial began, the charges against him were reduced to aggravated second-degree battery and conspiracy. The battery charge, however, was based on the idea that Bell used a "deadly weapon" during the assault. The lethal weapon? According to Walters, it was Bell's gym shoe.

Bell was soon found guilty by an all-white jury that included two people who were friendly with the Walters, and one who was a friend of the victim's father. Not only was the jury all-white, but the jury pool itself didn't contain a single African American.

According to the Jena 6 families, Bell's court-appointed defense attorney had been trying to cut a plea deal with the DA behind the scenes. The attorney didn't call a single witness in Mychal's defense or present any evidence on his behalf.

The charges against Jones, Shaw and Bailey were reduced to aggravated second-degree battery and conspiracy. Purvis has yet to be arraigned in the case and is the only remaining Jena Six member still charged with attempted second-degree murder.

Bell was originally scheduled to be sentenced on September 20, 2007, facing as much as 22 years in prison. But with the increased media attention and wave of activism around the case, new lawyers were able to overturn Mychal's conviction. The trial judge first threw out the conspiracy charge, and, later, Bell's battery conviction was overturned when an appeals court judge ruled that he should not have been tried as an adult.

The reversal of Mychal's conviction, however, doesn't affect the four other Jena 6 members charged as adults—because they were 17 at the time of the alleged crime and, under Louisiana law, are no longer considered juveniles.

Unequal "justice" is nothing new in Jena. Michael Kirkland, who runs a barbeque stand outside the Christian Saints Baptist Church on the road into town, has lived in Jena for the past 10 years, "It's a rough town," said Kirkland. "It's a good town, but it's rough. It's very segregated."

Kirkland rejects the idea that racism is a thing of the past in Jena. "It happens all the time," he says.

When the superintendent suggested that the hanging of the nooses was a "prank," Kirkland said, "It shocked the Black community. It didn't shock the white community because that was what they wanted him to do. He's their puppet on a string."

As for the incident with the shotgun, Kirkland says, "It was outrageous. This same guy who pulled the gun, he got away easy. But they charged the boy who took the gun from him with theft."

Gregory Gibbs, who was raised in Jena and attended Jena High, now lives in Alexandria. He speaks today of "getting through" and "getting out." Heywood Williams, who attended Jena High, too, and still lives in Jena, has the same feelings about the school.

According to Gibbs and Williams, it's not surprising that racial tensions would flare up at the high school, since kids in Jena attend separate, racially segregated elementary schools. White children, the men say, go to Nebo Elementary, while Black kids attend a separate school. Though the "whites only" tree at Jena High may be gone, there's still the "Nebo bench," the men say, where only students from Nebo—in other words, all whites—traditionally sit.

Blacks who have tried speaking out against racism in the past in Jena have found themselves retaliated against, Gibbs says. "If you get too outspoken here," he says, "you might show up at work in the morning and find you don't have a job. So that's what took it so long to come out."

Now, the conditions that Gibbs and others have endured are known around the world, thanks to the outrage of people who heard about the story—often on the Internet or through Black talk radio shows—and forced it into the mainstream media.

Even George W. Bush was forced to weigh in. Asked about the planned protest at a news conference, he said the "events in Louisiana have saddened me," and advised whoever is elected next year to "reach out to the African American community." In other words, don't look for any justice from Bush's Justice Department. Meanwhile, Louisiana's Democratic Gov. Kathleen Blanco had declared that the case was a "local matter," and she didn't have the jurisdiction to intervene.

But some Democrats are finding themselves on the hot seat for their failure to speak out. At a meeting in South Carolina, Jesse Jackson took Democratic presidential hopeful Barack Obama to task for failing to respond to Jena. "Jena is a defining moment, just like Selma was a defining moment," said Jackson.

The emotions stirred by the injustice in Jena were clear on September 20, the date that Mychal Bell had been scheduled to be sentenced, when tens of thousands of people made the trip to Jena—and demand that the charges against Mychal and the rest of the Jena 6 be dropped.

When the charges against Mychal Bell were finally overturned, Jena officials must have breathed a sigh of relief—figuring that the September 20 demonstration wouldn't draw a big turnout.

They were wrong. At least 50,000 people traveled to the out-of-the-way town, one of the largest civil rights demonstrations in 40 years.

The night before the protest, in Alexandria, Louisiana, a larger town 45 minutes south of Jena, every hotel and motel for miles around was sold out, filled with protesters preparing for the next day.

The next morning, buses and cars began arriving in Jena as early as 4:30 a.m. By 7:30 a.m., the two-lane road into town was backed up for at least a mile or more. Every available parking space for miles out of town was taken on both sides of the road.

Hundreds of people—nearly all dressed in black shirts in solidarity—began the long walk into town as more cars and buses continued on the road. The arrival of a contingent of hundreds of Black motorcycle riders—organized through Black bike clubs across the country—brought cheers and awe.

Days earlier, when it had become clear that there would be no stopping the protest, state officials declared a "state of emergency" in LaSalle Parish, where Jena is located, in order to ensure that some provisions would be made for protesters—portable toilets, emergency service, and so on. The Red Cross was on hand as well, to distribute water and Gatorade—a necessity, when the temperature climbed to 92 degrees by midday.

On the way into town, people's spirits were buoyed by the size of the turnout. Signs, banners and shirts bore witness to the distances people had traveled—from Washington, D.C., Chicago and Atlanta, and across Texas and Louisiana. Contingents from colleges and Black fraternities, churches and community groups, and civil rights organizations, continued to pour in—along with people who had simply heard about the case and been angered enough to come on their own or with a group of friends.

"Memphis supports the Jena 6," read one sign. "Atlanta supports the Jena 6: Until the six are free, never are we," read another, pasted on the side of a van full of men.

One of the van's passengers, Carnell, was cheering and pumping his fists as he rode on top of the van while it crawled along in the traffic. He said he and his friends decided to make the nine-hour drive after hearing about the case on talk radio. Disbelief gave way to outrage and the desire to do something to help win justice, he explained.

Johnny Williams, better known as "Big John" and a member of the Buffalo Soldiers motorcycle club in Alexandria, expressed the same sentiments. "When word got out, it wasn't any problem [getting people together]," he said. "I wouldn't be anywhere else today. I think it's very, very impressive. We need it."

On the way into town, a large highway sign pointed buses toward the Ward 10 Recreation Park, where thousands gathered for a rally featuring civil rights leaders and family members of the Jena 6, to be followed by a march through town later in the day.

But thousands felt compelled to go in the opposite direction—toward the center of town, to the LaSalle Parish Courthouse, where Mychal Bell was convicted, and farther down the road to the Jena High, to seek out evidence of the "white tree" and stand in defiance of racism.

The courthouse stands on a small hill that was soon packed with people, the overflow spilling onto the crowded streets below. As a small group of state police and—it appeared—town officials looked on with stony faces from the steps, protesters jeered or chanted with raised fists: "Free Mychal Bell," "No justice, no peace," "Enough is enough."

In the morning, Al Sharpton arrived on the courthouse steps with Marcus Jones, the father of Mychal Bell. "This is a march for justice," Sharpton said as the crowd broke out into cheers.

"[Martin Luther] King went to Selma. That wasn't the only place you couldn't vote. That was the point of action. They went to Birmingham. That wasn't the only place we didn't have public accommodations. It was the point of action. Jena is a point of action for the Jenas everywhere. There's Jenas in

Atlanta, there's Jenas in New York, there's Jenas in Florida, and there are Jenas all over Texas."

Later in the day, Jesse Jackson made the same point, drawing wild applause after leading a march from the Ward 10 park to the courthouse. "There's a Jena in every state in America," he said, mentioning police torture of African Americans under the watch of Commander Jon Burge in Chicago, the beating of Rodney King in Los Angeles and the use of prison slave labor today at Angola prison in Louisiana.

The message was the same at the high school, where protesters came to see where the "whites only" tree once stood. Shavette Wayne Jones from St. Louis remembered her years as a college student at Grambling State University—when she protested white supremacist David Duke running for governor of Louisiana.

"I just find it ironic that, here I am, coming back down here after that many years, to fight for justice to prevail again," she said. "I went to school in Louisiana for four years, so I know that not only is it here in Louisiana, but it's everywhere. Sometimes it's not as blatant as this, but all you have to do is live to experience it. It's alive and well."

Helen Comeaux drove five hours from Dallas with her friend Djuna LeBlanc to attend the protest. "I have seven grandkids, and it just scares me for them," she said. "We have to stand up now and fight. We have to. This happens everywhere. I think this is an eye-opener for everybody, not just Black people. It happens in small towns, big cities, everywhere."

Her friend Djuna added: "We want to let everybody know that we're tired, and we're not going to let our children be thrown away like that. Enough is enough."

To hear town officials tell it, the problem in Jena isn't racism, but "outsiders" stirring up trouble.

That certainly seems to be the attitude of Reed Walters, the district attorney. The day before the protest, Walters spoke at what Democracy Now's Rick Rowley called "one of the unfriendlier press conferences I think I've ever seen."

Walters began by blaming the media for supposedly finding examples of Southern racism where none existed. Jena, he seemed to suggest, was simply suffering from an irrational media bias against the small-town South.

"This case has been portrayed by the news media as being about race, and the fact that it takes place in a small Southern town lends itself to that portrayal," Walters said. "But it is not and never has been about race. It is about finding justice for an innocent victim and holding people accountable for their actions."

But Walters, who was also the lawyer for the school board when the nooses were hung, never described how white students were "held accountable" for their actions.

According to Rowley, "At the end, as someone asked Walters, 'Why are you trying to destroy these boys' lives with a stroke of your pen?' he picked up his folder and scattered microphones across the ground and said, 'It's obvious that this press conference is out of control.' And he turned around and ran back inside the courthouse."

After the demonstration, in an op-ed that appeared in the *New York Times*, Walters claimed that, had he the chance to do everything over, he would have done everything the same—except perhaps doing more to convince the media why the assault on Justin Barker was more serious. Defending his lack of action against those responsible for the hanging of the nooses, Walters wrote that "I am bound to enforce the laws of Louisiana as they exist today, not as they might in someone's vision of a perfect world."

Walters also stated, at a press conference days after the demonstration, that it was only divine intervention that had kept the largely Black demonstrators from becoming violent. "I firmly believe that had it not been for the direct intervention of the Lord Jesus Christ last Thursday, a disaster would have happened," he said.

Minnijean Brown-Trickey, one of the Little Rock Nine, who was expelled from Central High in 1958 in part for spilling food on a group of white boys who were harassing her, compared Walters' "outsiders" complaint to her own experience.

"The rhetoric is that 'our Negroes are fine, and y'all people are coming down here, riling them up,'" she told *Democracy Now*'s Amy Goodman in an interview the day of the Jena demonstration. "That's what it sounds like, and that's the tragedy. But I also think it's because of hearing that again that people feel such a sense of alarm."

For many of Jena's Black residents, the presence of "outsiders" is welcome. When Goodman asked the Jena 6 mother Caseptla Baily, "What do you say to those who say this is a bunch of outsiders coming in, everything was fine in Jena before they started marching on our town?" Bailey replied, "Well, I'd like to say that everything wasn't fine in Jena. That's why the outsiders are here, and that's why everything has gone so tremendously within the last few months.

"So I'd like to applaud those people that have come here from the outside—to come in and to support us and help us and assist us in this matter. I'd like to say, hats off to those persons."

Gregory Gibbs had the same reaction. "Thirty years late" was how he described the protest for the Jena 6. "It's been a long time coming," he said. "We've had so much injustice here. We happened to be raised in it, and we survived it. But they do it with the legal system now. They almost got away with it.

Heywood Williams agreed. "There's a level for the whites and a level for the Blacks," he said. "It's just like back in the '60s, like the way they had the water fountains—one for the colored, and one for the whites. That's the way our justice system is set up, on two levels—one for the colored, and one for the whites. That's the way our school system is set up."

"Living here in Jena," he added, "people get along for the most part, but when it comes down to treating each other fairly, the justice system is one-sided.

"And they let you know who you are. They let you know where you're from and where you're at. They let you know that you're in Louisiana and that you're down in the South. They let you know that they prefer their race to be the dominant race."

If Reed Walters and Jena officials get their way, things will stay the way they've always been. Though Walters, under heavy pressure, announced in October that he would not seek to retry Mychal Bell as an adult, he had not given any indication that the charges against the other defendants would be dropped or reduced.

Additionally, in a sore disappointment for supporters of the Jena 6, on October 11, it was announced that Mychal Bell's bail had been revoked at what was supposed to be a routine hearing. Bell was promptly sentenced to 18 months in jail on two counts of simple battery and two counts of criminal destruction of property. As an additional slap in the face, Bell's parents were ordered to pay court and witness costs. "He's locked up again," Marcus Jones,

Mychal's father, told the Associated Press. "No bail has been set or nothing. He's a young man who's been thrown in jail again and again, and he just has to take it."

Incredibly, state District Judge J.P. Mauffray Jr., the same trial judge who oversaw Bell's original trial in front of an all-white jury and inappropriate conviction on adult charges, decided Bell had violated his probation for an earlier case. A request to remove Mauffray from the case had been denied—despite the fact that Mauffray presided over a farce of a trial.

According to Al Sharpton, the revocation of Mychal Bell's bail was payback for the attention that has been focused on Jena and the justice system. "We feel this was a cruel and unusual punishment and is a revenge by this judge for the Jena 6 movement," Sharpton told the Associated Press.

A considerable racist backlash—both in Jena itself and elsewhere—has also emerged. On the evening of the September 20 demonstration, for example, two teens were arrested after driving a pickup through downtown Alexandria, with nooses hanging off the back. Both allegedly had been drinking, and a gun and brass knuckles were found in their truck.

A rash of noose hangings also occurred across the country in the wake of the case—at Andres High School in North Carolina and the University of Maryland, at the Hempstead Police Department locker room on Long Island, the Coast Guard Academy in New London, Conn., and, in the highest profile incident, outside the door of Madonna Constantine, an African American professor at Columbia University's prestigious Teachers College. That incident was labeled "Jena at Columbia" in a series of e-mails circulated by antiracist organizers.

More alarming, the families of the Jena 6 have been targeted for harassment by a neo-Nazi group that called on its Web site, after the September 20 demonstration, for its followers to "drag them out of the house." Some of the families' addresses and phone numbers were posted, "in case anyone wants to deliver justice."

Sharpton said in a statement that "[s]ome of the families have received almost around-the-clock calls of threats and harassment...[The fact] that some person could actually harm or even continue to harass these families with no effort by law enforcement, will further exacerbate the tensions around this case immeasurably."

Additionally, although later disavowing any knowledge of who they were speaking to, both Jena Mayor Murphy McMillan and the alleged victim in the case, Justin Barker, gave interviews to a Richard Barrett, the leader of the Nationalist Movement, a white supremacist group based in Learned, Mississippi.

When McMillan was asked by Barrett to "set aside some place for those opposing the colored folks." McMillan reportedly replied "I am not endorsing any demonstrations, but I do appreciate what you are trying to do. Your moral support means a lot."

Such a backlash shows that the struggle to win justice for the Jena 6 and challenge the racism that the case represents is far from over—but the protests on September 20 were an important step forward.

"People have been crying out for a long time for equal justice," said Heywood Williams." It took Al Sharpton and the coalition groups and Jesse Jackson and all the other people who came, and they got the world's attention. This small thing you see right here in Jena, if you allow it to continue, will spread. If they can get away with it now, they'll do it again.

"They were going to take those six kids' lives and just ruin them—just throw them away. That's what [Reed Walters] was intending to do. They've done it for years and years. That's how we were raised."

But things are different now that attention has been focused on Jena, says Williams. "I'm glad the people did come because it takes a movement," he said. "It takes a movement every time. And today we've seen it. They showed they whole world, and the whole world is showing this system down here that a change has got to come."

As Michael Kirkland put it, "I hope it's an eye opener—the attention of America on Jena. The whole world is watching now."

Chapter 36

TEXAS' UNREASONABLE WOMAN: AN INTERVIEW WITH DIANE WILSON

By Kelpie Wilson

DIANE WILSON IS THE author of *An Unreasonable Woman: A True Story of Shrimpers, Politicos, Polluters and the Fight for Seadrift, Texas* (Chelsea Green, 2005). It is a remarkable book, telling the story of Wilson's life as female shrimp boat captain and an environmental activist fighting devastating toxic pollution from chemical and plastics manufacturers on the Texas Gulf Coast.

But I have to confess, when the book was first recommended to me, I hesitated to read it. As an environmental activist, I have my own personal history of endless hours of research, boring meetings, scary confrontations, nasty intimidation and the infighting that goes along with these struggles, and I wasn't sure that I wanted to hear all the gritty details of someone else's pains and triumphs. Lois Gibbs, the courageous activist mother of Love Canal, said the same thing in her review of *An Unreasonable Woman* in *Orion* magazine. But like Gibbs, I was hooked after the first page. For one thing, the Texas Gulf Coast seems to be unlike any other place on the planet.

Molly Ivins and others have called *An Unreasonable Woman* a masterpiece of American literature, and I agree. First, there is the poetry of Wilson's language. I can only compare her to fiction writers like Cormac McCarthy and Annie Proulx. She wraps her tender descriptions of her beloved Lavaca Bay around poignant inner reflections, while rendering the home-grown dialogue and emotionally tense social ecology of her community with complete authenticity.

Then there is the excitement and exhilaration of working-class feminism that permeates Wilson's life. The first-person feminist voices we usually hear are those of academic or professional women speaking of their battles in the bedroom, the boardroom and the halls of power. We don't hear much about a lone woman, the first woman in her community to run a shrimp boat, relying on herself for both aid and comfort, fixing a broken engine with bailing wire and tape, satisfied with her own company through the long night, trawling for shrimp under the stars.

Finally, the best thing for me about Diane's book was getting to share her spiritual journey to a deeper humanity. So many things can tear you apart as an activist and it's a delicate balance you must maintain between your own passion and your compassion for your opponents, your victories and your failures. Diane has used the living sea itself as her spiritual role model:

"Risking one's life can be strangely liberating. That's what the sea counsels me. She still talks even though she's got a mercury Superfund on her left breast and vinyl chloride and phthalates on her right breast. She's a forgiving grandmother. Not unduly angry about the mix-ups and mess ups and the confounding fact of healing taking so long. She knows it is complicated. My intent will keep her, she says."

Diane was recently released from jail in Texas after serving time for an act of civil disobedience. I talked with her from her home in Seadrift, living in a tiny trailer she says she "paid no more than $500 for."

Kelpie Wilson: Diane, you just got out of jail. What were you in there for?

Diane Wilson: I was in several jails. I was arrested December 5th in Houston for disrupting Vice President Dick Cheney's speech at the Tom DeLay fundraiser. I was charged with possessing a fake document and spent five days in the Harris County Jail waiting on a trial that never materialized.

I was then transferred to the Victoria County Jail for an outstanding warrant. Back in 2002 I had climbed a 70-foot chemical tower at Dow Chemical in Seadrift, Texas, and chained myself to the top after dropping a twenty foot banner that read: "Dow—Responsible for Bhopal."

In October 2005, while on a book tour in the Northeast, I was told to go to jail for my 120 days, and I told the sheriff's department and DA that I wouldn't go to jail until Warren Anderson, former CEO of Union Carbide, went to jail for his outstanding warrant in India for the crime against Bhopal.

When I was arrested on December 5th in Houston, I spent the five days in Harris County Jail, then was transferred to Victoria County Jail, where I spent three months.

KW: I heard that the DA called you a "dangerous woman." Is that true? Who would you be dangerous to?

DW: The District Attorney in Calhoun County, Dan Heard, called me a "dangerous woman" during my trial and was speaking to the jury. I believe he said that because he thought my ideas were dangerous and that I had no fear of retaliation. He asked me once what they [the courts, the justice system] could do to make me stop fighting, and I told him there wasn't a thing they could do to stop me.

KW: Has anyone ever called you an eco-terrorist?

DW: Yes, when I was fighting Formosa Plastics' illegal discharge and attempted to sink my shrimp boat on top of the illegal discharge, the Coast Guard, who apprehended me and confiscated my shrimp boat, said I was a terrorist on the high seas. Another time, when I was trying to get DuPont to recycle their waste stream into the bay and I was on a 30-day hunger strike in front of their Delaware office, they said I was an eco-terrorist.

KW: You live in a community where many of your friends and relatives have died or are dying of cancer. What happened when you started to go to public hearings and speak up about the role of pollution in those cancers?

DW: At one meeting, a large delegation of politicians and industry leaders, the chamber of commerce, and the school system showed up. They said I was a fanatic and a nut and making stuff up. Or else I was a spy hired by Louisiana officials to disrupt economic development in Texas. A woman from the school district said she'd never heard of pollution causing cancer. She said her husband, who worked at Alcoa and died of cancer, got it because he was a smoker. Also the head of the American Cancer Society came down and urged me to *not* do a study on cancer in my community. He said if I *ever* contemplated doing a study I should call him first. He also showed me a copy of an *Earth First!* magazine and said I should bring down Earth First!ers and get them to protest (this was during the time that a bomb exploded in a car driven by Earth First!ers). He was trying to destroy my reputation in the community.

KW: I want to note that many times in your book you talk about the embryos and eggs of the shrimp and other sea life and how effluents from Formosa and Alcoa are killing them. Do you have any thoughts on the term "pro-life" that is so heavily used by Republicans and how that idea might apply to the situation where you are?

DW: I believe if the male of the species had babies there would be universal pro-choice. I think this idea of pro-life has more to do with control over the bodies and minds of women and is so hotly defended by the religious right because they consider the bodies of women and the body of the earth inherently evil. I don't think it is a coincidence that the killings at abortion clinics have sometimes been by Assembly of God (Pentecostal) members. I was raised Pentecostal so I've been a fly on that wall.

KW: When you were in jail in Victoria County, you wrote a letter to the Sheriff about deplorable conditions. You had several examples of terrible abuse by the withholding of medical treatment. The worst was the story of Shandra Williams. Can you tell that story briefly and also tell us your thoughts on how such a thing can happen in a Republican, "pro-life" state like Texas?

DW: I met Shandra on Christmas Eve after she had been picked up because she looked "suspicious." A year before, Shandra had been in the very same cell block after she had been picked up by the Victoria County cops for an outstanding warrant. Shandra was 6 or 7 months pregnant, and her file clearly stated that she was *not* to be picked up until after her delivery because she had a rare uterine condition and it was very problematic.

That mattered not a whit to the sheriff's department. The sheriff was running a re-election campaign and outstanding warrants don't look good on the campaign trail so in the cell she went. Due to the harsh conditions of cell life, Shandra's condition worsened and she started bleeding, but the guards and nurse said she was just trying to get out of jail and was a complainer and just wanted drugs, so she repeatedly had to "prove" her condition with a bloody pad. Eventually they stuck her in isolation, by herself, in a cold, cold room with nothing but a blue paper gown and a paper sheet. To keep her quiet they gave her Benedryl. Eventually she was placed back in the jail until her water broke, starting her labor. The nurse said she was hallucinating and trying to get drugs so they tried to place her back into isolation, which frightened Shandra. The guard said Shandra was going into isolation the "hard way or the easy way" and threatened to use the Taser on her. Fortunately, a startled guard gathered Shandra's belongings and got her into isolation before the guard tased her. Once in isolation again, Shandra went into labor. The baby was breech and started coming feet first. With a baby dangling to her knees, Shandra crawled about 60 feet to a call button and pressed it three times and yelled that she was in labor. Finally the guards and nurse arrived and they rushed her to the ambulance, but Shandra said her baby died en route.

In a state like Texas, unfortunately, there is no incongruence between stopping abortions and lack of health care for inmates. It's part of their disdain for all things that are "soft on crime." During the state Republican convention, the Attorney General and US Senate candidate John Cornyn joked about the differences between Republicans and Democrats. "If you've used the phrase 'protecting prisoners' rights,'" Cornyn said, "you might be a Democrat." Another Texas Attorney General noted Texas had big bad jails because they had big bad prisoners.

KW: What has been the effect of Hurricanes Katrina and Rita on the Gulf environment and the shrimpers and other fishermen?

DW: When Hurricane Katrina rolled in, the immediate impact was the Gulf of Mexico fisheries, and in fact the entire Gulf of Mexico was declared an official disaster. The Gulf of Mexico fisheries, especially the bays, were in dire straights before the hurricane, and now many are totally decimated. Another issue that will probably not be understood for a long time is the toll that pollution has taken on our gulf waters. Many, many chemical sites and waste sites were flooded. A man from my home town was working on a dredge boat that was doing salvage work near Beaumont and he dredged something up that triggered a heart attack. That's local knowledge but nothing the media knew about.

KW: Do you think the EPA is covering up the true extent of toxic contamination after the hurricanes?

DW: I have been involved in environmental issues for 17 years and in my opinion, the EPA and the chemical industry have been co-conspirators in their attempt to keep the extent of the pollution unknown. I had two investigators from the Texas state environmental agency give me internal documents about contamination, asking me to do something with it because they couldn't. There was a political bottleneck and nothing went higher up, they said.

KW: Turning back to your book, what made you think you wanted to write about it all?

DW: I am a closet writer. Always have been. I had a lot of anguish over my fight with Formosa and writing the story was the way I released it. I wasn't really thinking about publishing until I finished.

KW: Everyone who reads your story is overwhelmed by your courage and boldness. For instance, it must not have been easy being the first woman to run a shrimp boat by yourself. Was it the feminist movement that gave you the idea that you could do that?

DW: The feminist movement has not made it to the Gulf of Mexico. Never seen that movement. I became a boat captain because I loved the water and had been on a boat since I was eight. I captained the boat by myself because I liked being alone. Probably if I had a male deckhand on the boat he would have tried to gain control over the wheel. Running a boat isn't that hard. Just takes doing. Most or all women I ever knew were discouraged from running boats, but it was too late with me.

KW: Your father took you out shrimping as a youngster. Did he have a more liberated attitude? Did he encourage you to do a man's work?

DW: My daddy thought women were basically stupid, but he didn't mean that in a mean way. I was on the boat because I was good and I was a big help and I could patch nets and I could steer the boat without crying. It was a practical decision on my daddy's part.

KW: So what is it that gives you your strength?

DW: I am a mystic and am directed by an internal compass. I am not outer-directed.

KW: Tell me, what kind of dreams are you having these days?

DW: I was dreaming about my dead daddy. He was alive, he said, and couldn't I tell? He was making *coffee*—stupid!!!

Chapter 37

CRIMINALIZING ABORTION IN SOUTH CAROLINA: WHY DID GABRIELA FLORES GO TO JAIL?

By Michelle Bollinger

GABRIELA FLORES SAT IN a South Carolina jail for four months—just for having an abortion.

The 22-year-old immigrant farm worker and mother of three from Pelion, South Carolina, became pregnant and took Misoprostol, a medicine that is used in RU-486, to terminate her pregnancy. Flores' sister sent her the Cytotec tablets from Mexico.

Flores is charged with violating a state ban on "illegal" abortions—a law that is supposed to protect women from back-alley abortionists, not to send them to jail for having one. If convicted, Flores could face prison time and a costly fine.

Flores' case reflects a new level of madness among the anti-abortion bigots. According to a May 1 article in *The State* newspaper, state officials initially tried to charge Flores with murder—with the hope of seeking the death penalty, a source later said.

Eventually, this den of crackpots realized that a murder rap wouldn't stick—so the charges were reduced to the illegal abortion charge.

But no one can explain why Flores spent four months in jail with no assistance.

"I don't know how anyone could be forgotten like that," said Angela Hooton of the National Latina Institute for Reproductive Health.

The Flores case sharply reflects the racism, sexism and anti-immigrant fervor that South Carolina officials are known for. In 2001, South Carolina convicted a 24-year-old African-American woman, Regina McKnight, with homicide after her baby was stillborn—blaming her drug use for the death. She was sentenced to twenty years in prison.

And far from supporting a so-called "culture of life," Lexington County where Flores lives sends more people to the state's death row than any other county in the state.

A STATE WITHOUT CHOICE

Leading politicians, from Democrat Hillary Clinton to Republican Bill Frist, drone on and on about how "rare" they think abortion should be.

South Carolina grants them their wish. It is one of the most difficult places in the United States to obtain an abortion.

NARAL Pro Choice America granted the state an F in its 2004 report, "Who Decides? The Status of Women's Reproductive Rights in the United States." In South Carolina, 87% of counties have no abortion provider; married women are subject to a husband consent law; the state imposes biased counseling and mandatory delays on women seeking abortions and requires that only physicians perform abortions.

Flores' case illustrates the human cost of these restrictions. Estimated to have been sixteen weeks pregnant at the time, Flores could not have even gotten a surgical abortion in South Carolina.

Instead, she would have had to travel two-and-a-half hours away to Charlotte, North Carolina, just to receive services. Flores would have had to miss at least two days of work, jeopardizing her job as a migrant worker.

And to top it off—the cost for an abortion at that stage is around $700—essentially eliminating this as an option for Flores, who brought home about $150 a week picking lettuce at Rawls Farm in Pelion, SC. Her job did not provide medical benefits—denying her a full range of options in dealing with her pregnancy.

It's no wonder, then, that Flores used misoprostol, an over-the-counter medication that is inexpensive and easy to acquire in Mexico. So now, she faces imprisonment.

Jail time for trying to exercise her right to choose abortion—this is the real tragedy involving abortion today.

When Democratic Party politicians talk about seeking "common ground" with anti-choice bigots and—as Hillary Clinton has—condemn abortion as a "tragic choice," they aid in the criminalization of women like Gabriela Flores. Flores' story shames both Democratic Party politicians and the pro-choice lobbying groups that fund them.

But it is stories like these that illustrate the urgency behind building a new, grassroots movement to stop these attacks on our rights.

Chapter 38

WAR BREEDS STRANGER BEDFELLOWS: CLIMATE CHANGE IN ALABAMA, POLITICALLY

By David Underhill

MARCH, 2007

It's the wrong time of year for swooping Vs of migrating geese to be landing in Mobile. But that's what it sounded like for three hours on Saturday afternoon, March 17, 2007 at a midtown Mobile park as a honking chorus of support sprang from passing cars. While thousands marched on the Pentagon that day, dozens of familiar faces from Citizens for Peace and the Mobile chapter of Veterans for Peace, plus several new folks, lined the perimeter of the park with a generally welcomed anti-war poster parade.

When W launched his war on Iraq four years ago, the air around this park was thick with hostility. Some drivers stopped in the street to scream curses and call us traitors. Now it appears the majority are traitors, although most of Alabama's supposed representatives in congress continue to shuffle along in a zombie conga line behind their Pied Piper.

A year ago this same park was the first pause on a national Veterans for Peace march that began in downtown Mobile and ended in New Orleans. Their banners and buttons said: Every Bomb Dropped on Iraq Explodes Along the Gulf Coast. The march called on America to devote its talents and resources to rebuilding the hurricane wreckage instead of wrecking another country.

This year Veterans for Peace came to that park again. In mid-March a caravan began at Ft. Bragg in North Carolina en route to a volunteer rebuilding project in the zone still lying in ruins a year and a half after Katrina. They stopped at several military bases along the way.

After spending Saturday the 24th at civil rights history sites in Montgomery, they pulled into the Mobile park about noon on Sunday. The caravan comprised a motorcycle, several cars, and two painted busses: one festooned in American flag colors, the other in doves hovering around scenes and poems of peace.

The usual crew from Veterans and Citizens for Peace was there to greet them. Reinforced by the caravanistas, we lined the edge of the park with signs and received the usual response of honks, answered this time by rumbling basso blasts from the busses' horns.

Then we shepherded the caravan through west Mobile's mallville sector, giving agog shoppers something to contemplate besides bargain sales of shoddy merchandise. The destination was the Mobile office of Rep. Jo Bonner, where the caravan would picket with us for a couple hours before departing for their reconstruction project.

Bonner has fervently endorsed W's every shifting explanation of the reasons for the Iraq war, every appropriation he desires, and every escalation that sends more soldiers to be maimed and killed—while claiming to Support the Troops. And the congressman is not inclined to meet with people who think otherwise.

In July of 2006 Citizens for Peace began calling his Mobile office requesting a meeting. But somehow he could never find time to talk about stopping a war, although his grinning face often appeared in the news convening with others throughout his district about all manner of other topics.

Then a couple of weeks ago, after nine months of mulling whether he ought to speak with those he represents, his mental womb labored and brought forth a finger capable of dialing the president of Citizens for Peace. But he reached her on the job at a moment when she couldn't halt to talk with him. So we didn't know whether he was calling to offer an appointment or to fudge and dither further.

Besides, after waiting since July without a response from Bonner, we'd already decided to go to his office with Veterans for Peace. Nobody would likely be inside on a Sunday, but we figured that didn't matter, since he hadn't met with us on any other days either.

We hoisted signs along the street in front of the office complex housing his suite. The bus horns echoed the familiar serenade from passing vehicles.

The picketers included Vivian Beckerle, who ran as the Democratic candidate against Bonner in the 2006 election. Also present was a resident of a FEMA trailer from the swath of Katrina waste along the shore south of the city.

Her involvement with last years' Mobile to New Orleans march by Veterans for Peace had brought her into contact with various local groups working on hurricane recovery and environmental issues. They later helped her gather materials and volunteers to begin rebuilding her ruined house. As a result of all these links, she left church early to join the others at Rep. Bonner's office that Sunday.

Her individual story is an emblem of what's happening statewide, slowly but steadily. As the war in Iraq continues and bulges toward Iran, as it consumes ever more lives and money, as local needs are neglected to nourish imperial urges, people who scarcely knew each other previously and rarely or never worked together are now doing so.

Their loose coalitions are coming together stitch by stitch. And the consequences of this are becoming evident in the political maneuvers at the capitol in Montgomery.

This is merely a trend, hardly a movement with momentum yet. But, like global warming, it could be inching toward a tipping point. Then the honkers driving by will stop and join the pickets.

We gathered into an irregular column and threaded through the complex to the locked door of Bonner's dark quarters. The tinted glass of the door had a mail slot.

In went an Appeal for Redress brochure about the legal right of military personnel to convey their views to their representatives in congress. It calls for "…the prompt withdrawal of all American military forces and bases from Iraq. Staying in Iraq will not work and is not worth the price. It is time for U.S. troops to come home."

The slot was also wide enough for one hand to enter. In went a rolled up poster. By an act of prestidigitation the hand unrolled the poster and fluttered it face up to the floor. From outside its bold lettering was legible: DROP BONNER, NOT BOMBS.

Chapter 39

INSIDE THE TEXAS DEATH HOUSE: A CRUEL AND UNUSUAL REALITY

By Lily Hughes

"I DIDN'T DO IT." Those were the words that Michael Dewayne Johnson scrawled in his own blood as he died from a self-inflicted slashed neck—hours before he was scheduled to be put to death in the Texas death chamber.

Johnson's horrific suicide highlights the physical and mental cruelty inflicted on the men and women on death row in America's execution capital.

Since the reinstatement of capital punishment in 1977, Texas has accounted for over one-third of all executions carried out in the U.S. The number of executions throughout the U.S. and in Texas gas been on a downward trend for the past several years, but the Texas execution machine still runs at an assembly-line pace, with one execution running up against another some months.

Johnson was to be the 22nd execution victim in Texas this year—put to death for a murder that he insisted was committed by another man charged in the crime, who testified against Johnson and is free today after serving eight years in prison.

But in the face of this barbarism, death row prisoners in Texas are organizing against brutal and inhumane conditions. Six prisoners are on a hunger strike that is close to a month old, and another group—which calls itself DRIVE, or Death Row Inner-Communalist Vanguard Engagement—is gaining recognition for its campaign of resistance from on death row.

Much of the grievances are focused on conditions on the Polunsky Unit—the "state-of-the-art" prison in Livingston, Texas, where death row was moved in 1999. In the new facility, inmates live in 23-hour administrative segregation inside 60-square-foot cells with sealed steel doors.

They have lost all group recreation, work programs, television access and religious services. There are also no contact visits allowed at Polunsky. Prisoners are only allowed one five-minute phone call every six months, their mail is often censored, the quality of food is low, and they have inadequate health and dental services.

This intolerable situation has prompted some prisoners to organize for better conditions—and to link their fight to the larger struggle against the death penalty.

The five DRIVE members—Kenneth Foster Jr., Rob Will, Gabriel Gonzalez, Reginald Blanton and Da'mon Simpson—say in their Web site statement that they are committed to "non-violently protest against this inhumane scheme called the Death Penalty."

Protest tactics include distributing literature, addressing their issues with guards, and occupying day rooms, showers and visitation chambers. Prisoners are encouraged to protest on days when executions are scheduled, and to protest against their own executions by refusing to walk to the van that takes them to the Ellis Unit, where executions still take place; refusing last meals; and refusing to walk to the execution chamber.

As Gabriel Gonzalez puts it in his diary, "Many times, we have addressed the problems with conditions and suggested reasonable solutions to the problems, which would not cause any breaches in the security of the prison, nor cost the state any money—but to no avail, because our verbal and written grievances fell on the deaf, indifferent ears of a sadistic administration that enjoys torturing and treating us like any thing but human.

"Yet how do you physically, psychologically and spiritually torture and treat people like animals and expect them to act civil and humane? Those of us here who still have a sense of self and humanity have had enough of the state-induced carnage and the brutal rape of our human rights and constitutional rights! Therefore, with this nonviolent protest, we have drawn a line and decided to physically and nonviolently resist the oppression."

Meanwhile, six other death row prisoners went on hunger strike on October 5. The men—Travis Runnels, Steven Woods, Richard Cobb, Kevin Watts, Justin Hall and Stephen Moody—went without food until January 1.

"For the past several years, I and a few hundred others have been living out what can easily be called a nightmare," explained Steven Woods. "After the injustice of being sentenced to death by a corrupt legal system, we are shorn of our dignity and our identity, caged and treated like animals. We spend these years stored in the Polunsky Unit in a segregated housing facility that has been designed to house over 500 people in a complete indefinite isolation."

The hunger strikers' demands include better meals, cell maintenance, adequate health care and proper hygienic and laundry necessities. They are also calling for a halt to the excessive punitive measures used against death row prisoners, especially those making protests.

One of the worst retaliatory practices used on protesting prisoners is gassing. Prisoners occupying day rooms and other areas are met by SWAT teams that use tear gas and pepper spray to remove them.

One of the hunger strikers, Steven Woods was gassed on October 9. "A smoke grenade was dropped on the outside yard, which filled it to the top with smoke," DRIVE member Kenneth Foster wrote in his diary. "Steve endured that, and no less than 10 minutes later, another was dropped...My god, we thought they'd killed him. All this for a man who weighs 140 pounds. This was an overuse of chemical agent. I truly believe they are trying to kill us with the gas."

That these prisoners are wiling to endure this abuse to fight for their basic human rights should be a wake-up call to the people of Texas and to the world. They need our support.

"We are neither violent or passive," writes Foster. "We are combative. We are resisters. We are diverse activists, but more than anything else may we be looked upon as men that embraced the sacredness of life and sought to assert the full measure of their humanity in the face of those that would seek to destroy it."

Chapter 40

BORN AGAIN: CAN KING'S LEGACY BE RECLAIMED FROM ITS ABUSERS?

By Kevin Alexander Grey

EVERY YEAR THIS TIME people pull out Martin Luther King's "I Have a Dream" or "Mountaintop" speeches with corresponding video footage. Generally speaking, King is presented at two times in his life, at the beginning and end of his career and life. Rarely is there a discussion or education on his beliefs.

King's image is misused by just about everybody. So much so there needs to be a rescue operation to save his legacy and the civil rights agenda. Politicians throw King or "civil rights" in a sentence and they're done. In the aftermath of the Trent Lott confession, white politicians—Republican and Democratic—have fallen all over themselves to say they are for "civil rights." Presidential candidate and North Carolina Senator John Edwards said he was for "civil rights" which could mean either "I like black people" or "I want black votes."

Whites are not alone in the misuse. Many blacks think King's image or a King-like speech substitutes for substance. Here in South Carolina in the past campaign year, the Democrats mailed out flyers with a picture of King on one side and it's two statewide black candidates on the other. Under the King picture were the words "Someone we can trust." Steve Benjamin, the candidate for state Attorney General (one of the men pictured on the King mailer) ran as a pro-gun, pro-death penalty, tough on crime conservative. He said he would further limit paroles in a state where the adult prison population is 65% black and the youth population is 85% black. He traveled to Charleston on Labor

Day to speak to workers but refused to support the right of garbage workers to bargain collectively. How's that for irony given that King died while organizing garbage workers?

As for the hip-hop generation, they are often chided for being irreverent of King and unfeeling towards the civil rights struggle as well as what civil rights means. Not being one for idolatry, I am not upset with Cedric the Entertainer's jibs in the movie *Barbershop* nor did I agree with the calls to have the Jesse Jackson, Rosa Parks and King comments cut from the movie. Still, as I watched the movie and heard the King quip I thought, Robert Kennedy, J. Edgar Hoover and the FBI spent thousands of dollars and man hours to destroy this man even suggesting he kill himself over his infidelity. So, is the hip-hop generation movie promoting the government's and haters' line or just "flippin the script?"

Some argue that King supporters accept him flaws and all, which was the point of the controversial *Barbershop* scene. King was not perfect but he lead a great movement. I would like to believe that blacks are more forgiving than most. Still, we can't expect a movie whose primary purpose is to entertain—to educate.

Politicians and movies aside, what King was trying to accomplish still needs doing. In "Where do we go from here" King said "the movement must address itself to the question of restructuring the whole of American society " or, in preacher terms, "America must be born again!" His 1967 speech is clear as to where we are today and why. He reminds us "the problem of racism, the problem of economic exploitation and the problem of war are all tied together. These are the triple evils that are interrelated."

Clearly, the goal of the human and civil rights movement remains far undone. The sad reality is that at this point there is no movement and no organization at the grassroots level to make a movement happen. That's not to say a movement isn't on the horizon but it's going to take building. And in both movements and wars, old people send young people do most of the marching, fighting and dying. And the hip-hoppers of color will die in George Bush's war in greater numbers than most. So, building a peace movement is in their interest. It's a matter of life or death, freedom or imprisonment, ignorance or transformation and enlightenment.

As for where King might be on war with Iraq—in 1968, King entertained running as an independent candidate for president with Dr. Benjamin Spock as Vice-president to oppose the Vietnam War. King supported peace. He was against killing. So maybe amidst the misuse and cynicism there is room for optimism as opposition to war is high in the black community. In the 2002 National Opinion Poll of African Americans conducted by David Bositis of the Joint Center for Political and Economic Studies, less that 19 percent of blacks supported going to war with Iraq. The poll highlights the economy and employment as the main concerns of blacks.

As was King's mission we must organize the just and peaceful society. Those seeking peace should oppose all other forms of state-sponsored killing to include the death penalty.

Environmentalism is a peace option. It means being against the production of nuclear bomb material at the Savannah River Plant here in South Carolina.

A peace and justice agenda involves transforming a society where one in three black men are under some type of criminal justice supervision. Being for peace means being against the "war on drugs." That is unless we want that ratio to be 4 out of 4?

When you are for peace you reject the exploitation of workers and the corporate-manufactured (and most often racist) animosities between them. It means the rejection of unjust social, political and economic conditions that lead to war, death, hurt or exploitation.

So, where do we go from here? First, the task to restructure must be fought at every level but most importantly at the grassroots level using a variety of tactics and methods. We can't all just go off to a big march in Washington or a march once a year on King's birthday and that's it. From here on out we have to muster the resources to run and support candidates with a human rights agenda. We have to do local teach-ins, start freedom schools and create structures to challenge government, status quo politics and inhumane policies. It means thinking differently about things and helping others to do the same. It means changing values. Fundamentally, restructuring means dismantling white privilege and supremacy.

Now, more than ever, we must educate the public not just about King, but what he believed in and what we all claim to believe in when we raise him name up. We must organize and make change happen. We live in dangerous times. If we don't mobilize, our children's lives, our lives and future is in peril. We must act.

Chapter 41

EAT, FIGHT, FUCK, PRAY:
AN INTERVIEW WITH JOE BAGEANT

By Joshua Frank

JOE BAGEANT IS AUTHOR of *Deer Hunting With Jesus: Dispatches from America's Class War* published by Random House Crown. Here he speaks with Joshua Frank about his controversial book, religion, rednecks and what it's like to serve beer to an underage horse.

Joshua Frank: So Joe, what the hell is going on with the redneck strain of the working class anyway? Why do they seem more apt to embrace evangelism rather than a labor union? Is it, as psychologists would say, learned helplessness?

Joe Bageant: Well, Josh, that's a pretty broad brush you're painting with there. In fact, it's too broad to be answered, but that will not stop me from responding with my usual shrillness and tin drum noise punctuated by flatulence. Let me start by saying the term redneck does not apply especially to southerners. I have found indigenous redneck culture and communities in Maine, Oregon Kansas, New York, Massachusetts, and California ... in virtually every state and in large numbers. Among loggers, cowboys, Poles, Germans, and even Latino rednecks.

Really. Don't you think beer and low riders and macho sports aesthetic of Latinos, the heterosexual, patriotic Jesus focused Catholic is that much different from their Jesus focused Baptist Dixie and Midwestern counterparts? The low riders of LA are the same as beer and muscle cars of the south. In fact the first rednecks were probably the striking miners at the Ludlow, Colorado massacre, who wore red bandanas and were seen as tough, surly, angry working class people who had to be kept down. The sun on the neck definition is another more recent one that got applied especially to Southerners, during the civil rights era I suppose.

We have been taught to use these ethnic, regional and racial labels to cover up the real issue in America that the rich want keep hidden another 200 years—that we are a classist country. That one class owns pretty much the whole country these days and that all the rest are left to suck hind tit and pretend they are all members of something called "the middle class." The only real middle class is that thin layer of commissars, lawyers, teachers, journalists, and other caterers to the empire, those people necessary to manage it and count the beans, dumb down the kids and lock up enough people to keep the privatized gulags in business.

Anyway, I assume you are referring the heartland white working class people who attend fundamentalist churches. Ever since around 1800 about one-third of white America has been fundamentalist Christians, about one-third of Americans have had a born again experience. The thing that is different now is that these churches have access to political power. They were welcomed across the church-state wall of separation by cynical GOP strategists to whom giving the Republicans another chance to sack Washington, loot the national kitty and maybe pull off a good oil raid in the Middle East, was more important than our Constitution. Now that they've let John Calvin's wooly beast into to tent, we find it chewing on the Constitution and generally stinking up the joint—it's not going to leave without a fight.

As to the last parts of your question: When it comes to embracing the church instead of a labor union, I can remember a time when the churches stood behind the labor unions. Have we learned to be helpless? Man, we are helpless. Capitalist conditioning has replaced citizenship with consumerism. I mean, what are we doing? I write a book so the global publishing chain of Bertelsmann makes more money. There are far better alternatives. We could grab some axe handles and heat up the tar bucket and start to burn some shit down. That still works you know.

JF: I've always thought that'd work.

JB: But we won't. Because we are all programmed to participate through purchase, whether it is my book at Barnes and Noble or the software that enables us to read *CounterPunch*. Or choose the candidate that has been preselected and purchased in advance by the people who have essentially made Americans into a nation of iPod implanted pizza drivers and well dressed lawn jockeys sitting in front of monitors on the empire's electronic plantations.

JF: So how can we change this political myopia?

JB: Our involvement with politics, our political lives, are merely as spectators who listen to commercials for three years before the magical moment before we "cast our vote" by simply going shopping in the tiniest shopping space of all—the voting booth—with the most limited choices possible that can still be called a choice: two twin parties whose parents, the corporations, have to display them against different colored backgrounds so people can get a clue as to their difference. ("I am for fighting the war until the last dog is dead," as opposed to "I am for pulling the troops out, but not until a few hundred thousand more dogs are dead. I don't wanna be seen as weak on the dead dog thing." Or my favorite, "We can't leave now or there will be chaos." What the fuck is it we have created there now?) Right now the owning class Westchester Country Club Democrats is offering us two flavors, Hillary Clinton (bitter vanilla) and Barack Obama (mocha hope.)

Soooo ... What's going on politically with the great beery redneck nation? Nothing. We don't think about politics until the last half hour before time to vote. Then a sort of a heartburn grips our chests, and all the negative campaign ads, and the sound of Bill O'Reilly's voice and last night's beer and bratwurst and Hillary's stern beady eyes drill in on us ... preachers call down lightening bolts and fighter planes do a double roll over the desert ... then suddenly an acidic clot curdles in our throat, we close our eyes and we projectile vomit all our fears and suspicions and prejudices and state injected messages in the direction of the party making the most noise right up until the last minute. That's what we do down here.

What do ya'll do?

JF: Well, I grew up in Montana with rednecks aplenty. Most of my own family is made up of small farmers and poor German sharecroppers who were forced to move to the little towns in the area because of the onset of industrial agriculture. They lost the land they worked. Most of them are still proud rednecks. I respect the work ethic, but not all the close-minded culture that goes along with it. Up in Big Sky country, folks know politicians lie, so they put their trust in God instead.

Pick up trucks. Gun racks. Elk hunting. Beer drinking. It's a way of life there. I enjoy most of it. It takes some pretty damn rough times before people stand up and say, enough is enough! You'd think they'd be screaming from the mountaintops by now. But they haven't because they don't think they can do a damn thing about their lot. And that's where you get a lot of that anti-government sentiment. The Freeman and the Unabomber. It resonates quite well. As it should. The state doesn't stand up for the little guy, but for the big corporations with all their subsidies and bailouts, and they know it. The elites, however, always seem to capitalize off of their collective weakness—mainly our inability to stand up in the face of power.

JB: I lived in northern Idaho for years and had a lot of truck with Montanans like yourself. And to me they are among the best people in this country, tough uncomplaining people, kinda like Southerners, but with far less racism (unless you happen to be an Indian in some cases). Once when I was trending bar on the reservation, a Montana cowboy led his horse right into the place and demanded a beer for his steed. He had been drunk for two days, driving south toward New Mexico with his horse trailer, down from Alberta, Canada, and was obviously looking for a good old time tension-releasing brawl. "Well sir," I told him. "That horse ain't old enough to drink." "That horse is 18," he replied. I peeled back the horse's lips and checked his teeth. I had horses of my own and knew how to check their age. "That horse is nine years old," I said. "Just about the age a good cow pony starts getting some real sense." He threw back his head and laughed. The situation was defused and we sat there in the Bald Eagle Bar, you'd like that place, and we jawed until closing time. A good, tough, brave man of the kind America doesn't make anymore. Tipped me ten dollars, then went off to wrap himself in a blanket and sleep in his truck until first light.

At the same time though, there is a belief in authority, a reverence even, that is so typically American. America has never been a nation of true dissenters. Even during the Sixties. You're damn young. Don't let the old newsreels fool you. You gotta remember that when those kids were gunned down at Kent State, one half of America was cheering and an even larger portion did not give a shit. But the footage was so shocking, and we actually had a rather liberal media back then, and so, like Twin Towers footage, it was shown over and over and written about until the message finally soaked in. But Americans for the most part are on the side of their own oppressor and like it that way. Heartland Americans were happy when the working man was shot down at Ludlow, and happy when the Bohunk and Pollack miners were gunned down at the Latimer mines (again, the rewriters of history have made it seem otherwise). The good people of the heartland were happy with the kangaroo courts that framed and murdered Joe Hill and Sacco and Venzetti. And today they are happy when they see police in black Kevlar beating down young radicals in Seattle and old Jewish women in Miami protesting turning that city into a free trade zone labor gulag.

JF: Your book has been put out by a major publishing house. As you note, Random House is in the business of making money, and I'm assuming they wanted to make your book palatable to the run-of-the-mill liberal audience. What was that process like?

JB: For lefties it can be infuriating. My publisher, Random House, is owned by owned by Bertelsmann, the former Nazi German publisher that made massive profits from Jewish slave labor and published anti-Jewish propaganda for Hitler. It also owns Doubleday, Bantam, and a slew of other media around the world. So today we see the irony of scores of Jewish editors etc working for Bertelsmann, but this time instead of tattoos, they are sporting blackberries, worrying about theater tickets and treating their Salvadorian nannies like shit.

Anyway, big publishers like Random House roll the ball right down the middle of the aisle looking for a strike to sell the most books to the broad middle class. No leftie gutter balls. Let Seven Stories have'em. On the other hand, Crown publishes Anne Coulter, which tells you something about the real middle road and what sells. Everyone must do that to keep their jobs and climb the ladder of the company, which constitutes the corporate brand allegiance that is their lives, livelihood and personal identity in the Empire. Their lives are the brand. The brand is their lives. As in, "I am an editor at Harper Collins, the one who did the Martini Book of Common Wisdom," or "Hillary's book," or whatever.

At one end, you have the editors, many of whom care about the life of the mind but have internalized capitalist market driven values, and thus feel courageous when they really are not. At the other end you have the company management, who see all books merely as units. Naturally, in a system like that, the pull is always rightward toward profit driven and non-risky thinking. Consequently, the American reading public for idea based books, which is small as hell, thinks it is expanding its knowledge through reading when they buy books, when actually, all most want to do is see their viewpoints reaffirmed. But what really happens is that they are drawn more rightward by the narrowness of available choices in a marketplace that loves the homogeneity and standardization of thought which makes marketing much easier.

In all fairness though, I would be the first to say that a publisher like Random House seems to put energy, resources and talent behind you, once they are committed. Frankly, they put in more than I really care to deal with sometimes. But when I hear the horror stories of some very good writers working with small publishers and their limited resources, I know I have been fortunate that way. Lucky to have the editor, publicist and agent I have. Most writers would kill for what sort of landed in my lap, given that I was not looking to write a book in the first place. I try not to be an ingrate, but at the same time I am not at all impressed with this stuff. I might have been at your youthful age, but not now. Thankfully, it has come too late. It's rather like a beautiful woman coming to the bed of an 85-year old man. Delightful to behold, but no distraction from the path that took so long to hew through the jungle of false thinking and ill-focused passions.

I had the good standard middle class New York Jewish editor. She had the job of reconciling my cranky agrarian based redneck leftist thinking with the publishing environment and the marketplace as it is. I am a rather uncontrolled writer given to free association and distracting rants. When it comes to something as long as a book, I absolutely need an editor for guidance. Someone to say, "That sucks. It's unreadable," and make suggestions. Without her work, it would not be getting the glowing reviews it is getting so far.

Writer/editor relationships can get very personal as you know, and we had class issues, given was the chasm between our backgrounds. But I must say the editor made every effort to bridge that gap, once she got around to my book, when, at times, I simply refused to. Mostly when drunk and depressed by the glacial process by which books are published. To compound matters, time was running out for me. I was very ill with my lung disease at the time and was diagnosed as having about 18 months to live, which turned out to be somewhat wrong; I've got a few more years in me yet. So here I was sneezing blood, working 55 hours a week at a straight gig, and trying to write a book too while my editor had put me on the back burner so she could work on Barack Obama's book. Needless to say, I was a very miserable camper during much of the process.

At the same time, the entire grisly process brought my editor and I closer together as human beings, and I now consider her among my good friends, even if our backgrounds have forever conditioned us in different directions. I shudder for the fate of her children in this world.

JF: What do the folks of your town, of which you write so frankly, think about the book?

JB: Not much so far. The working class people in the book, who never buy or read books at all, seem rather mystified when someone exposes them to parts of it. They relish figuring out who is who and generally agree with its message about class in America. The town's old families are pissed. Some have called me. One asked why I wrote such "mean things about this town's leading families." Leading families! Can you imagine that? Another told me there is "no such thing as class in Winchester. We are all happy and equal." I just about choked on that one. They tell me the local newspaper is oiling up its guns for an attack. And some upper crust family is bound to try and sue me.

JF: So when is this class war you write about going to come to a head, or has it already? Will there ever be a true class revolt in the United States, or will any sort of militant dissent be stopped dead in its tracks?

JB: I don't think that will ever happen, but that doesn't mean we shouldn't keep up the fight. I think so-called terrorism and ecocide may tear down the system for us, though. Danger has no favorites. The good old days of "the teeming masses," that sweat soaked, beer farting mob of working class Americans who didn't have a pot to piss in, much less a credit card, but instinctively knew fascism when they saw it, are over. Seattle in 1999 may not happen in the states again. We have all become an artificial product of corporately "administrated" modern life.

Chapter 42

A FERAL DOG HOWLS IN HARVARD YARD: HANG THE PROFESSORS BUT SAVE THE EUNUCHS FOR LATER

By Joe Bageant

It is time to close America's universities, and perhaps prosecute the professoriat under the RICO act as a corrupt and racketeering-influenced organization. American universities these days have the moral character of electronic churches, and as little educational value. They are an embarrassment to civilization.
—Fred Reed, American expatriate writer and "equal-opportunity irritant."

IF THERE IS ONE bright spot in the bleak absurdity of slogging along in our new totalist American state, it is that ordinary working Americans are undisciplined as hell. We are genuine moral and intellectual slobs whose consciousness is pretty much glued onto an armature of noise, sports, sex, sugar and saturated fats. Oh, we nod toward the government bullhorns of ideology, even throw beer cans and cheer when told we are winning some war or Olympic sports event. But when it comes right down to it, we could generally give a rat's ass about government institutions and are congenitally more skeptical of government than most nations, especially nations that get things like good teeth and free higher education for their tax dollars.

Surely, there are governmental facts of life no working American can escape, like the IRS, but no ordinary person is dumb enough to actually trust political parties, banks, the courts or the news media. Born with the organizational instincts and global awareness of a box turtle, we take the most torpid political path—we call it all bullshit, pay lip service, vote occasionally, then forget about our government altogether until April 15th of the next year.

As inhabitants (you couldn't really call what we practice citizenship) of a nation that is essentially one big workhouse/shopping compound, American life is simultaneously both easy for us and rather dangerous to the rest of the world. For instance, when the corporate state's CBS-ABC-CBS-FOX-NBC-XYZ television bullhorns told us some warthog named Saddam Hussein blew up the World Trade Center and probably fixed the NFL ratings too, Tony the electrician said, "Well, OK then. Sure, go ahead and bomb the fucker." Then he flicked to the Home and Garden Channel, where the guy in the plaid shirt is explaining how to get a skylight installed without leaking. Thanks to American industrial molecular science, there's yet another new sticky stuff miracle from DuPont, a tube of which costs about as much as the entire friggin roof. After the obligatory DuPont public relations sponsored tour of the plant where the goo is cooked up, plaid shirt guy gives "application instructions," meaning he tells you how to squirt it out of the tube. And somewhere along the line, between the plant tour and watching the goo dry, Tony gave "informed consent" to the war in Iraq without even knowing it, or for that matter, giving a shit.

This sort of life has its advantages, such as never having to analyze the institutions that manage us—not that we'd know how even if we cared to. That's what television is for. Right? Given our short attention spans, compliments of the business state's 100-channel national nerve system (three minutes into the show and the blonde hasn't taken her bra off or killed anybody yet, CLICK!) diversion fills the void of understanding as a nation of clueless mooks knocks around the new American emptiness, wandering the mall food courts, and maybe half-heartedly looking for a pair of size XXXL 50-inch waist long wicking NBA shorts (they actually make 'em), but generally is just bored.

But hold yer drawers there, hoss, because we nevertheless do possess a seed of existential angst, however tiny, this despite the liberal intellectual managing class' and leftist profs' claims to the contrary. And that makes us potentially unmanageable politically speaking, potentially dangerous even (it's the length of the fuse that is deceiving.) We may be being lead around by our stomachs and our dicks with our eyes taped shut, but we're not total ideological slaves yet. Because even the worst ideology requires at least a modicum of thought, and as a people with no authentic intellectual culture, we haven't enough collective intellect or education these days to pull it off.

Meanwhile, when it comes to pulling off, that small American class in charge of all things intellectual are doing just that, jerking off a whole nation. Admittedly, it's an unenviable job, but there are people selfless enough to do it. These poor intellectual bastards constitute the most servile class in America—the Empire's house slaves. It is their job to maintain the semblance of ideological control over the pizza gobbling herd (America eats 126 acres of pizza a day!) for the Corporate States of America, which entertains no breach of official ideology, that collection of clichés and things that sound as if they ought to be true, according to our mercantile mythology and conditioning. So it is the American intellectual's gig to weave some philosophical and ideological basket of American Truth out of mercantile folklore and smoke in such a way as to appear to hold water when viewed at great distance by the squinting millions out there in the burboclaves, office campuses, construction sites and fried chicken joints. If the result were not so abysmally eye glazing, tedious and predictable, it would be an act of pure alchemy, truly spinning gold from chaff, turning mud bricks into bullion. Like we said, somebody's gotta do it, but the question remains as to why anyone would choose to. Answer: It beats working.

> *"Blessed are the thinking classes, for theirs is the kingdom of tenure."*
>
> —Jesus to the Boston University Philosophy Department

Though they never admit it, and especially to each other, these professors, book editors, intellectual critics, and social and economic "theorists" are very class conscious, privileged and understand that they occupy their desk chairs at the pleasure of The Corporation. You don't have to stand back very far to see they have been the spin masters of the business class from the outset, and have either held America together, or kept the fuck job going from the beginning, depending upon the class from which you are viewing American history.

Of course they are only human. Like any group of people with a class advantage, they prefer to keep on drinking cognac and pissing it out upstream from the rest of the Pepsi swilling herd destined for bladder cancer. So this class sticks together, despite its prissy intellectual disputes in journals and critical publications. They produce "criticism" for the for the *New York Times*

Book Review, or *The National Review,* etc., which, though it may even be lively at times, and often full of that vacuous wit that garden variety liberals so love because it revolves around a few threadbare names and dead ideas they learned during their college days or masters degree indoctrination.

But the thinking classes' main job is to serve as intellectual hit men for the ruling elites, the business class, which doesn't come all that hard for them, having been all stamped out of the same dough on the Corporate system's university conveyor belt. Most are utterly convinced they are original and think-· ing for themselves, which in the university scheme of things means absorbing vast amounts of text, fermenting it in some sort of a second stomach and regurgitating it as a concentrated cud, supposedly unique because they alone coughed it up. The few who understand that this in no way resembles original thought usually keep mum, and keep their jobs in publishing or academia. Or flee screaming in despair once·they figure out what is going on.

Then too, there is a huge number for whom America's university system is a sheltered workshop; people who simply could not survive in the real working world, which, miserable as it may be, nevertheless demands a modicum of practicality and some scant ability to socialize. I once dated a university professor with a doctorate in linguistics who, honest to god, let her Irish wolfhound shit all over the house and completely destroy every piece of furniture in her place until she was forced to sleep in the attic crawlspace in a sleeping bag, and actually did not understand why nobody ever accepted her dinner party invitations. She was not, by the way, brilliant or eccentric. Just completely helpless and out of it in her own little corner of academic goo-goo-land. Yet out there on the plains of Washington State University hers was a reasonably respected intellect.

Now you can skin the cat (or that goddamned wolfhound) any way you choose, but if you want to be a really respected intellectual, you must serve business and power. You must serve the only apparatus capable of allowing you exposure enough to make a lunge at respect, which after all, merely amounts to being allowed to create something scientifically useful to the Empire's goals, or in other cases, achieve that weird localized hothouse plant celebrity as an intellectual one finds on every campus. Either way, you'll never make as much money as say, Ann Coulter, who is infinitely more useful to the Empire and the business class that runs it than any intellectual can ever hope to be.

PISTOL WHIPPED WITH THE "BUSINESS END" OF A GOOD EDUCATION

The United States has the most obsessive business class in the world. This would be no big deal if it did not direct the minds of the nation's population thorough its public relations indoctrination industry. This is a matter of life and death for the financial pickle vendors, sub-prime mortgage shysters and CitiBank, Morgan Stanley and other high financiers who have come to actually own this country. There is only one threat to their empire of debt: people acting in the interests of ordinary society—which in the rest of the world is known as socialism. Consequently, we have no socialist politicians and no socialist journalists in our entire press and media, which is simply unimaginable in most civilized places like Europe. It is important that the working class thinks it has the self-determination they learned about in high school civics classes designed in the universities, that they feel any kind of individual power at all, which basically comes down the tepid power of consumer choice, which makes them malleable, and intolerant of any voice that suggests otherwise. But if even one iota of class awareness were allowed to flourish here, well, much of the American business class and the entire Yale University faculty would be hiding out in Argentina.

Without class interests and class awareness there can be no genuine politics or political parties. So, to the everlasting relief of the business classes, and with thanks to our university system's poli-sci, history and social science departments, we have neither. Despite all the media's political white noise, we have a depoliticized society. It may be that the Internet is changing things. It surely is the most refreshing opportunity to come along maybe in all of modern American history, and it does put heat on some political campaigns. No arguing that it influences certain influencers in society, to the degree that anything besides advertising influences anybody in the consumer republic. Problem is though, how do you create critical political mass in a depoliticized society? Most people don't vote and when it comes to actual participation in politics, opportunity is zilch. If you are not from the relatively privileged political and business segments, what the hell access is there for the individual to participate, except in one of the two business based and supported parties offered? Even at the local level. Anyone who has tried to affect one of these parties locally knows you either play entirely by the party line or stand isolated, over in the corner of the Holiday Inn meeting room with your paper plate of stale salami and Triscuits and keep your mouth shut and let the Rotary Club's big dogs bark. "Save the class dissidence bullshit for your next Al-Qaeda cell meeting, buddy!"

It is 1958 and I am twelve years old, living on the edge of niggertown in Winchester, Virginia and hiding out in the Handley Public Library from the redneck bully kids. I am reading a somewhat pompous but erudite biography of a Harvard dean and wondering how such a mythical magical being could possibly exist in the same country and on the same planet as me. A place where my dad came home from the gas station every night, skin penetrated by and forever smelling of motor oil and cigarettes. Yet this man in this book, this Harvard dean who apparently ate fish eggs called caviar (I looked it up in the dictionary), was a bulwark against something called McCarthyism, hated some people called communists and was friends with a fellow named John Kennedy. His name was McGeorge Bundy, which meant absolutely nothing to me, neither at the time, nor even later when he became one of the Kennedy administration's gurus who launched the Bay of Pigs and then cranked up Vietnam War. Still, reading about him beat the hell out of being bloodied by the red-faced inbred yokels who plagued the 10-block walk home from school. That same year I read Allen Ginsberg's "Howl," a copy of which was given me by an older kid, a fellow habitué of the decaying old Southern library, the queer son of the local insurance agent. It changed my life forever:
America when will you be angelic?
When will you take off your clothes?
When will you look at yourself through the grave?

Learning is a fickle thing. You never know which parts of it will turn out to be important and you don't really need any credential or even much literacy to begin the journey. After reading Howl I was pretty sure I was a class dissident, even though the word was not even in use yet. Before a word is born, there is a mumbling in the heart that cries for a name.

All these years later I find great comfort in that there are any number of genuine class dissidents and original thinkers still nested within the university system, nursing happy-hour pitchers, writing poetry, formulating perfectly rational antidotes to our national delusions, even though they serve now as mere manikin proof of the great academy's tolerance for diverse ideas. They have been rendered eunuchs, but at least they are dissident eunuchs with health insurance. But I have always enjoyed living in or visiting major university communities. Just last week I had one of the most meaningful evenings in ages with the dissident crowd at the University of Pennsylvania in Philly. Thankfully, such dissidents prefer to congregate there instead of, say, Bob Jones Cult College or wearing the secret Mormon underwear of Brigham Young University. It felt like old times. It felt free. Sort of. Still though, there was a nagging feeling that these people were an endangered species. And also that they were actually philosophers and bards and artists, noble pursuits once esteemed by universities and the intellectual class, but somehow now fall under the category of dissents—which in America is code for terrorist sympathizing malcontents.

> *From the viewpoint of university administrators, my puny philosophy department, and even the entire humanities division, looks rather like some vestigial organ... The business school is the heart, the natural sciences are the brain, and we, who read Plato and Descartes, Homer and Montaigne, are the appendix, just waiting to be excised once and for all.*
> —Justin E. H. Smith, Concordia University philosophy professor.

Meanwhile, until appendectomy happens, there are the nation's intellectual hall monitors to deal with. Most of America's intellectual class, like any privileged one that expects to maintain privilege, the intellectual class must be self-policing. So real dissidents and original thinkers are ignored and we watch B. F. Skinner's extinction behavior practice put into action. Smile and ignore the dissident to death professionally. Sometimes though, in spite of the best pest eradication efforts in the garden of academe, there sprouts a weed so completely antithetical to the great lie that he or she cannot be ignored. And if the offending party is particularly unlucky, he or she may be discovered by one of the political hacks sponsored to "elected office" by the Corporation, usually a Republican congressman looking for threats from within this very republic of eagles under god. Then all hell breaks loose. First the dissident is publicly discredited and demonized by an organized media lie campaign. After that, an appointed academic committee somehow discovers that his or her credentials, even after 25 years in the university system, are fraudulent and that there are some serious questions about his or her sexual appetites, not to mention his or her whereabouts on September 11.

I once thought I understood the ways in which America removes those who would point to the essential global criminality by which all Americans draw their ration of bread. But as I watched this process be conducted on my friend Ward Churchill, I realized how the extraction of these people from society has become an exquisitely brutal form of public surgery, certainly chilling on the face of it, but even more horrifying for the entertainment value it provided for the cheap seats in the Coliseum. I've known Church for over 30 years and though I've never completely agreed with what I considered his somewhat violent take on things, I agree with him now. Not simply because the system took out another of my dissenting friends, but because for the first time I could see how the dismemberment of a thinking citizen's identity and life is conducted, tissue by tissue, through carefully sharpened lies and fraudulent moral and intellectual charges. In his starkest truth telling about the genocide perpetrated upon indigenous peoples, and in his now infamous description of the Empire's "little Eichmanns" occupying the World Trade Center towers, Church came too close to the truth about the kind of psychic violence that underpins The American Way, the unacknowledged kind that is executed by America's most servile class, the bureaucratic, managerial and intellectual classes that maintain a system which could never survive the light of truth or anything resembling real justice.

It is because of guys like Church that the American intellectual establishment must conduct the self-policing of their own class. So a carefully nurtured and sustained system of intellectual critics finds faults, finds problems in the basic thesis or critical thinking or premise of any writer or thinker whose observations do not match the national hallucination being sold by the system's elites (to whom they must cater without appearing to cater.) Even the supposed intellectual left does this. In fact, probably does it best of all through its staunch assertions of the evils of free market capitalism, even though free market capitalism does not even exist and has never been practiced (more on that later). Most born into the establishment's intellectual class are born blind, rather like kangaroos or possums inside safe dark middle or upper middle class marsupial pouches where they experience nothing except what feels good as defined by the moist darkness of their nurture. And when they emerge they feel entitled to be where they are and honestly cannot see the system itself, never giving it a thought until they go off to college and, between spring breaks and beer parties, learn to experience and define reality through texts.

Those who do see the system for what it is are either worn down by the sheer mass of our institutions, or construct elaborate mental architecture to bridge over and avoid the truth. While their efforts are often applauded taken up by fellow intellectuals—post modernism has been the latest of these, and like all such constructions, contains a maybe one or two fly-shit sized specks of truth—they are utterly lost in the national machinery of fabrication. Text is not reality. Hell, reality isn't even reality in this country.

It is not too hard to grasp why unlettered but intuitive—and not a little bit vengeful—Chinese peasants in their revolution killed, humiliated and imprisoned the intellectuals. If Mao got one thing right it was that those intellectuals who pretend to ignore the existence of class, or refuse to live at the level of the most common class, are actually class exploiters, and entertain the pretense at their own eventual peril. No amount of text, no amount of ideology or pretense can ultimately protect us from reality, something which Americans are about to learn the hardest way possible.

When it comes to the state sanctioned American intellectual establishment's support of charade and pretense, the biggest fraud of all has been the notion of capitalism and free markets. There never was a free market, and, as Howard Zinn has so often demonstrated, every single industrialized nation was built on protectionism from the beginning. Even a cursory study of economic history shows that not a single developed nation in the world has ever followed the rules of free market capitalism. Not one. Early America built its textile industry on protectionism from the British. A hundred years later our steel industry came about the same way.

That is not to say the rules of free market capitalism are never observed. The rules of free market economics are for ramming down the throats of Third World or otherwise uncooperative peoples. Especially those tracking crude oil through the marketplace on the soles of their sandals. Yet there is scarcely a college or university, or business or school of that mumbo jumbo ritual called "economics" in this nation that does not teach "free market history" and free market "solutions" to such problems as the devastating eco collapse in progress, or that millions of babies shit themselves to death from dysentery or die for lack of a plain old drink of clean water.

WATCHING DOOMSDAY ON HBO

Free market capitalism may have been a fraud from the git-go, but at least there was once a version which accepted the notion that any market needed customers. Once upon a time business in the industrialized world needed its citizen laborers as customers, as consumers, which implied they be paid at least enough to buy the products of the businesses and corporations that beat their asses into submission along America's assembly lines and hog slaughtering plants. That was called American opportunity and prosperity and it looked pretty damned good to millions of war ravaged Urpeen furiners trying to decide whether to eat a wharf rat or the neighbor's cat for dinner. As for the Third World, they could eat dirt and do native dances for what few tourists existed then (otherwise called the rich), but mainly they should stay out of the way of "our" natural resources in their countries.

At any rate, when the citizen labor force, by their sheer numbers, held most of the dough in their calloused mitts, there was no avoiding them by the business classes. But now that so much of not just this nation's, but the world's wealth, has become concentrated in the hands of so few, that is no longer a problem for the rich. People are cheaper than ever and getting more plentiful by the minute. So work'em to death, kill'em, eat'em if you want to. Who the fuck cares? The international rich, the managers and controllers of the new financial globalism and the world's resources and the planet's labor forces, whether they be Asian "Confucian capitalists," masters of Colombian narco state fortunes or Chinese tongs, New York or London brokerage and media barons, or Russian oligarchs, hold increasing and previously unimaginable concentrated wealth. They look to be a replacement for the mass market, indeed even a better one with fewer mass distribution problems, higher grade demand and at top prices.

Until then however, the real dough is still in the energy game, the big suckdown of hydrocarbons, that plus convincing Americans to burn up their own seed corn. Academics, economists and scientists offer "free market solutions," such as ethyl alcohol from corn—which most readers here know requires more petroleum to grow than energy it produces, and will deprive the rest of the world of much needed food—just so Americans may continue motoring the suburban savannah lands, grazing on Subway Cold Cut Combos and Outback's Kookaburra Chicken Wings.

But even when the last Toyota Prius is forever moldering in the globally warmed deserts of Minneapolis, we proles will not be totally unprofitable creatures. Yesterday I read a gem of an economic paper asserting that in the emerging information, amusement, service, and "experience and attention economy," it is vital that "private business capture ownership and control of the public's knowledge and its attending rent streams." Apparently it's not bad enough that we become a third rate gulag of impoverished nitwits. They are going to charge us for the privilege.

Oh, dammit to hell anyway. Like a lady in Philly told me last week, "Joe, you're always so grim about these things." She's right. It's not the end of the world. Just the opening act. There is still quite a bit of this ugly little drama to be played out. But I can say one thing with certainty: This may be, as the economic intellectuals assert, the new American "attention economy," but I sure as hell ain't gonna to pay to watch.

CODA

Chapter 43

BREAKING AWAY:
THE NEW SECESSIONISTS

By Kirkpatrick Sale

SECESSION STRIKES MANY PEOPLE as an outlandish idea at first, but on serious consideration, and compared to other kinds of political action in this failed and boughten nation, it becomes a reasonable, even powerful, alternative. That's what a group of people discovered at a meeting in Middlebury, Vermont, in November 2004. Let me tell you how it went.

For a whole day we thought through the possible strategies open to an American interested in working for a fundamental alteration of the national government we suffer under and creating societies responsive to basic human needs .

We began with elective politics, the idea of voting for the same old Democrats and Republicans, but it didn't take long to reject that as futile: *they* were the ones we wanted to change, after all, they had proved time and again how beholden they were to the corporate masters who pay for their campaigns, and votes. And we took no time in rejecting the reformist lobby-Congress trap that so many environmental and liberal-cause groups spend so much money and effort on, since that was, after all, trying to change those same elected officials.

Next we considered the third-party alternative, thinking of Perot's and Nader's influence on national politics, and concluded that they did so poorly, despite considerable money and media attention, because the two major parties had essentially rigged the system so that outsiders couldn't win. Besides, launching a party and fighting an election on a national scale involves getting money and support from the same kinds of people and organizations that contribute to the other parties, and in the process becoming beholden to them.

So if reformism in all its guises is rejected, what other means of action for serious change? There's always revolt and revolution, of course, but it didn't take much deliberation to decide that there was no way, even if there were trained militia bands and some weaponry smuggled in by separatist sympathizers in Canada, a serious revolution could be mounted in this country today. And no reason to doubt that Washington would use its most potent weaponry to crush it if it arose.

And that leaves secession—instead of reforming or attacking the corrupt and corporatist system, leave it. At first glance, it seemed like a crazy idea to many, and maybe as dangerous as a revolution—after all, the last time anybody in this country tried secession, they were ruthlessly attacked and eventually destroyed. But the more we considered it, it seemed like a *doable* option, particularly if it was done peaceably and openly.

It is in the grand American tradition—the war of the colonies against the British empire was not a war of revolution, for no one wanted to take over London, but of secession, leaving the empire; and there was even a peaceable tradition, for Maine seceded from Massachusetts peaceably, Tennessee from North Carolina, and Kentucky and West Virginia from Virginia.

It could justifiably be seen as legal and constitutional, since three of the colonies wrote provisions allowing them to secede before joining the Union, there is nothing in the Constitution forbidding it, and the fact that Congress considered passing a law against it in 1861 but failed to do so indicates it was not then considered unlawful.

It is more practical as a political goal than the age-old attempt to eliminate capitalism and its institutions, a project that has generally failed even where it succeeded—and has no chance whatever of becoming a political reality in this country. Secession does not demand a wrenching alteration of basic American forms and ideas and systems, or the creation of new kinds of people.

It could be done practically and democratically, either by a vote among all citizens of voting age with, say, a two-thirds majority, or by a two-thirds (or other large) vote of the legislature of a state. Upon such a vote and a declaration of independence delivered to Washington, a seceding state could immediately appeal to the world, apply to the United Nations, and seek diplomatic support particularly from the fifteen republics that seceded from the Soviet Union and the seven nations that seceded from Yugoslavia, and Norway (which seceded from Sweden), Belgium (from France), plus all the colonies that declared independence from European empires.

And its especial appeal would be that not only does it allow a state (or region) to remove itself from the taxes, regulations, entangling alliances, bloated bureaucracy, and corrupting forms of governance of the national government, it allows a state to regain some measure of democracy, some hands-on control over the decisions that effect its life.

We ended that November meeting with a strong feeling that secession was a very powerful tool for promoting self-determination, democracy, and independence, but also a powerful idea that could spread widely throughout this continent, as it has spread widely throughout the world since 1945. (The U.N. began with 50 nations—it now has 194.) And if it took hold in even a half-dozen likely places (Alaska, Hawaii, Puerto Rico, Texas, the South, Vermont, New Hampshire), it would rapidly create a great change in the American empire and the way it works, probably leading to its eventual demise.

The final act of the conference was to issue a Middlebury Declaration, the final part of which read:

There is no reason that we cannot begin to examine the processes of secession in the United States. There are already at least 28 separatist organizations in this country and there seems to be a growing sentiment that, because the national government has shown itself to be clumsy, unresponsive, and unaccountable in so many ways, power should be concentrated at lower levels. Whether these levels should be the states or coherent regions within the states or something smaller still is a matter best left to the people active in devolution, but the principle of secession must be established as valid and legitimate.

To this end, therefore, we are pledged to create a movement that will place secession on the national agenda, encourage nonviolent secessionist organizations throughout the country, develop communication among existing and future secessionist groups, and create a body of scholarship to examine and promote the ideas and principles of secessionism.

That meeting was effectively the beginning of the conscious continental movement for secession that has blossomed over the succeeding years. There were secessionist groups before then, to be sure—particularly in Alaska, Quebec, Puerto Rico, and since 1994 in parts of the South—but they were isolated and not communicating. What has happened in the last few years is that groups have started right across the U.S.—not all have lasted, but most have—and begun getting in touch with each other., culminating in two continental conventions with delegates from two dozen active organizations.

Let me suggest some of the ways in which we can gauge the growth and influence of the new secessionists.

• A poll taken by the University of Vermont in February 2007 that found that 13 per cent of the state's residents came right out and said "it would be a good idea for Vermont to secede from the United States and become once again an independent republic as it was from 1777 to 1791." Thirteen per cent—that may not seem a lot at first, but it is up significantly from 8 per cent the year before and translates to 64,400 people of voting age in the population at large—and Vermont has only 625,000 people.

Vermont has had a secession movement for the last four years, made up of what is now a think-tank called the Second Vermont Republic, a newspaper called *Vermont Commons,* and various groups, most recently FreeVermont.Net, hoping to put the question of secession on the agenda of the state's 230 town meetings by the year 2010. But only recently has it begun to get media notice, with an AP article that ran nationwide in June 2007, and articles in the *Burlington Free Press, Los Angeles Times,* and *Philadelphia Enquirer,* among others, and interviews on Fox News, CNN, BBC, CBC, and dozens of radio stations across the country. The Vermont effort was also a featured part of articles in *Orion* and *Good* magazines in 2007.

And another question from the UVM poll indicates that there is fertile ground for it. When asked, "Has the United States government lost its moral authority," a surprising 74.3 per cent said yes, an indication that attachment to the Federal government is clearly eroding. It was the loss of moral authority that played a large part in the downfall of the apartheid government in South Africa, the communist regimes in Eastern Europe, and the Soviet Union itself. When the center cannot hold—allegiance, loyalty, moral authority—things fall apart.

• An independent think tank called the Middlebury Institute—born at the Middlebury meeting—has been established "to study separatism, secession, and self-determination" both globally and within North America. It has issued a half-dozen papers exploring the issues related to secession and, most important, has sponsored two continental conventions, one in Vermont in 2006 and a second in Tennessee (co-sponsored with the League of the South) in 2007; a third will be held in South Carolina in 2008.

The conventions attracted more than 40 representatives from 20 secessionist organizations in 26 states (including particularly strong showing from Hawai'i, Alaska, Cascadia, Texas, Louisiana, South Carolina, Tennessee, Virginia, Vermont, and New Hampshire), and an additional 100 observers. That such events were held at all is pretty remarkable, but the fact that they drew serious people from across the land for days of reports and meetings indicates that there is something that can fairly be called a secessionist movement. The second convention, partly because it was co-sponsored by a northern and a southern group, joining Blue states and Red, grew worldwide attention, and an AP story on it was carried by more than 100 U.S. papers and a dozen overseas.

• The *Washington Post* in April 2007 carried an op-ed article by Ian Baldwin, publisher of *Vermont Commons,* and Frank Bryan, a professor at UVM, entitled "The Once and Future Republic of Vermont," laying out the case for Vermont being an independent republic as it was from 177 to 1791. According to an editor there, it was the second-most read piece in the entire Sunday paper (12,000 hits on-line) and garnered more than 200 emails, considered a high rate of response. It was syndicated cross-country and exploded with 21,000 entries on the internet.

• A poll taken by the Opinion Research Corporation in the fall of 2006 and broadcast by CNN on October 23, 71 per cent of Americans agreed that "our system of government is broken and cannot be fixed, and another 7 per cent agreed it was broken but might be fixed.

• A *Daily Kos* poll in April 2007 asked, "Should states be allowed to secede from the union peaceably?" and 65 per cent answered affirmatively—which is interesting especially because it is conventional liberals, of the kind that this blog mostly attracts, who usually believe in working within the system and are not often fans of secession. A previous poll in 2005 showed only 53 per cent in favor of secession

• An online petition recently posted on its website by the League of the South, one of the oldest secessionist groups, asks support for "the South's right to secede from the current regime and form its own government." It had been signed by 2,615 people as of January 2008, and gets around one signature a day.

There are a number of other active secessionist organizations in North America.

The Alaska Independence Party has swung in electoral support from 5 per cent when it began in 1986, up to 38.8 per cent in 1990 (when Walter Hickel was on the ticket and won the governorship), down to 13 per cent in 1994, and it has hovered around 1-2 per cent in elections since then. (Still, 2 per cent is nearly 10,000 voting-age people, a real constituency.) It recently installed new leadership and it has nominated serious candidates for statewide elections in 2008. "The people of Alaska are fed up," according to AIP vice-chair Dexter Clark, "and if ever there was a time ripe for change, this is it."

The Puerto Rico Independence Party has varied from 1 per cent in referendums for statehood vs. independence in 1967 to 4.4 per cent in 1993, 2.5 per cent in 1998, and 2.4 per cent in 2004. (But even that represents a 648,000 voting-age population.) It recently got a boost from an endorsement by a "Panama Proclamation" passed unanimously at the Latin American and Caribbean Congress meeting in November 2006 urging that Puerto Rico "become a free and independent nation."

Hawai'i is a special case. Several votes and polls have shown wide support for sovereignty: 73 per cent in an election in 1996, 63 per cent in a *Honolulu Advertiser* poll in July 2006. (Percentages like these amount to roughly 900,000 people.) The trouble with the campaign there is that it is divided into a half-dozen different groups with different agendas and tactics, and it hasn't yet been able to translate what is obviously popular support into a coherent movement.

One other interesting area is the South, where professional polls seem to suggest support, as one leading pollster put it, only "in the high single or low double digits." A poll said to be fairly typical, by the University of North Carolina in 1992, found that 8.4 per cent agreed that "if it could be done without war, the South would be better off as a separate country today," and 16.8 per cent said that "the South would be a lot better off it had won the War Between the States." The League of the South, the strongest secession group in the South, boasts chapters in 16 states and a dues-paying membership said to be close to 4,000; a new secessionist organization, the Southern National

Congress, was started last year and plans an inaugural convention for later this year.

The other strong secession movement in North America is the Parti Quebecois in Montreal, which has come within a hair (in 1995) of winning a referendum on separation from Canada. Its latest showing in this spring's election was third, but only 11 seats behind the leading Liberals, with 28 per cent of the vote, which represents something like 2.2 million people, so it still plays an important role in Quebec politics.

The latest group to emerge on the secession scene are the Lakota Sioux Indians, representatives of whom in December declared the tribe's status as a sovereign nation, no longer under the jurisdiction of the United States and no longer bound by any treaties signed with it. It is not clear what this will mean on the ground, though the representatives have said there will be no Federal income taxes and even welcomed non-Indians who want to avoid taxes onto the reservation (if they renounce their U.S. citizenship), so there is every likelihood of a clash with the IRS some time in the course of the next year or two.

The leader of the breakaway Indians is Russell Means, a longtime American Indian Movement activist, and he has a substantial following for his secession. There are some people on the reservation, and some Lakota in surrounding communities, who are not convinced that this move will actually provide the Lakota with real self-government free of the U.S. Bureau of Indian Affairs. Means has insisted that independence will be real and said his group is ready to "negotiate with any American political entity." They have established a website at Lakotafreedom.com.

It is still too early to know what will become of the new secession movement, but it is clear that it gives expression to many thousands of people grown dissatisfied with the American empire and longing to have control over the decisions that effect their lives. The spirit encapsulated by Thomas Jefferson is alive and well: "Whenever any form of government is destructive of these ends [of consensual government] it is the right of the people to alter or to abolish it, and to institute new government...as to them shall seem mostly likely to effect their safety and happiness." That spirit conquered once, and it might once again.

CONTRIBUTORS

Rose Aguilar is a journalist writing a book about her experiences in "red states."

Justin Akers Chacón, along with Mike Davis, is the author of *No One is Illegal*. He was born and raised in Mexico. His reports from the border war first appeared in the *Socialist Worker*.

Kevin Gray is a *CounterPunch* contributer and civil rights organizer who resides in Columbia, South Carolina.

Joe Bageant is the author of the best-selling *Deer Hunting With Jesus: Dispatches from America's Class War*. He was raised in Winchester, Virginia.

Julene Bair is author of *One Degree West: Reflections of a Plainsdaughter*. She lives in Kansas.

John Blair is president of the environment health advocacy group, Valley Watch and earned a Pulitzer Prize for News Photography in 1978. He lives in Indiana.

Alan Bock is Senior Essayist at the *Orange County Register*. He is the author of *Ambush at Ruby Ridge*. He is also author of the new book *Waiting to Inhale: The Politics of Medical Marijuana*.

Michele Bollinger writes for the *Socialist Worker*.

Nicole Colson is a contributor to *CounterPunch*.

Carrie Dann is a member of the Western Shoshone tribe and has been active in the movement to recover millions of acres of land that originally belonged to the Shoshone peoples but was seized by the U.S. government as part of the 1863 Treaty of Ruby Valley.

Roxanne Dunbar-Ortiz is an American professor of ethnic studies. In addition to many scholarly books and articles, she has published three memoirs, *Red Dirt: Growing Up Okie*; *Outlaw Woman: A Memoir of the War Years*, 1960–1975; and *Blood on the Border*. Dunbar-Ortiz was raised in rural Oklahoma.

Julie Fishel is a lawyer for the Western Shoshone Defence Project.

Jordan Flaherty is an activist and an editor of *Left Turn Magazine*. He lives in New Orleans.

Joshua Frank, co-editor of Dissident Voice, a regular contributor to *CounterPunch*, is the author of *Left Out! How Liberals Helped Reelect George W. Bush* and with Jeffrey St. Clair of the forthcoming *Green Scare: The New War on Environmentalism*. He was born and raised in Montana.

Steve Higgins is editor of *The Bloomington Alternative*.

Lily Hughes writes for the *Socialist Worker*.

Dean Kuipers writes for the *Los Angeles Times* and is the author of *Burning Rainbow Farm*.

Josh Mahan edits Lowbagger.org, the web's most un-PC environmental rag. He lives in Montana and rides the roaring rivers of the West whenever he can.

Bob Moser is a *Nation* contributing writer. His book about Democrats and the South will be published in Summer 2008. His essay on antiwar activists in Kentucky first appeared in the *Nation*.

Greg Moses is the editor of the *Texas Civil Rights Review* and author of *Revolution of Conscience: Martin Luther King, Jr. and the Philosophy of Nonviolence*. He lives in Texas.

Ted Nace is the author of the best-selling *Gangs of America: The Rise of Corporate Power and the Disabling of Democracy*. Nace is the founder of Peachpit Press, the world's leading publisher of books on computer graphics and desktop publishing. Prior to that he worked as a freelance writer and served as staff director of the Dakota Resource Council, helping rural communities deal with the impact of strip mines and power plants. He was raised in North Dakota. His essay on populist rebellion in North Dakota first appeared in *Orion*.

Brenda Norrell has been a news reporter in Indian country for 23 years, working as a staff reporter for *Navajo Times* and *Indian Country Today* and as an AP correspondent during the 18 years she lived on the Navajo Nation. She is currently a freelance writer based in Tucson and a contributor to *CounterPunch*.

Andrea Peacock is the author of *Libby, Montana: Asbestos and the Deadly Silence of an American Corporation* and co-author, with Doug Peacock, of *The Essential Grizzly*. She lives in Montana.

Bill Quigley is a human rights lawyer and law professor at Loyola Law School in New Orleans.

Mike Roselle, "Man Without a Bioregion," is cofounder of Earth First!; the Rainforest Action Network and the Ruckus Society and has been instrumental in virtually every famous GreenPeace stunt. His dispatches from the road can be read on Lowbagger.org.

Eric Ruder is a writer for the *Socialist Worker* where his border reports first appeared.

Kirkpatrick Sale is the author of twelve books, including *Human Scale*, *The Conquest of Paradise*, *Rebels Against the Future*, and *The Fire of His Genius: Robert Fulton and the American Dream*.

Jeffrey St. Clair is co-editor of *CounterPunch* and author of 11 books, including the best-sellers *Whiteout: the CIA, Drugs and the Press*; *Al Gore: a User's Manual*; *Five Days That Shook the World*; and most recently *Born Under a Bad Sky*. St. Clair was born and raised in Indiana.

David Underhill was a radio talk show host for many years in Mobile, Alabama until he was fired after repeated failures to rectify his persistent political incorrectness.

Jesse Walker is the managing editor of *Reason* and the author of *Rebels on the Air: An Alternative History of Radio in America*. His essay herein first appeared in *Reason*.

Kelpie Wilson is the environmental editor for Truthout.org.

INDEX

FRIENDS OF AK PRESS

Help sustain our vital project!

AK Press is a worker-run collective that publishes and distributes radical books, audio/visual media, and other material. We're small: ten individuals who work long hours for short money, because we believe in what we do. We're anarchists, which is reflected both in the books we publish and in the way we organize our business: without bosses.

AK Press publishes the finest books, CDs, and DVDs from the anarchist and radical traditions—currently about 18 to 20 per year. Joining The Friends of AK Press is a way in which you can directly help us to keep the wheels rolling and these important projects coming.

As ever, money is tight as we do not rely on outside funding. We need your help to make and keep these crucial materials available. Friends pay a minimum (of course we have no objection to larger sums!) of $25/£15 per month, for a minimum three month period. Money received goes directly into our publishing funds. In return, Friends automatically receive (for the duration of their membership), as they appear, one FREE copy of EVERY new AK Press title. Secondly, they are also entitled to a 10% discount on EVERYTHING featured in the AK Press distribution catalog—or on our website—on ANY and EVERY order. We also have a program where individuals or groups can sponsor a whole book.

PLEASE CONTACT US FOR MORE DETAILS:

AK Press
674-A 23rd Street
Oakland, CA 94612
akpress@akpress.org
www.akpress.org

AK Press
PO Box 12766
Edinburgh, Scotland EH8, 9YE
ak@akedin.demon.co.uk
www.akuk.com